Trading and Hedging with Agricultural Futures and Options

Trading and Hedging with Agricultural Futures and Options

James B. Bittman

McGraw-Hill

New York   Chicago   San Francisco   Lisbon   London   Madrid
Mexico City   Milan   New Delhi   San Juan   Seoul
Singapore   Sydney   Toronto

Library of Congress Cataloging-in-Publication Data

Bittman, James B.
    Trading and hedging with agricultural futures and options / by James B. Bittman.
      p. cm.
    ISBN 0-07-136502-8
    1. Commodity futures.   2. Options (Finance)   I. Title.

   HG6046 .B48   2001
   332.64'41—dc21
                                      00-054626

McGraw-Hill

A Division of The McGraw·Hill Companies

1 2 3 4 5 6 7 8 9 0   DOC/DOC   0 9 8 7 6 5 4 3 2 1

P/N 137790-5
Part of
ISBN 0-07-136502-8

Printed and bound by R. R. Donnelley & Sons Company.

McGraw-Hill books are available at special quantity discounts to use as premiums and sales
promotions, or for use in corporate training programs. For more information, please write
to the Director of Special Sales, Professional Publishing, McGraw-Hill, Two Penn Plaza,
New York, NY 10121-2298. Or contact your local bookstore.

This book is printed on recycled, acid-free paper containing a minimum of
50% recycled, de-inked fiber.

Dedicated to my wife, Laura,
whose support and encouragement
helped make this book possible.

Contents

Foreword

One lesson from my 40 years in agricultural research is that economic analysis guides decision making and reduces risk but does not eliminate all uncertainty. The perfect complement to agricultural research, therefore, is a tool that not only implements research but also increases flexibility. Options are such a tool.

Trading in options on agricultural futures contracts began with authorization by the Commodity Futures Trading Commission in 1982. Since that time, trading volume has expanded dramatically, providing clear testimony by traders and risk managers in an increasingly volatile world market environment that options add value.

Options on agricultural futures expand the strategies available to agricultural market participants for managing market risk and capturing trading opportunities. When used in combination with cash forward contracts and futures contracts, options on futures allow agricultural market participants to change the nature of business risks. Agricultural producers, merchants, brokers, food manufacturers, food distributors, and food service providers can use options to alter the profile of risks for sales revenues, raw material costs, and business margins. For traders, options offer more alternatives to take advantage of a forecast.

Having pointed out the growth in trading volume and the reasons that options are important hedging and trading tools, it also must be stated that we are looking at a business in its infancy. Agricultural business strategies incorporating options are often avoided by hedging managers, or applied incorrectly, for several reasons. First, there is still a lack of understanding of how options work and how they can be used. Second, the thinking process for using options is substantially different than that for using futures contracts, and that thinking is also not well understood. Third, the nature of option prices and option price changes is more complex than for futures contracts. Fourth, strategy trade-offs involving risk avoidance, opportunity loss and strategy costs for options are harder to learn than for strategies involving only futures. Fifth, misinformed members of the media have repeated misconceptions about options for many years and continue to do so today. Finally, much of the existing literature concerning options is oriented to the financial markets for equities, currencies, and interest rates. It has been difficult for an agricultural risk manager to find, in literature, a practical and organized combination of options theory and application specifically focused on agriculture.

Jim Bittman has filled this long existing need with a thoughtful and easy-to-read treatment of this seemingly complex subject. Jim has taught courses at Sparks since 1994. In those classes, he uses practical examples and exercises to teach the mechanics of options, their price behavior, and how they can be used to hedge agricultural price risks. His step-by-step teaching approach has been transferred nicely to this text.

There are hands-on exercises involving straightforward calculations and graphic illustrations. The discussion of option price theory is conceptual, not mathematical. Not only is option price theory explained with a focus on practical applications, those applications are explained in detail for both agricultural risk managers and traders. Bittman also conveys a clear understanding of each concept before moving on to the next one.

When should a manager choose to use options to manage the risks inherent in a decision to purchase commodity raw materials? Bittman clearly delineates the trade-offs between strategies using options and strategies using futures. Variations of option strategies that are available to decision makers also are explained. In 1995, when we at Sparks forecast a rise in corn prices, a price rise that in fact turned into one of historic proportions, we advised our clients to use options strategies, including the more advanced techniques explained in Chapter 10. These advanced strategies are especially valuable because they illustrate techniques that minimize the cost of the use of options in specific circumstances.

Bittman also explains strategies for stagnant markets. The selling options strategies explained in the hedging strategies section and Chapter 13 in the "Trading Strategies" section suggest opportunities to improve margins and add price protection. Who knows when the next drought, the next Chernobyl, or the next Southeast Asian typhoon will be? Certainly no one wants to pay for expensive protection against such unlikely events. All the more reason, therefore, to know about the low- to zero-cost disaster insurance strategies discussed in Chapters 8, 9, and 10.

How does a risk manager's forecast for futures prices affect strategy selection? *Trading and Hedging with Agricultural Futures and Options* makes the choices clear. The similar and related decisions facing agricultural producers and marketers are treated in thorough detail as well.

Jim Bittman further provides business risk managers and traders with a simple and effective computer program, OP-EVALF™. The program calculates prices for both single options and spread positions. It also has a graphic capability that enhances the learning process. For those who have already mastered the necessary skills of manually graphing basic option strategies, the computer program provides a powerful tool to swiftly and accurately analyze more complex applications. OP-EVALF™ will become a useful companion for option traders and risk managers who follow the thinking process explained in the exercises in the section on trading. In particular, the impact on option prices of changing time and changing volatility will become crystal-clear.

A firm grounding in the fundamentals of options gained from reading *Trading and Hedging with Agricultural Futures and Options*, will be valuable immediately to any market participant and will become even more valuable in the future. Agricultural markets worldwide continue to see lower trade barriers and diminished government interference in the processes of supply and demand. Free of the buffering effect of government actions, prices of agricultural commodities affect the world's producers and consumers to a greater extent than ever before. Agricultural commodity price movements have tended to become more volatile over time, increasing both opportunities and applications for option strategies.

As greater volumes have been traded, a more complex market has arisen in which contract dealers and market makers have offered customized over-the-counter (OTC) instruments. From the basic swap, OTC products quickly have expanded to include option contracts with terms differing significantly from exchange-traded options on futures. A great variety of negotiated instruments are now in use. However, they are all based on the options theory and applied concepts thoroughly explained in *Hedging and Trading with Agricultural Futures and Options*. A diligent reader and student of this book will be well prepared to extend this knowledge to the expanding world of trading and risk management. I believe that anyone who is intrigued by commodities markets will enjoy this book.

Willard R. Sparks
Sparks Companies, Inc.
Memphis, Tennessee

Acknowledgments

I would like to thank all the people at Sparks Companies who helped make this book possible. The encouragement of Willard Sparks was instrumental, and the assistance of his team of top-notch agricultural research professionals was invaluable. My many years of trading at the Chicago Board of Trade did not give me the in-depth knowledge of hedging strategies that I have learned from Rob Westmoreland since our association began in 1994. Rob read the text as it was being prepared and suggested several improvements and clarifications. Bruce Sherr provided technical advice as well as encouragement. Rosamary Posey also offered valuable assistance. Her organizational skills helped me in many ways, and her pleasant personality made it fun at the same time. I would also like to thank Carroll Brunthaver who started my relationship with the Sparks companies.

James Karls wrote the OP-EVALF™ program. Ingenious in its simplicity and ease of use, it offers everything that most hedgers and traders will ever need.

I would also like to thank my friends at the Chicago Board of Trade, Peter Alonzi (now with Dominican University) and Alice Koza. They have been very supportive of my teaching efforts over the years. Chris and Cari Manns of Traders Group, Inc. also provided valuable assistance by introducing me to delegations from all over the world. One organization worthy of note is The Federation of Swedish Farmers (LRF) and their leader Leif Zetterberg. The efforts of Chris and Cari and Leif to educate farmers and other agricultural industry participants is testimony to the need for this kind of book.

A special note of thanks is due to Debra Peters, CBOE Vice President and Director of the Options Institute. She has been very encouraging in all the projects I have undertaken, and she has given other OI staff members and me the necessary freedom to stretch our personal limits.

Disclosures

T he examples in this book are hypothetical. They do not represent and are not intended to represent real people, real situations, or actual hedging or trading advice. The examples presented here are meant to be realistic, but they are for illustrative purposes only.

To simplify computations, commissions and other transaction costs, margin requirements, and bid-ask spreads have not been included in the examples used in this book. These factors will affect the outcome of futures and options strategies and should be considered in real-world situations. Futures and options involve risk and are not suitable for everyone. Hedgers and traders considering futures and options should ask a tax adviser how taxes may affect the outcome of contemplated transactions.

Introduction

IS THIS BOOK FOR YOU?

T his book is written for hedgers and traders who want to use commodity futures and options. Hedgers will learn how options work and how to think in a new way about price-management planning. Setting goals, two-step thinking, and understanding trade-offs are what the successful use of futures and options in hedging requires. Traders will learn about option price behavior and the differences in market forecasting that trading options requires relative to trading futures. Traders will also learn how to analyze more than one strategy for a given situation.

RISK EXISTS

Farmers who plant crops in the spring do not know what the price will be when it is time to sell in the fall. Processors who need a steady flow of supplies throughout the year constantly face an unknown future of fluctuating prices. Markets in commodity futures and options on futures arose out of a need to deal with, or manage, these risks.

MARKET PARTICIPANTS

Markets are created by the interaction of three different types of participants: hedgers, traders (or speculators), and arbitrageurs. Hedgers have a real business interest in the underlying commodity. They either produce the commodity, such as farmers who plant and grow grain, or use it, such as bakers who use grain to make bread. Some hedgers are both producers and users. Soybean crushers,

> **Three different types of market participants**

for example, are users of soybeans and producers of soybean meal and soybean oil. Some hedgers do not fall neatly into either the producer category or the user category. Grain elevators, for example, provide a middleman function by purchasing grain from farmers and storing it until it is sold to a user. Without futures and options, hedgers would be limited in their ability to manage the risks of price fluctuations.

Traders, or speculators, have no business interest in the underlying commodity. They only have opinions about the direction of prices, and they hope to profit from those opinions. Traders are an important part of commodity markets because, as additional participants, they make it easier for others to enter into new positions or close out existing positions. Traders perform an essential function known as *adding liquidity*. Generally speaking, the more liquidity in a market, the narrower the spread between bid and ask prices. This means that total costs are lower for entering and exiting positions.

Arbitrageurs are the third type of market participant. They attempt to earn profits from price discrepancies. If corn is trading at $2.50 per bushel on the East Coast and $3.00 on the West Coast, and if it costs 20 cents per bushel to ship corn across the country, there is an arbitrage opportunity. An arbitrageur would buy corn at $2.50, ship it across the country, and sell it at $3.00. The result, in this simplified example, would be a profit of 30 cents per bushel. By attempting to make profits in this manner, arbitrageurs provide the function of *market parity*, which sometimes is described as "keeping prices in line." Arbitrageurs perform the function of leveling the playing field so that commodity buyers and sellers in different parts of the country (and the world) pay or receive approximately equal prices adjusted for time and distance.

In the commodity futures and options markets, there are several arbitrage-pricing relationships. There is a relationship between cash market prices and the prices of futures contracts. There are also relationships between option prices and the prices of the underlying futures contracts. Arbitrageurs therefore play an important role in agricultural markets, and that role is too frequently misunderstood.

WHAT YOU WILL LEARN

The chapters in this book are designed to help hedgers and traders understand, (1) how options work, (2) how they can be used to pursue stated goals, and (3) what the pros and cons of using them are. With this understanding, hedgers and traders should be able to incorporate options into their activities.

For hedgers, this book will first explain the theory of hedging strategies. It then will discuss the thinking and planning process that using options requires. Perhaps the biggest challenge for hedgers is adapting to a new way of thinking. Using options in risk management planning is different from using futures!

Commodity buyers can use options to lock in maximum prices and still be free to pay a lower price if prices decline. Commodity sellers can use options to lock in a minimum price and still be free to sell at a higher price if prices rise. Both buyers and sellers can use options to enhance income in sideways-trading markets.

While these hedging concepts may be enticing, it is important not to get too excited too soon. The successful use of options as hedging tools requires the development of realistic expectations about what can be accomplished with options, what the costs are, and, equally important, what is not possible. Setting and achieving hedging pricing targets also involves many subjective elements; the use of options makes the job no less subjective.

Realistic expectations are important

For traders, the discussion of option price behavior is extremely valuable. Understanding how option prices change with changes in the underlying futures price, changes in the time to expiration, and changes in volatility makes it possible to select trading strategies that are consistent with a market forecast. Traders must also learn to analyze more than one trading alternative.

It is the hedger's job to research available information and make subjective predictions in selecting hedging strategies. Options add value for hedgers, because they increase hedging alternatives. The alternatives that options make possible are not necessarily "better"; instead, they offer different trade-offs—different sets of positives and negatives. Given a hedger's specific circumstances and market opinion, an option alternative may be deemed better by that person, but the option strategy will not be better in an absolute sense.

What do options give hedgers?

Each option strategy should be understood in terms of the trade-off it offers. Sometimes, for a specific person making a subjective decision, the option trade-off will be preferable; and the option strategy will be selected. On other occasions, the trade-off of buying or selling the commodity in question in the cash market at the current market price will be preferable, and that strategy will be selected.

> Options
> do not solve
> all problems

This book does not assert that options are the answer to all hedging and trading situations. Rather, it is the contention of this book that options help some of the time, offer good alternatives to consider, and add an essential diversity to hedging and trading tools. To use options wisely and efficiently, however, hedgers and traders must understand the trade-offs they offer and how and when those trade-offs fit into the subjective decision-making process.

BOOK OUTLINE

This book is divided into three parts: "The Basics of Futures and Options," "Hedging Strategies," and "Trading Strategies."

Part 1 thoroughly explains the vocabulary, the mechanics of futures and options, and the important concepts of why futures and options have value. This section is essential for beginners. Chapter 1, "The Terminology of Futures and Options," is important because industry terms sometimes are used in a way that differs from everyday usage. Chapter 2, "Diagrams of Basic Trading Strategies," is also important for beginners. This chapter illustrates in great detail how profit and loss diagrams are created. These diagrams illuminate potential profit and potential risk. These factors become especially important in later sections, when market opinion and hedging or trading objectives are matched with strategy trade-offs. Chapter 3, "Diagrams of Basic Hedging Strategies," takes profit and loss diagrams to the next level. Hedgers have a real interest in the underlying commodity and therefore cannot think in options-only terms. They must include their need to buy or sell the underlying commodity in the diagram of the strategy. Chapter 4, "Why Futures and Options Have Value," explains conceptually the components of value for these instruments. Chapter 5, "Option Price Behavior," explains how option prices change before the expiration date. To say the least, the behavior of option prices seems counterintuitive to many beginners, and this chapter provides an essential introduction to the trading strategies that are presented later in the bank. Chapters 6 and 7 go beyond the basic discussion of price behavior in Chapter 5 to discuss the important subject of volatility and more advanced option pricing topics. Beginners in options may want to skip these chapters initially and come back to them after reading Part 3, "Trading Strategies."

Part 2, "Hedging Strategies," starts with Chapter 8, "Strategies for Long Hedgers." Four strategies are presented in a step-by-step process. First, the mechanics of the strategy are explained, and, then theoretical advantages and disadvantages are discussed. Then a realistic example that includes rising price and falling price scenarios is presented. Then, the forecast that justifies selecting the strategy is explained. Finally, the psychology behind using the strategy is discussed. Chapter 9 uses the same five-step process to present four strategies for short hedgers. Chapter 10, "Advanced Hedging Strategies," explains six multiple-part strategies and the thinking process that is required to use them.

Part 3, "Trading Strategies," shifts the focus and examines short-term strategies in which an understanding of option price behavior is of the utmost importance. Chapter 11 introduces the computer program, OP-EVALF™, which comes with this book. Trading options requires realistic expectations about how option prices change, and this easy-to-use tool helps develop those expectations and analyze trading alternatives. The remaining chapters in Part 3 work through, in step-by-step detail, some short-term trading situations, examining the important decisions that must be made. They also illustrate how OP-EVALF™ can be used to assist in the process. The software, of course, does not make trading decisions, and it does not in any way guarantee success. The purpose of the program is to get consistent information that can help improve the decision-making process. Chapter 12, "Buying Options," focuses on long option strategies. Managing trading capital and the use of OP-EVALF™ to develop realistic expectations about various alternatives are important topics in this chapter. Chapter 13, "Selling Options," explains the differences in market forecasting, trade planning, capital management, and risk monitoring for strategies involving short options. Chapters 14 through 16 discuss vertical spreads, straddles and strangles, and ratio spreads, respectively. In these chapters a strategy is defined first, and then its mechanics at expiration are reviewed. The delta, gamma, vega, and theta of the strategy are discussed next so that the strategy's short-term price behavior can be anticipated. Chapter 17 summarizes the important topics developed throughout this book. If you have any questions or would like to discuss topics of particular interest, feel free to contact the author at *bittman@cboe.com*, or write to him care of OP-EVAL, Suite 200, 2501 North Lincoln Avenue, Chicago, IL 60614.

Trading and Hedging with Agricultural Futures and Options

Part 1

The Basics of Futures and Options

One

The Terminology of Futures and Options

T his chapter defines the terminology that hedgers and traders need to know. As experienced traders will see, however, not every term associated with futures and options is covered. Frankly speaking, one of the reasons why futures and options are frequently considered more complicated than they actually are is that technical words are used incorrectly or with conflicting meanings. There are, in fact, many technical terms that most hedgers and traders do not need to know. The following list of terms will be used throughout this book as defined in this chapter:

Futures contract	American-style exercise
Call option	European-style exercise
Put option	Effective purchase price
Long futures	Effective selling price
Short futures	Option buyer
Long call	Option writer
Short call	In-the-money, at-the-money, out-of-the-money
Long put	
Short put	Premium
Strike price (exercise price)	Intrinsic value
Delivery date	Time value
Expiration date	Initial margin
Exercise (and exercise notice)	Maintenance margin
Assignment (and notice of assignment)	Margin call
	Mark to the market

If you are familiar with these terms, you may skip ahead to Chapter 2. If you wish to read through the following definitions, keep in mind that they are written on a basic level. The nuances will be explained in later chapters.

This chapter will first discuss futures contracts, then call options, and then put options. At the end of the chapter some questions (with the answers following) will help reinforce your understanding.

FUTURES CONTRACTS

The Delivery Date

A *futures contract* is an agreement between two parties, a buyer and a seller, to exchange a standardized good, the commodity, for an agreed-upon price at a specific date in the future, the *delivery date*. The agreement is made through representatives of the parties, commodities brokers, on the floor of an organized futures exchange. The exchange guarantees the performance of both parties. The specifications and delivery procedures of the standardized good are detailed in the futures contract. Unless a futures contract is closed out before the delivery date, both the buyer and the seller are obligated to fulfill their sides of the transaction.

> **Buyers of futures are obligated to buy**

It is the standardized nature of a futures contract and the exchange guarantee that distinguish a futures contract from a forward contract, which is a unique negotiated agreement between two parties. An example of a forward contract occurs when Party A agrees to buy 12,600 bushels of soybeans from Party B on October 9. The advantage of a negotiated forward contract is that the buyer gets exactly what is needed when it is needed.

> **Sellers of futures are obligated to sell**

The seller of a forward contract gets a desired price and a desired delivery schedule. One disadvantage of a forward contract is that both parties assume performance risk. In this example, Party A assumes the risk that Party B will deliver soybeans of the specified grade on the specified date, and Party B assumes the risk that Party A will accept delivery and pay. Another disadvantage of forward contracts is that neither party can get out of the contract, even at a loss, without the permission of the other party. If Party A wants to cancel the contract but Party B refuses, Party A must find a third party, acceptable to Party B, to buy exactly 12,600 bushels of the specific grade of soybeans on October 9. This is known as an "illiquid" contract.

Futures contracts, however, have the advantage of being very liquid. Unless extraordinary market conditions exist in which a futures contract has reached its upper or lower price limit for a particular trading session, futures contracts can be traded freely. Also, futures contracts involve neither performance risk nor the expenses of negotiation. Futures contracts are generally far less costly to administer than are forward contracts.

Standardization is the major disadvantage of futures contracts. If a contract covers 5,000 bushels, for example, it is impossible to get 12,600 bushels delivered through the exchange's delivery mechanism. A buyer must purchase either two or three contracts in that case. Nevertheless, the growth of futures markets indicates that many market participants find that the advantages outweigh the disadvantages.

Margin Accounts and Margin Deposits

After entering into a futures contract, both the buyer and the seller must deposit funds in an account with the broker to demonstrate that they are financially capable of fulfilling the terms of the contract. The deposit is known as a *margin deposit* and the account is known as the *margin account.* The actual risk borne by the parties is usually substantially larger than the margin deposit. Users of futures and options need to be aware of margin account procedures because different strategies have different margin requirements.

Initial Margin, Maintenance Margin, and Margin Call

Initial margin is the minimum account equity required to establish a position. Initial margin requirements for futures and futures options frequently are expressed in absolute dollar terms. The initial margin for a soybean futures position, long or short, for example, might be $900. If a position loses money, the account equity, i.e., the margin, will decrease. *Minimum margin* is the level, expressed as an absolute dollar amount, at or above which the account equity must be maintained. If account equity falls below the minimum margin level, the brokerage firm will notify the trader in a *margin call* that the account equity must be raised to the maintenance level. *Maintenance margin* is the level of account equity to which an account balance must be raised when a margin call is received. Maintenance margin is typically less than initial margin. Upon receiving a margin call, a trader may either deposit additional funds or securities or close the position.

Mark to the Market

A process that ensures that buyers and sellers of futures contracts are in compliance with the minimum margin requirements established by the exchange is known as *marking to the market*. By this process, the margin account balances of both the buyer and the seller are adjusted daily to reflect changes in the price of the futures contract.

Assume, for example, that on day 1 John buys one wheat futures contract from Ramona. Assume also that this contract covers 5,000 bushels of wheat, the price is $3.00 per bushel, and the margin requirement is $1,000. This means that both John and Ramona must deposit $1,000 in accounts with their brokers.

Now consider the risks that John and Ramona are assuming. John has agreed to buy 5,000 bushels at $3.00 each for a total commitment of $15,000. In theory, if the price of wheat were to drop to zero, John would be obligated to pay $14,000 in addition to the $1,000 already in his account, and his total loss would be $15,000.

Ramona's risk is different. If Ramona has 5,000 bushels of wheat ready to deliver, she has no risk other than opportunity risk, the risk that the price of wheat could rise and a higher price could have been received. In this case, in which Ramona has 5,000 bushels of wheat, she simply waits until the delivery date and then delivers her wheat in accordance with exchange-specified procedures. Upon delivery she receives $15,000.

If Ramona does not have any wheat, however, she is assuming an unlimited risk, because the price of wheat could rise indefinitely.

Now consider how a change in the price of the futures contract and marking to the market affect John's and Ramona's account balances. If on day 2 the price of wheat rises 10 cents to $3.10, the value of 5,000 bushels rises to $15,500. Ignoring the fact that John will feel good and Ramona will feel bad, the price rise has increased John's creditworthiness and decreased Ramona's. John's commitment to purchase wheat at $3.00 is now backed by his $1,000 deposit plus the $500 increase in value of the futures contract. Ramona, however, has only $500 of "free and clear margin," because $500 of her $1,000 deposit is now an unrealized loss.

Something now happens in the futures business that does not happen in a normal purchase and sale transaction. Given the 10-cent price rise indicated above, the exchange will instruct Ramona's broker to transfer $500 cash from her account to John's broker for deposit to John's account. Such cash transfers occur every

MARK TO THE MARKET
Cash transfers
are made daily

day in the futures business. When prices rise, cash is transferred from holders of short positions to holders of long positions. When prices fall, the opposite happens.

These daily cash transfers are an important element of the creditworthiness of the futures system. First, they assure that every futures position is backed by the exchange-required minimum deposit of cash or cash equivalents. Second, they provide assurance to every trader with an unrealized profit by covering that unrealized profit with cash.

In the example above in which $500 is transferred out of Ramona's account, her equity, or margin account balance, is reduced to $500. As long as her balance is above the exchange's minimum requirement, no action need be taken. If an account balance drops below the minimum, however, then the broker will notify the customer that additional funds must be deposited or the position must be closed. This notification is known as a margin call. If the customer does not deposit the required funds and does not close the position, the broker has the authority to close the position without the customer's permission.

Should a trader who receives a margin call deposit more money or close the position? This is a decision that only the trader can make, and there is no right or wrong answer. The important point is that every open futures position is backed by at least the exchange's minimum margin requirement. If Ramona deposits sufficient additional funds, the exchange minimum is met. If she closes her position by purchasing a contract in the marketplace, another party will make the required deposit. In either case, both the long and short sides of all open futures contracts are backed by at least the minimum margin balance required by the exchange.

CALL OPTIONS

A *call option* is a contract between the call buyer (or owner) and the call writer (or seller). A call option gives its owner the right, but not the obligation, to buy some underlying instrument from the call writer at a specified price until a specified date. The writer, however, is obligated to deliver the underlying if instructed to do so. It is "the right, but not the obligation," of the buyer that distinguishes an option contract from a futures contract. A futures contract, remember, obligates both the buyer and the seller. The underlying instrument may be a stock, a bond, a physical commodity, or a futures contract. In this book, it is assumed that one futures contract is the underlying instrument for each option. Options that have one futures contract as the underlying instrument sometimes are described as "options on futures" or "futures options."

This distinguishes them from "stock options," "index options," and other types of options.

Strike Price and Expiration Date

The *srtike price* (or *exercise price*) is the price specified in the option contract at which the underlying futures contract is traded if the call is exercised. The *expiration date* is the date specified in the option contract, and it is the date after which the right contained in the option ceases to exist. The expiration date for options on futures is generally the Saturday following the Friday before the last full week before the first notice day for delivery of the underlying futures contract. For example, if July 1, a Wednesday, is the first notice day for July futures, options on those July futures will expire 11 days earlier, on Saturday, June 20. Options expire on a Saturday for technical reasons related to trade clearing and error resolution. The last day options can be traded and exercised is typically a Friday, which is the last business day before the Saturday expiration.

Premium

The term *premium* simply refers to the price, or cost, of an option. An option's premium is paid by the option buyer and is received by the option seller. At futures exchanges in the United States, option buyers have no margin requirement after they pay for an option. Option sellers, however, do have margin requirements, and those requirements change as prices of the underlying futures contracts change.

Rights and Obligations

Call owners have the right to buy

Call writers have the obligation to sell

The buyer of one September 2.80 Wheat Call has the right, but not the obligation, to purchase one September Wheat Futures contract from the call writer at a price of $2.80 (per bushel) at any time up to the expiration date. The call writer, in contrast, has an obligation to deliver one September Wheat Futures contract. The obligation is a contingent obligation until the call owner exercises the right to buy. If the call owner exercises, however, the call writer must deliver the contract.

Long Call and Short Call

The call buyer is described as having a *long call* position. "Long," in this context, means "own." As experienced traders know, it can also mean "bullish," as in "long the market."

The call writer is described a having a *short call* position, and in this context, "short" means "open written position" or "obligation." It can also mean "bearish."

Exercise (and Exercise Notice) and Assignment (and Notice of Assignment)

Exercise occurs when the call owner declares the right to buy a futures contract from the call seller and makes the proper notifications. *Assignment* occurs when a call writer is notified that a call owner has exercised the right to buy and that a futures contract must be sold. The process by which exercise and assignment occur is as follows. When a call owner decides to exercise, the first step is to notify the brokerage firm. The brokerage firm then submits an *exercise notice* to the clearing corporation of the exchange where the option is traded. It is the clearing corporation that guarantees the performance of option con-

> **Option owners exercise**
>
> **Option writers are assigned**

tracts. The clearing corporation then makes a random selection of a brokerage firm with a short call position that matches the long call being exercised. That brokerage firm in turn selects at random a customer with a short call position and notifies that customer, through an *assignment notice*, that the option has been assigned. At this point, a futures transaction has occurred: The call owner is the buyer of the futures contract, and the call writer is the seller. The price of this transaction is the strike price of the option (plus or minus commissions).

A call option ceases to exist after one of two events occurs. First, if the call owner exercises the right to purchase, the call writer must fulfill the terms of the contract. After exercise, the option no longer exists, but a futures contract has been purchased. If an August 8500 Feeder Cattle Call is exercised, for example, the exerciser purchases an August Feeder Cattle Futures contract at 85 cents per pound and must make the appropriate margin deposit. Second, a call ceases to exist if it is not exercised before expiration. In this case, the option is said to "expire worthless."

Position after Exercise and Assignment

Both the call owner and the call writer will have changed positions and margin requirements after a call is exercised. Figure 1–1 summarizes the changes. For the call owner, an exercised call creates a futures purchase transaction (one contract per option). If there was initially no futures position, exercising a call creates a long futures position at the strike price of the call, and an appropriate margin must be deposited. If, however, a short futures position existed on a one-for-one basis with the long calls, exercising a call purchases futures contracts that offset the short futures position, and the result is no position.

For the call writer, assignment of a call means that a futures sale transaction is created. If the call writer had no futures position, assignment of a short call creates a short futures position at the strike price of the call, and appropriate margin must be deposited. If, however, a long futures position existed on a one-for-one basis with the short calls, the assigned call writer sells futures contracts that offset the long futures position. The result is no position.

Figure 1–1 Call Options: Changed Positions after Exercise or Assignment

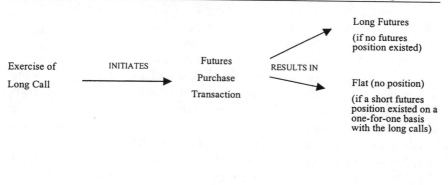

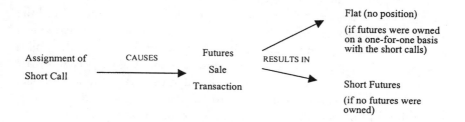

Effective Purchase Price and Effective Selling Price

The price at which the call was bought and sold is significant, because it is an important factor in the ultimate price of the futures transaction. The *effective purchase price* is the price of purchasing a futures contract that takes into account the price of the option. The *effective selling price* is the price of selling a futures contract which takes into account the price of the option. The following example illustrates this point.

> **FOR CALLS**
> Effective purchase price =
> strike plus call premium =
> effective selling price

If a 2.50 Corn Call that was purchased for .20, or 20 cents, is exercised, the effective purchase price of the corn futures transaction is 2.70. This price is calculated by adding the call price to its strike price on a per-unit basis. For the assigned call writer, the effective selling price of the futures is also 2.70: .20 was received for selling the call, and a short futures position at 2.50 is created when assignment occurs. The general formula — strike price plus call premium — applies equally to the call writer as the effective selling price and to the call buyer as the effective purchase price.

American-Style Exercise and European-Style Exercise

An option subject to *American-style exercise* is one in which the right granted by the option may be exercised at any time before the expiration date. An option subject to *European-style exercise*, however, may be exercised only on the last trading day before established deadlines. In the United States, all futures options are American-style.

> **AMERICAN OPTIONS**
> Early Exercise: YES

> **EUROPEAN OPTIONS**
> Early Exercise: NO

In-the-Money, At-the-Money, and Out-of-the-Money

The relationship of the futures price to the strike price determines whether an option is in-the-money, at-the-money, or out-of-the-money. An *in-the-money call* has a strike price below the current futures price. If a futures is trading at 6.00, for example, the 5.75 Call is in-the-money. To be precise, it is 25 cents in-the-money. This call, however, is not necessarily trading for 25 cents. In fact, it is very likely to be trading for more than 25 cents. Why options trade for more than the in-the-money amount is discussed in Chapter 4.

An *out-of-the-money call* has a strike price above the current futures price. For example, with futures trading at 6.00, the 6.25 Call option is out-of-the-money. Specifically, this call is out-of-the-money by 25 cents.

At-the-money means the futures price is equal to the strike price. This term has both a strict definition and a looser common usage. Theoretically, the 6.00 Call is at-the-money only when the underlying futures is trading exactly at 6.00. The rest of the time, it is either in-the-money or out-of-the-money. In practice, however, the 6.00 Call is designated as an at-the-money call when the futures price is closer to that strike price than it is to another strike price. With a futures trading at 5.94 or 6.08, for example, it is common practice to refer to the 6.00 Call as the at-the-money call.

In-the-money, at-the-money, and *out-of-the-money* are dynamic terms. As futures prices rise, out-of-the-money calls become at-the-money and then in-the-money. As futures prices fall, the opposite happens: In-the-money calls become at-the-money and, subsequently, out-of-the-money.

Intrinsic Value and Time Value

As was noted earlier, the term *premium* refers to the price of an option. This premium, or price, consists of two parts: intrinsic value and time value. *Intrinsic value* refers to the in-the-money amount of an option's price, and *time value* refers to any portion of an option's price that exceeds intrinsic value. Consider a situation in which the following prices exist:

	Price (per bushel)
Futures	6.00
5.75 Call	.32
6.00 Call	.18
6.25 Call	.09

An analysis of each option's premium (or price) will illustrate the concepts of intrinsic value and time value. First, examine the 5.75 Call, which is an in-the-money call. The futures price of 6.00 is 25 cents above the strike price. Consequently, the 5.75 Call is 25 cents in-the-money and therefore has 25 cents of intrinsic value. The premium (or price) of the 5.75 Call, however, is 32 cents. The difference of 7 cents is the time value.

The 18-cent premium of the at-the-money 6.00 Call consists entirely of time value. The premium of the out-of-the-money 6.25 Call —

Figure 1–2 Call Options: Intrinsic Value and Time Value

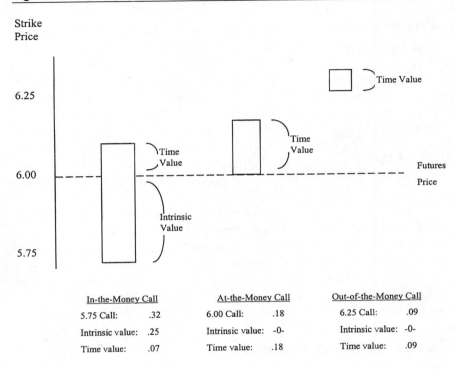

In-the-Money Call		At-the-Money Call		Out-of-the-Money Call	
5.75 Call:	.32	6.00 Call:	.18	6.25 Call:	.09
Intrinsic value:	.25	Intrinsic value:	-0-	Intrinsic value:	-0-
Time value:	.07	Time value:	.18	Time value:	.09

9 cents — also consists entirely of time value. Figure 1–2 illustrates intrinsic value and time value for in-, at-, and out-of-the-money calls.

Competition in the market makes it extremely unlikely that in-the-money options will trade for less than intrinsic value. Assume, for example, a soybean futures price of 6.10. If the 6.00 Call were trading for .05, traders could buy the call, exercise it immediately, and sell the futures for 6.10. Since the effective purchase price of the futures in this example is 6.05 (strike, 6.00, + call premium, .05), the result would be an immediate profit of 5 cents (not including transaction costs). A profit opportunity of this nature would attract many professional traders. Competition between professional traders would force the call price up and/or the futures price down, reducing the 5-cent profit to an amount slightly greater than transaction costs. Since transaction costs for professional traders are very low, options rarely trade below intrinsic value. When they do, it is very near to the expiration date and the amount below intrinsic value is only one-eighth or one-quarter of a cent.

PUT OPTIONS

Put owners have the right to sell

Put writers have the obligation to buy

A *put option* gives the put buyer (or owner) the right, but not the obligation, to sell a futures contract to the put writer (or seller). The put writer, in contrast, has an obligation to buy the contract. The obligation is a contingent obligation until the put owner exercises. If the put owner exercises, however, the put writer must buy the contract. In the case of put options subject to American-style exercise, the right to sell may be exercised at any time before the expiration date. In the case of European-style options, the right to sell may be exercised only on the last day of trading before established deadlines. Do not forget that option owners can close their position on any business day by selling their options in the marketplace. As was stated earlier, all futures options in the United States are subject to American-style exercise.

The put buyer is described as having a *long put* position, and the put seller is described as having a *short put* position. The process by which puts are exercised and assigned is identical to that for calls described above.

Position after Exercise and Assignment

As with calls, put owners and put writers will have changed positions after a put is exercised. Figure 1–3 summarizes the changes. For the put owner, an exercised long put creates a futures sale transaction, and a short futures position is created if there is no existing long futures position. If, however, the put owner has a long futures position on a one-for-one basis with the puts, the put exercise sells the futures contracts and leaves the former put and futures owner with no position.

For the put writer, assignment of a short put creates a futures purchase transaction. If no position existed initially, assignment of a short put creates a long futures position. If, however, a short futures position existed on a one-for-one basis with the short puts, the put assignment purchases futures contracts that offset the existing short position. The result in this case is no position.

Effective Purchase Price and Effective Selling Price

The price at which a put is transacted is significant, because it is an important factor in the ultimate price of the futures transaction. Consider a 2.50

Figure 1–3 Put Options: Changed Positions after Exercise or Assignment

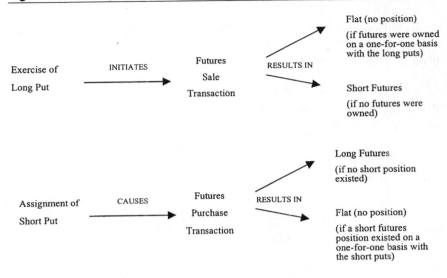

Put that is purchased for .15, or 15 cents. For the put owner who exercises this put and, consequently, sells futures, the effective selling price is 2.35. The futures contract is sold at 2.50 in accordance with the terms of the put option contract, but .15 was paid for the put, and this reduces the net amount received to 2.35. Similarly, for the assigned put writer, the 15 cents received lowers the effective price paid for the futures from 2.50 to 2.35. The general formula — strike price minus put premium — applies equally to the put writer as the effective purchase price and to the put buyer as the effective selling price.

> **FOR PUTS**
> **Effective purchase price =
> strike minus put premium =
> effective selling price**

In-the-Money, At-the-Money, and Out-of-the-Money Puts

The relationship to the strike price of at-the-money puts and out-of-the-money puts is the opposite of that for calls. An *in-the-money put* has a strike price above the current futures price and an *out-of-the-money put* has a strike price below the current futures price. Consider a situation in which a futures is trading at 3.80. The 4.00 Put is in-the-money; specifically, it is 20 cents in-the-money. The 3.60 Put is out-of-the-money by 20 cents. The 3.80

Put is at-the-money. The term *at-the-money* applies to puts in a similar way that it applies to calls. If the futures price is at or very close to the strike price of the option, that option is referred to as an *at-the-money put.*

Intrinsic Value and Time Value

As with calls, *premium* refers to the price of a put, and it consists of two parts: intrinsic value and time value. Consider a situation in which the following prices exist:

	Price (per bushel)
Futures	3.80
3.60 Put	.06
3.80 Put	.13
4.00 Put	.25

Figure 1–4 Put Options: Intrinsic Value and Time Value

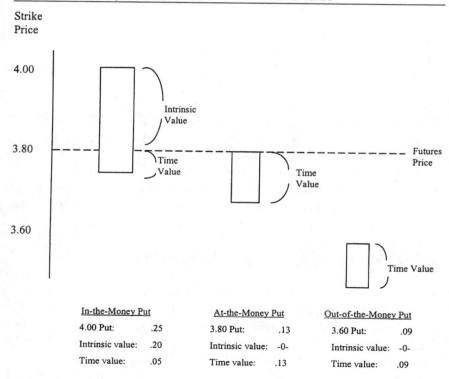

Strike
Price

In-the-Money Put	At-the-Money Put	Out-of-the-Money Put
4.00 Put: .25	3.80 Put: .13	3.60 Put: .09
Intrinsic value: .20	Intrinsic value: -0-	Intrinsic value: -0-
Time value: .05	Time value: .13	Time value: .09

The 4.00 Put is 20 cents in the money. It therefore has 20 cents of intrinsic value and 5 cents of time value. The 3.80 Put premium of 13 cents consists entirely of time value, and the 6-cent price of the out-of-the-money 3.60 Put also consists entirely of time value. Figure 1–4 illustrates intrinsic value and time value for in-, at-, and out-of-the-money puts.

SUMMARY OF DEFINITIONS: A QUIZ

This chapter concludes with the following quiz. Match the terms with their correct definitions – that is, fill in the number of the appropriate definition in the space provided next to each term. Note that some terms may have the same meaning as other terms, and some definitions may be used twice. The answers appear immediately after the definitions.

Terms

Long futures	_____	In-the-money put	_____
Short futures	_____	At-the-money put	_____
Long call	_____	Out-of-the-money put	_____
Short call	_____	Initial margin	_____
Long put	_____	Minimum margin	_____
Short put	_____	Maintenance margin	_____
Strike price	_____	Margin call	_____
Delivery date	_____	Premium	_____
Exercise price	_____	Intrinsic value	_____
Expiration date	_____	Time value	_____
Exercise	_____	Effective purchase price: long call	_____
Exercise notice	_____	Effective selling price: short call	_____
Assignment	_____	Effective purchase price: short put	_____
European-style option	_____	Effective selling price: long put	_____
American-style option	_____		
In-the-money call	_____		
At-the-money call	_____		
Out-of-the-money call	_____		

Definitions

1. A form presented to the clearing corporation of an exchange by a broker demanding that the terms of an option contract be fulfilled

2. A position which involves the obligation to buy a standardized good for an agreed-upon price at a specific date

3. A put option with a strike price above the current futures price

4. The process by which a short option position is selected as the one to make good on its contingent obligation

5. A call option with a strike price equal to the current futures price

6. The total price of an option

7. The portion of an option's total price that is in excess of the intrinsic value

8. Strike price minus premium

9. A call option with a strike price below the current futures price

10. A put option with a strike price equal to the current futures price

11. A call option with a strike price above the current futures price

12. Strike price plus premium

13. A position that involves the obligation to buy an underlying instrument at a specified price on or before a specified date if an assignment notice is received

14. An option that may be exercised only on the last trading day before established deadlines.

15. The portion of an option's total price that is equal to the in-the-money amount

16. A put option with a strike price below the current futures price

17. The deposit required when establishing a futures position that demonstrates the financial ability to fulfill the terms of that position

18. A position which involves the right, but not the obligation, to buy some underlying instrument at a specified price before a specified date

19. The level, expressed as an absolute dollar amount, at or above which account equity must be maintained

20. A position which involves the right, but not the obligation, to sell some underlying instrument at a specified price before a specified date

21. The price specified in an option contract

22. Demand that the terms of an option contract be fulfilled

23. A notice from a brokerage firm that the account equity must be raised to the maintenance level or the position will be closed

24. An option that may be exercised at any time before the expiration date

25. The date specified in a futures contract when the standardized good must be transferred from the seller to the buyer

26. The date after which an option ceases to exist

27. A position that involves the obligation to sell some underlying instrument at a specified price before a specified date if an assignment notice is received

28. The level of account equity to which an account balance must be raised when a margin call is received

29. A position which involves the obligation to sell a standardized good for an agreed-upon price at a specific date in the future

Answers

Out-of-the-money call	11	Effective selling price: long put	8
At-the-money call	5	Effective purchase price: short put	8
In-the-money call	9	Effective selling price: short call	12
American-style option	24	Effective purchase price: long call	12
European-style option	14	Time value	7
Assignment	4	Intrinsic value	15
Exercise notice	1	Premium	9
Exercise	22	Margin call	23
Expiration date	26	Maintenance margin	28
Exercise price	21	Minimum margin	19
Delivery date	25	Initial margin	17
Strike price	21	Out-of-the-money put	16
Short put	13	At-the-money put	10
Long put	20	In-the-money put	3
Short call	27		
Long call	18		
Short futures	29		
Long futures	2		

TWO

Diagrams of Basic Trading Strategies

A requirement for understanding and using futures and options success-fully is the ability to draw profit and loss diagrams. Although many readers already have seen the graphs explained in this chapter, there is a difference between seeing them and truly understanding them. If you are not sure of your ability to draw these diagrams, you must take the time to study this chapter. Anyone who can draw expiration profit and loss diagrams is well on the way to understanding futures and options. A firm grasp of the concepts presented in this chapter, will greatly enhance your abil-ity to match strategies with objectives. The skills developed in this chapter will serve you well throughout your hedging and trading career. This chapter explains futures-only and options-only strategies. Later chapters discuss hedg-ing strategies and more advanced trading strategies that combine the two.

FUTURES VERSUS OPTIONS

Although there are some similarities between hedging and trading with options and hedging and trading with futures, the differences are significant. One similarity is that the decision to initiate an option or futures position involves a consequence on the expiration date (the delivery date in the case of futures), assuming that the position is not closed before that time. A dif-ference, however, is that, for options, the consequence depends on the underlying futures price. Another similarity is that both futures and options have limited time frames, and positions must be established with a keen awareness of time. Another difference is that option strategies involve many risk-reward trade-offs, while futures contracts involve only one. Option strategies, in fact, open a range of hedging and trading alternatives; the pos-itives and negatives of these alternatives will be discussed throughout this book. Another difference is that option strategies have different break-even points than do futures strategies.

WHAT A DIAGRAM IDENTIFIES

Strategy analysis begins with the basics. When completed, an expiration profit and loss diagram reveals many things about a strategy, such as profit potential, risk potential, and break-even points. Hedgers and traders also need to know what futures position is created if an option is in-the-money at expiration. An in-the-money long call at expiration, for example, is assumed to be exercised and thus to create a futures purchase transaction. These are important things to know because, looked at as a whole, they illustrate the trade-off a strategy offers. A trade-off involves benefits and risks, and an understanding of trade-offs will lead to strategy comparisons and thus, improve the decision-making process by clarifying choices.

> **P/(L) diagrams reveal many aspects of a strategy**

PROFIT AND LOSS DIAGRAMS: BASIC STEPS

A profit and loss diagram can be created by following six basic steps.

Step 1   Describe the opening transaction completely.

Write down in words the transaction you want to diagram, for example, "buy a November 6.00 Call for 28 cents" or "sell a March 2.10 Put at 4 ¼." It is not sufficient to write "buy a call" or "sell a put," because you will not have enough information to complete the diagram.

Step 2   Start a grid and a profit and loss table.

A profit and loss diagram is drawn on a grid that shows the profit or loss of a strategy over a range of possible futures prices. The vertical grid line represents profit (+) or loss (–). The horizontal grid line represents a range of futures prices. When making a grid, start with the option strike price or the futures entry price in the middle of the horizontal grid line and work out in each direction. Figure 2–1 shows a sample grid.

Profit and loss calculations are easily made and clearly presented if a table such as Table 2–1 is used. The leftmost column indicates the range of futures prices that appear on the grid. Tables for simple option strategies contain only one column that indicates the profit or loss of the strategy at each futures price at expiration. Tables for more complicated strategies have columns for the profit or loss of each component of the strategy and a column for the strategy's total profit or loss. Table 2–1 is an example of a table used for a strategy with two components.

Figure 2–1 Sample Profit and Loss Grid

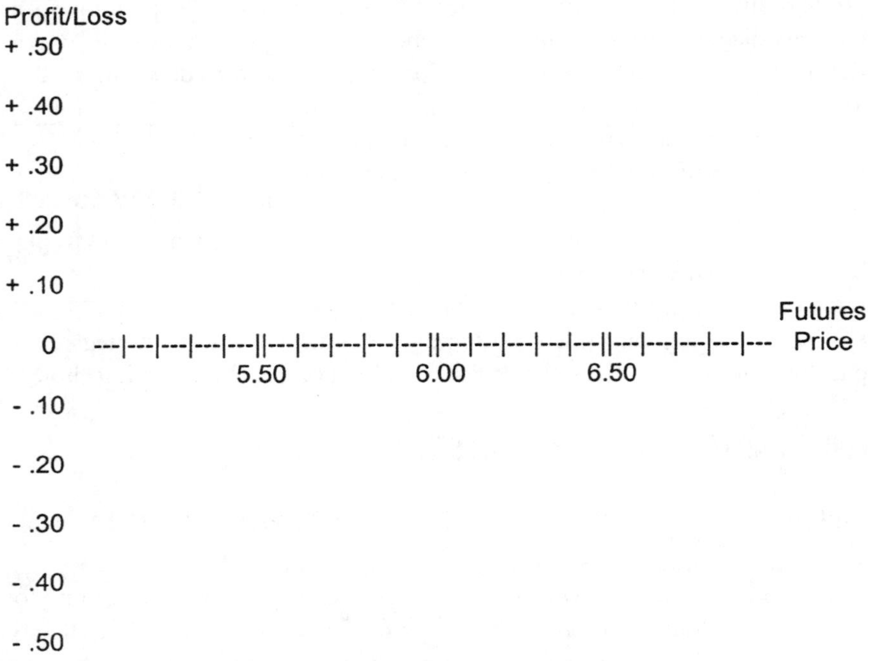

Profit/Loss

+ .50

+ .40

+ .30

+ .20

+ .10

                                                                    Futures

  0   ---|---|---|---|---||---|---|---|---|---||---|---|---|---|---||---|---|---|---|--- Price

                5.50   6.00   6.50

- .10

- .20

- .30

- .40

- .50

Step 3   Select a futures price and calculate the option's value at expiration.

At expiration, an option will be worth either the intrinsic value (the in-the-money amount) or zero. Intrinsic value was introduced in Chapter 1. If the futures price is 5.76, for example, the September 5.50 Call is worth .26 at expiration. If the futures price is 5.44, this call is worth zero at expiration. To start your profit and loss calculations, choose a futures price within the range of prices on the grid and the table and determine the value of the option.

Step 4   Calculate the profit or loss.

For an option that is purchased, calculate the profit or loss by subtracting the purchase price of the option from its value at expiration as determined in step 3. A 5.50 Call, that is purchased for .12 with an expiration value of .26 will show a profit of .14 (value of .26 minus the purchase price of .12). The same call with an expiration value of zero will show a loss of .12 (value of -0- minus the purchase price of .12). For an

Table 2–1 Sample Table for a Two-Component Option Strategy

Futures Price at Expiration	Option Position 1 Profit / (Loss)	Option Position 2 Profit / (Loss)	Total Strategy Profit / (Loss)
6.40			
6.30			
6.20			
6.10			
6.00			
5.90			

option that is sold, the profit or loss is calculated by subtracting the value at expiration from the selling price. A 2.80 Put that is sold at 8¼ with the futures price above 2.80 at expiration has a value of zero and will yield a profit of 8¼. The same put with an expiration value of .12, with the futures price at 2.68, will show a loss of 3¾.

Step 5 Chart the profit or loss.

Place a dot on the grid above (if a profit) or below (if a loss) the selected futures price at a point even with the profit or loss calculated in step 4. Figure 2–2 shows the placement of a profit of .10 taken from Table 2–2. In this example, the 6.00 Call was purchased for .20 and, with a futures price of 6.30, had an expiration value of .30.

Step 6 Repeat steps 3, 4, and 5 until the diagram is complete.

Steps 3, 4, and 5 should be repeated over the range of futures prices on the grid. As dots are placed on the grid, a complete profit and loss diagram will emerge. The dots can be connected and will always form straight lines, although sometimes different segments of the lines will have different slopes.

Diagrams of basic futures positions are presented first. It is always helpful to start on familiar ground! Single-option strategies are presented second, and then four two-option strategies are diagrammed. More complicated strategies will be presented in later chapters.

Long and Short Futures

Figure 2–3 illustrates the strategy of buying futures at 6.00. Table 2–3 contains the profit and loss results on a per-bushel basis. This is how the prices

Figure 2–2 Charting a Profit or Loss

6.00 Call was purchased for .20
Futures price at expiration is 6.30
Profit is .10

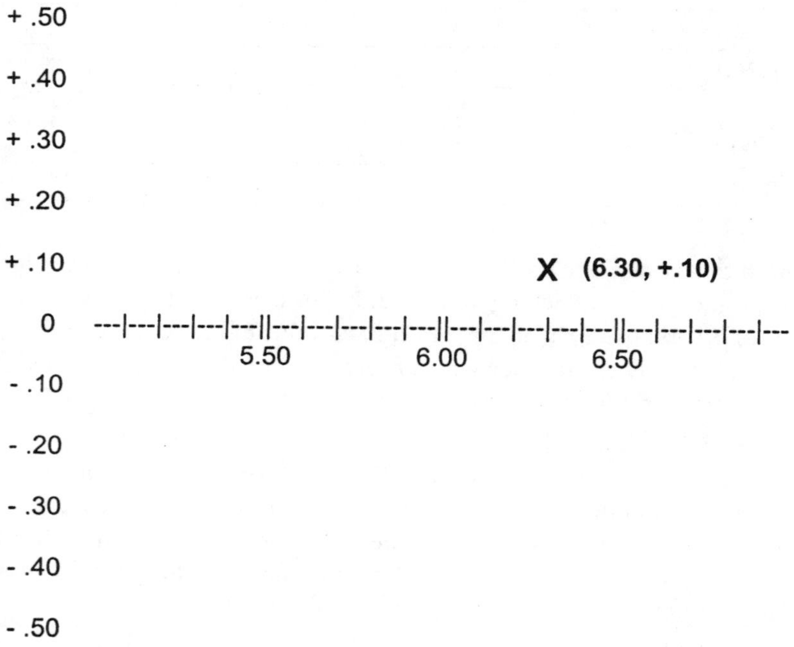

+ .50

+ .40

+ .30

+ .20

+ .10   **X (6.30, +.10)**

  0   ---|---|---|---|---||---|---|---|---|---||---|---|---|---|---||---|---|---|---|---
                  5.50   6.00   6.50
 - .10

 - .20

 - .30

 - .40

 - .50

Table 2–2 Illustration of Profit Entered in Table

6.00 Call Purchased for .20

Futures at 6.30 at expiration

Profit of .10

Futures Price at Expiration	Long 6.00 Call at .20 Profit / (Loss)
6.40	
6.30	+ .10
6.20	
6.10	
6.00	
5.90	
5.80	

Figure 2–3 Long Futures at 6.00

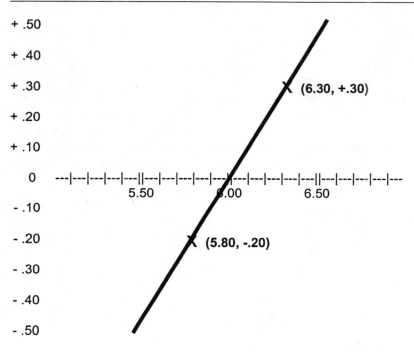

Table 2–3 Long Futures at 6.00: Profit and Loss Calculations

Futures Price at Expiration	Long Futures at 6.00 Profit / (Loss)	Futures Price at Expiration	Long Futures at 6.00 Profit / (Loss)
6.50	+ .50	5.90	− .10
6.40	+ .40	5.80	− .20
6.30	+ .30	5.70	− .30
6.20	+ .20	5.60	− .40
6.10	+ .10	5.50	− .50
6.00	.00	5.40	− .60

of agricultural futures contracts and options on those contracts typically are quoted. The potential results are straightforward: Buying futures will result in a profit if the price rises and a loss if the price falls. The two marks on the line in Figure 2–3 correspond to two rows in Table 2–3: 6.30 and 5.80. A 30-cent profit results if the futures is sold at 6.30. A 20-cent loss is realized if the futures is sold at 5.80. The slope of the line in Figure 2–3 is 1 × 1, the profit or loss changes by 1 cent for every 1-cent change in the futures price.

Figure 2–4 illustrates the strategy of selling futures short at 6.00, and Table 2–4 contains the profit and loss results. Selling short results in a profit if the futures price falls and a loss if the price rises. The line in Figure 2–4 has a –1 × 1 slope; the profit or loss changes by 1 cent in the opposite direction for every 1-cent change in the futures price.

Figure 2–4 Short Futures at 6.00

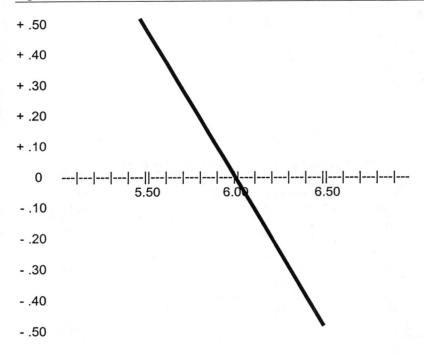

Table 2–4 Short Futures at 6.00: Profit and Loss Calculations

Futures Price at Expiration	Short Futures at 6.00 Profit / (Loss)	Futures Price at Expiration	Short Futures at 6.00 Profit / (Loss)
6.50	− .50	5.90	+ .10
6.40	− .40	5.80	+ .20
6.30	− .30	5.70	+ .30
6.20	− .20	5.60	+ .40
6.10	− .10	5.50	+ .50
6.00	.00	5.40	+ .60

Basic Option Strategies

We are now ready to tackle option strategies. Profit and loss diagrams for four single-option strategies will be presented first and then four two-option strategies will be diagrammed. For each strategy, the important price points will be identified and the strategy characteristics will be discussed.

Unless otherwise stated, the price of the underlying futures contract is assumed to be 6.00 when the option position is established. It is also assumed that each futures contract covers 5,000 bushels.

Strategy: Long Call

Example: Buy a 6.00 Call at .20

Step 1   Describe the opening transaction completely.
Buy a 6.00 Call at .20.

Step 2   Start a grid and a profit and loss table.
Use a grid like the one in Figure 2–1 and a table like Table 2–1.

Step 3   Select a futures price and calculate the option's value at expiration.
With the futures at 6.00 at expiration, the 6.00 Call is worth zero.

Step 4   Calculate the profit or loss.
Loss of .20 (0 value minus .20 purchase price = .20 loss).

Step 5   Chart the profit or loss.
Figure 2–5A shows a dot indicating a .20 loss at the strike price of 6.00.

Step 6   Repeat steps 3, 4, and 5 until the diagram is completed.
Profit and loss results over a range of futures prices from 5.40 to 6.50 are presented in Table 2–5. Figure 2–5B shows a second dot indicating a profit of .20 at 6.40, and Figure 2–5C shows a third dot indicating a loss of .20 at 5.60. Figure 2–5D shows the completed profit and loss diagram.

Observations About the Long Call

Break-even point:	6.20. This is calculated by adding the premium paid for the call to the strike price. In this case, 6.00 + .20 = 6.20.
Maximum risk:	This is limited to .20 (per bushel). No matter how much the futures price declines, purchasing the 6.00 Call can result in losing only the premium paid for the call.
Profit potential:	This is unlimited. If the futures price rises dramatically, the option value will rise as well.
Position created if option is in-the-money:	The long call becomes a long futures contract if the futures price is above the strike at expiration. (In expiration profit and loss diagrams, it is assumed that all in-the-money long options are exercised.)
Trade-off:	The positive aspect is that risk is limited to .20 per bushel. This is positive relative to owning a futures contract that has the theoretical risk of the futures price falling to zero and the entire 6.00 per bushel being lost. The negative aspect is a higher break-even point, 6.20, for buying the call compared to 6.00 for buying futures in this example.
Desired price price action:	Bullish. A profit, at expiration, occurs only if the futures rises above 6.20.

Figure 2–5 Long 6.00 Call at .20

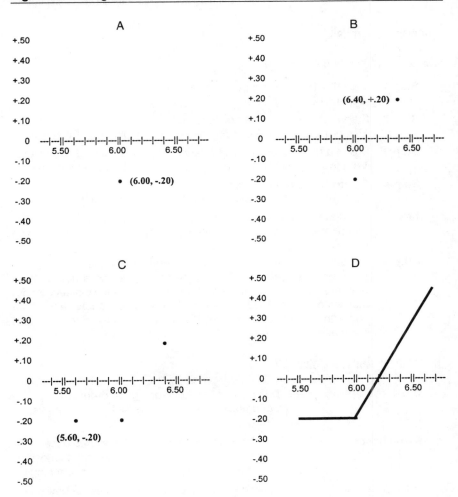

Table 2–5 Long 6.00 Call at .20: Profit and Loss Calculations

Futures Price at Expiration	Long 6.00 Call at .20 Profit / (Loss)	Futures Price at Expiration	Long 6.00 Call at .20 Profit / (Loss)
6.50	+ .30	5.90	− .20
6.40	+ .20	5.80	− .20
6.30	+ .10	5.70	− .20
6.20	.00	5.60	− .20
6.10	− .10	5.50	− .20
6.00	− .20	5.40	− .20

Strategy: Short Call

Example: Sell a 6.00 Call at .20

Step 1   Describe the opening transaction completely.
Sell a 6.00 Call at .20.

Step 2   Start a grid and a profit and loss table.
Use a grid like the one in Figure 2–1 and a table like Table 2–1.

Step 3   Select a futures price and calculate the option's value at expiration.
With the futures at 6.00 at expiration, the 6.00 Call is worth zero.

Step 4   Calculate the profit or loss.
Profit of .20 (.20 sale price minus 0 value = .20 profit).

Step 5   Chart the profit or loss.
Figure 2–6A shows a dot indicating a .20 profit at the strike price of 6.00.

Step 6   Repeat steps 3, 4, and 5 until the diagram is completed.
Profit and loss results over a range of futures prices from 5.40 to 6.50 are presented in Table 2–6. Figure 2–6B shows a second dot indicating a loss of .20 at 6.40, and Figure 2–6C shows a third dot indicating a profit of .20 at 5.60. Figure 2–6D shows the completed profit and loss diagram.

Observations About the Short Call

Break-even point:	6.20. This is calculated by adding the premium received for selling the call to the strike price. In this case, 6.00 + .20 = 6.20.
Maximum risk:	The potential risk is unlimited. As the futures price rises, the value of the 6.00 Call will rise, and the loss from a short call position will increase correspondingly.
Profit potential:	This is limited to .20 per bushel. Regardless of how much the futures price falls, the option value at expiration can drop only to zero, earning a profit of .20 per bushel.
Position created if option is in-the-money:	The short call becomes a short futures contract if the futures price is above the strike at expiration. (In expiration profit and loss diagrams, it is assumed that all in-the-money short options are assigned.)
Trade-off:	The positive aspect is a higher break-even point, 6.20 for the short call versus 6.00 for the short futures position in this example. The negative aspect is that profit potential is limited to the call premium received, while a short futures position has the theoretical profit potential of the futures price falling to -0-.
Desired price action:	Neutral/bearish. Profit potential in a neutral market is significant, because this aspect of some option strategies cannot be achieved with futures contracts alone.

Figure 2–6 Short 6.00 Call at .20

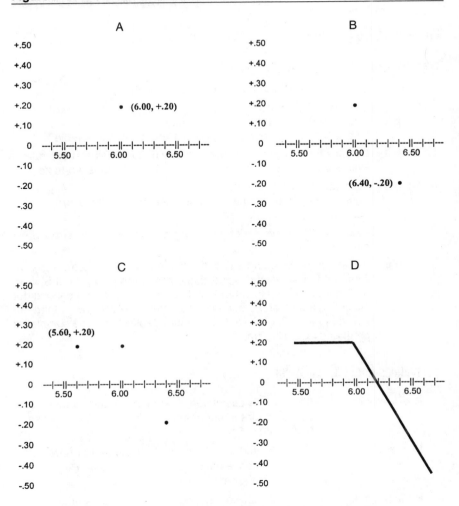

A

```
+.50
+.40
+.30
+.20                    • (6.00, +.20)
+.10
  0  ---|---||---|---|---|---|---||---|---|---|---|---||---|---|---
        5.50          6.00          6.50
-.10
-.20
-.30
-.40
-.50
```

B

```
+.50
+.40
+.30
+.20                    •
+.10
  0  ---|---||---|---|---|---|---||---|---|---|---|---||---|---|---
        5.50          6.00          6.50
-.10
-.20      (6.40, -.20) •
-.30
-.40
-.50
```

C

```
+.50
+.40
+.30      (5.60, +.20)
+.20         •          •
+.10
  0  ---|---||---|---|---|---|---||---|---|---|---|---|---||---|---|---
        5.50          6.00          6.50
-.10
-.20                          •
-.30
-.40
-.50
```

D

```
+.50
+.40
+.30
+.20
+.10
  0  ---|---||---|---|---|---|---||---|---|---|---|---||---|---|---
        5.50          6.00          6.50
-.10
-.20
-.30
-.40
-.50
```

Table 2–6 Short 6.00 Call at .20: Profit and Loss Calculations

Futures Price at Expiration	Short 6.00 Call at .20 Profit / (Loss)	Futures Price at Expiration	Short 6.00 Call at .20 Profit / (Loss)
6.50	– .30	5.90	+ .20
6.40	– .20	5.80	+ .20
6.30	– .10	5.70	+ .20
6.20	.00	5.60	+ .20
6.10	+ .10	5.50	+ .20
6.00	+ .20	5.40	+ .20

31

Strategy: Long Put

Example: Buy a 6.00 Put at .20

Step 1   Describe the opening transaction completely.
Buy a 6.00 Put at .20.

Step 2   Start a grid and a profit and loss table.
Use a grid like the one in Figure 2–1 and a table like Table 2–1.

Step 3   Select a futures price and calculate the option's value at expiration.
With the futures at 6.00 at expiration, the 6.00 Put is worth zero.

Step 4   Calculate the profit or loss.
Loss of .20 (0 value minus .20 purchase price = .20 loss).

Step 5   Chart the profit or loss.
Figure 2–7A shows a dot indicating a .20 loss at the strike price of 6.00.

Step 6   Repeat steps 3, 4, and 5 until the diagram is completed.
Profit and loss results over a range of futures prices from 5.40 to 6.50 are presented in Table 2–7. Figure 2–7B shows a second dot indicating a loss of .20 at 6.40, and Figure 2–7C shows a third dot indicating a profit of .20 at 5.60. Figure 2–5D shows the completed profit and loss diagram.

Observations About the Long Put

Break-even point: 5.80. This is calculated by subtracting the premium that was paid for the put from the strike price. In this case, 6.00 − .20 = 5.80.

Maximum risk: This is limited to .20 (per bushel). No matter how high the futures price rises, purchasing the 6.00 Put can lose only the premium paid.

Profit potential: This is limited to 5.80, because the futures price cannot fall below zero.

Position created if option is in-the-money: The long put becomes a short futures contract if the futures price is below the strike at expiration. (In expiration profit and loss diagrams, it is assumed that all long options are exercised.)

Trade-off: The positive aspect is that risk is limited to the premium paid, .20 per bushel in this example. This is positive relative to a short futures position, which has unlimited risk. The negative aspect is a lower break-even point, 5.80 for the long put compared to 6.00 for short futures in this example.

Desired price action: Bearish. A profit at expiration occurs only if the futures declines below 5.80 at expiration.

Figure 2–7 Long 6.00 Put at .20

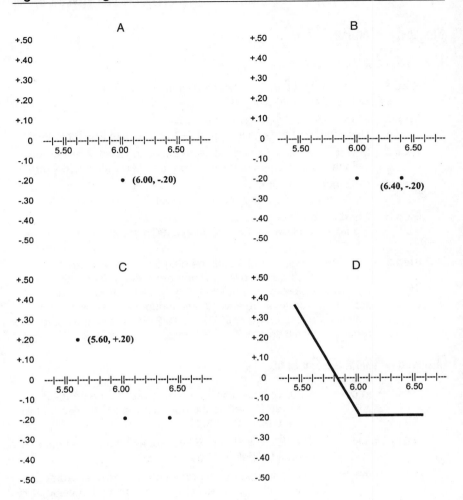

Table 2–7 Long 6.00 Put at .20: Profit and Loss Calculations

Futures Price at Expiration	Long 6.00 Put at .20 Profit / (Loss)	Futures Price at Expiration	Long 6.00 Put at .20 Profit / (Loss)
6.50	− .20	5.90	− .10
6.40	− .20	5.80	.00
6.30	− .20	5.70	+ .10
6.20	− .20	5.60	+ .20
6.10	− .20	5.50	+ .30
6.00	− .20	5.40	+ .40

Strategy: Short Put

Example   Sell a 6.00 Put at .20

Step 1   Describe the opening transaction completely.
Sell a 6.00 Put at .20.

Step 2   Start a grid and a profit and loss table.
Use a grid like the one in Figure 2–1 and a table like Table 2–1.

Step 3   Select a futures price and calculate the option's value at expiration.
With the futures at 6.00 at expiration, the 6.00 Put is worth zero.

Step 4   Calculate the profit or loss.
Profit of .20 (.20 sales price minus 0 value = .20 profit).

Step 5   Chart the profit or loss.
Figure 2–8A shows a dot indicating a .20 profit at the strike price of 6.00.

Step 6   Repeat steps 3, 4, and 5 until the diagram is completed.
Profit and loss results over a range of futures prices from 5.40 to 6.50 are presented in Table 2–8. Figure 2–8B shows a second dot indicating a profit of .20 at 6.40, and Figure 2–8C shows a third dot indicating a loss of .20 at 5.60. Figure 2–8D shows the completed profit and loss diagram.

Observations About the Short Put

Break-even point: 5.80. This is calculated by subtracting the premium received for selling the put from the strike price. In this case, 6.00 – .20 = 5.80.

Maximum risk: The risk is limited to 5.80, because the futures price cannot fall below zero.

Profit potential: This is limited to the premium received. Regardless of how much the futures price rises, the option value at expiration can drop only to zero, earning a profit of .20 per bushel in this example.

Position created
if option is
in-the-money: The short put becomes a long futures position if the futures price is below the strike at expiration. (In expiration profit and loss diagrams, it is assumed that short in-the-money options are assigned.)

Trade-off: The positive aspect is a lower break-even point, 5.80 for the short put versus 6.00 for the long futures position in this example. The negative aspect is that profit is limited to the put premium received, while a long futures position has an unlimited profit potential.

Desired price
action: Neutral/bullish. This is the second example of an option strategy that can make money in a neutral market. (The short call was the first example.)

Figure 2–8 Short 6.00 Put at .20: Profit and Loss Calculations

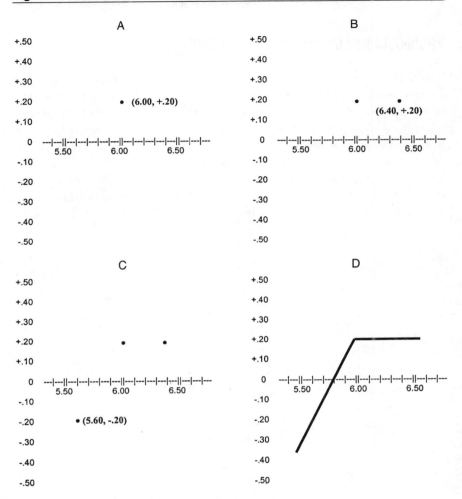

Table 2–8 Short 6.00 Put at .20: Profit and Loss Calculations

Futures Price at Expiration	Short 6.00 Put at .20 Profit / (Loss)	Futures Price at Expiration	Short 6.00 Put at .20 Profit / (Loss)
6.50	+ .20	5.90	+ .10
6.40	+ .20	5.80	.00
6.30	+ .20	5.70	− .10
6.20	+ .20	5.60	− .20
6.10	+ .20	5.50	− .30
6.00	+ .20	5.40	− .40

INTRODUCTION TO MULTIPLE-PART STRATEGIES

The ability to draw profit and loss diagrams for the six basic strategies just covered — long and short futures, long and short call, and long and short put — is essential for moving forward. The next step is to combine two basic strategies to create more advanced strategies. This process increases the number of strategies available to both hedgers and traders. Two strategies involving puts and calls will be presented first: the long straddle and the short straddle. The third and fourth strategies involve only calls: the bull call spread and the bear call spread. These four strategies will be diagramed and analyzed in the same manner as the basic strategies just presented.

Strategy: Long Straddle

Strategy defined: Buy both a call and a put with the same underlying, the
same strike price, and the same expiration date.

Example: Buy one 6.00 Call at .20 and buy one 6.00 Put at .20

Step 1   Describe the opening transaction completely.
Buy one 6.00 Call at .20, and buy one 6.00 Put at .20.

Step 2   Start a grid and a profit and loss table.
Preparation of a grid for a multiple-part strategy is no different than
for a single-option strategy. Use a grid like the one shown in Figure
2–1, but adjust the price range of the horizontal axis and the profit
and loss range of the vertical axis. Tables for multiple-part strategies require one column for each component of the strategy and
one column for the total or net profit. For a straddle, use a table with
three columns.

Step 3   Select a futures price and calculate the value of each option at
expiration.
With the futures price at 6.00 at expiration, both the 6.00 Call and
the 6.00 Put are worth zero.

Step 4   Calculate the profit or loss of each option and add the results
together.

Total loss of .40
(the call: -0- value minus .20 purchase price = .20 loss
the put: -0- value minus .20 purchase price = .20 loss
total: .20 loss on call plus .20 loss on put   = .40 loss)

Step 5   Chart the total profit or loss.
Figure 2–9A shows a dot indicating a .40 loss at 6.00.

Step 6   Repeat steps 3, 4, and 5 until the diagram is completed.
Profit and loss results over a range of futures prices from 5.00 to
7.00 are presented in Table 2–9. Figure 2–9B shows a second dot
indicating a profit of .40 at 6.80, and Figure 2–9C shows a third dot
indicating a profit of .40 at 5.20. Figure 2–9D shows the completed
profit and loss diagram.

Figure 2–9 Long 6.00 Straddle at .40

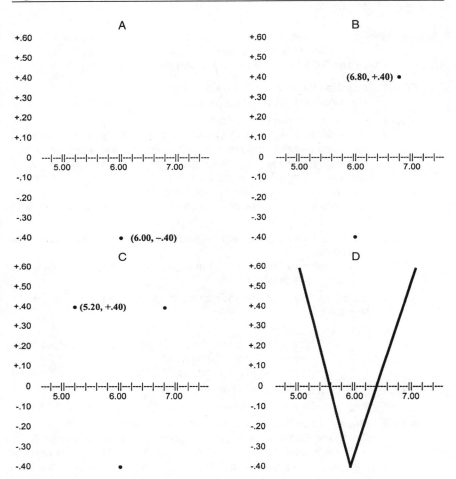

Table 2–9 Long 6.00 Straddle at .40: Profit and Loss Calculations

Futures Price at Expiration	Long 6.00 Call at .20 Profit / (Loss)	Long 6.00 Put at .20 Profit / (Loss)	Combined Profit / (Loss)
7.00	+ .80	–.20	+ .60
6.80	+ .60	–.20	+ .40
6.60	+ .40	–.20	+ .20
6.40	+ .20	–.20	.00
6.20	.00	–.20	– .20
6.00	–.20	–.20	– .40
5.80	–.20	.00	– .20
5.60	–.20	+ .20	.00
5.40	–.20	+ .40	+ .20
5.20	–.20	+ .60	+ .40
5.00	–.20	+ .80	+ .60

Observations About the Long Straddle

Break-even points: 5.60 *and* 6.40. This is the first example in which there are two break-even points. In this case, the upper break-even point is equal to the strike price plus the total premiums paid and the lower break-even point is equal to the strike price minus the total premiums paid.

Maximum risk: Risk is limited to the total premium paid, .40 in this example. If the futures price exactly equals the strike price at expiration, both options will expire worthless.

Profit potential: This is unlimited. Profit is realized at expiration if the futures price is above 6.40 or below 5.60.

Position created if the option is in-the-money: Either long futures or short futures, depending on the futures price at expiration. If the futures price is above the strike price, the long call is exercised and the position becomes a long futures contract. If the futures price is below the strike, the long put is exercised and the position becomes a short futures.

Trade-off:	The positive aspect is that profit can be realized with a futures price change in either direction. This is positive relative to purchasing only a call or a put. There are two negative aspects: The cost is two premiums, and the break-even points are farther from the strike than is the case with a single-option strategy.
Desired price action:	Large movement either up or down. This is known as a "high-volatility" strategy, because a large move is desired, but direction is not important.

Strategy: Short Straddle

Strategy defined: Sell both a call and a put with the same underlying, the
same strike price, and the same expiration date.

Example: Sell one 6.00 Call at .20 and sell one 6.00 Put at .20

Step 1   Describe the opening transaction completely.
Sell one 6.00 Call at .20 and sell one 6.00 Put at .20.

Step 2   Start a grid and a profit and loss table.
Use the grid shown in Figure 2–9 and use a three-column table
like Table 2–9.

Step 3   Select a futures price and calculate the value of each option at expiration.
With the futures price at 6.00 at expiration, both the 6.00 Call and
the 6.00 Put are worth zero.

Step 4   Calculate the profit or loss of each option and add the results
together.

Total profit of .40
    (the call: .20 sales price minus -0- value   = .20 profit
    the put: .20 sales price minus -0- value   = .20 profit
    total: .20 profit on call plus .20 profit on put = .40 profit)

Step 5   Chart the total profit or loss.
Figure 2–10A shows a dot indicating a profit of .40 at 6.00.

Step 6   Repeat steps 3, 4, and 5 until the diagram is completed.
Profit and loss results over a range of futures prices from 5.00 to
7.00 are presented in Table 2–10. Figure 2–10B shows a second
dot indicating a loss of .40 at 6.80, and Figure 2–10C shows a third
dot indicating a loss of .40 at 5.20. Figure 2–10D shows the completed profit and loss diagram.

Figure 2–10 Short 6.00 Straddle at .40

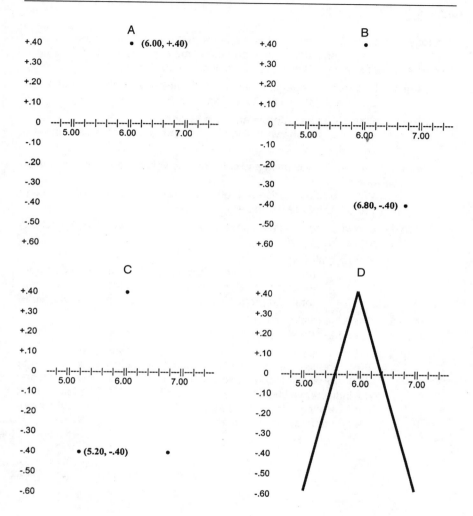

Table 2–10 Short 6.00 Straddle at .40: Profit and Loss Calculations

Futures Price at Expiration	Short 6.00 Call at .20 Profit / (Loss)	Short 6.00 Put at .20 Profit / (Loss)	Combined Profit / (Loss)
7.00	− .80	+ .20	− .60
6.80	− .60	+ .20	− .40
6.60	− .40	+ .20	− .20
6.40	− .20	+ .20	.00
6.20	.00	+ .20	+ .20
6.00	+ .20	+ .20	+ .40
5.80	+ .20	.00	+ .20
5.60	+ .20	- .20	.00
5.40	+ .20	- .40	− .20
5.20	+ .20	- .60	− .40
5.00	+ .20	- .80	− .60

Observations About the Short Straddle

Break-even points: 5.60 *and* 6.40. The upper break-even point is equal to the strike price plus the total premiums received, and the lower break-even point is equal to the strike price minus the total premiums.

Maximum risk: Risk is unlimited. A loss occurs at expiration if the futures price is above 6.40 or below 5.60.

Profit potential: This is limited to the total premiums received, .40 in this example.

Position created if option is in-the-money: Either long or short futures, depending on the futures price at expiration. If the futures price is below the strike price, the short put is assigned and the position becomes a long futures. If the futures price is above the strike, the short call is assigned and the position becomes a short futures.

Trade-off: There are two positive aspects: The amount received is two premiums, and the break-even points are farther from the strike than is the case with a single-option strategy. The negative aspect is that a loss can be realized with a large change in the futures price in either direction.

Desired price action: No movement. This is known as a "low-volatility" strategy, because a large move either up or down could cause a loss.

Strategy: Bull Call Spread

Strategy defined: Buy a call and simultaneously sell another call with the
                     same underlying and the same expiration date but with a
                     higher strike price.

Example: Buy one 6.00 Call at .20 and sell one 6.25 Call at .10

Step 1   Describe the opening transaction completely.
              Buy one 6.00 Call at .20 and sell one 6.25 Call at .10.

Step 2   Start a grid and a profit and loss table.
              Adjust the grid shown in Figure 2–9 so that two strike prices, 6.00
              and 6.25, are centered on the horizontal axis. Use a three-column
              table like Table 2–9.

Figure 2–11 Bull Call Spread at .10

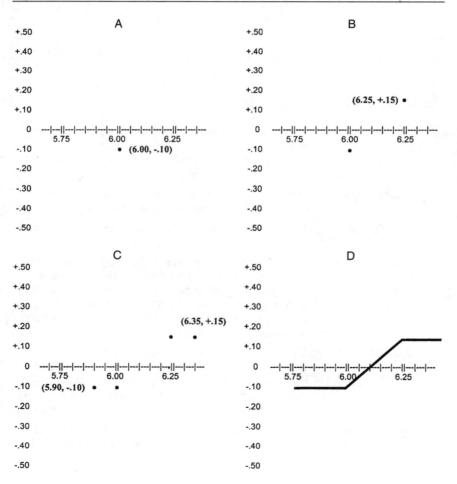

Table 2–11 Bull Call Spread: Profit and Loss Calculations

Futures Price at Expiration	Long 6.00 Call at .20 Profit / (Loss)	Short 6.25 Call at .10 Profit / (Loss)	Combined Profit / (Loss)
6.40	+ .20	− .05	+ .15
6.35	+ .15	.00	+ .15
6.30	+ .10	+ .05	+ .15
6.25	+ .05	+ .10	+ .15
6.20	.00	+ .10	+ .10
6.15	− .05	+ .10	+ .05
6.10	− .10	+ .10	.00
6.05	− .15	+ .10	− .05
6.00	− .20	+ .10	− .10
5.95	− .20	+ .10	− .10
5.90	− .20	+ .10	− .10

Step 3 Select a futures price and calculate the value of each option at expiration.

With the futures price at 6.00 at expiration, the 6.00 Call is worth zero and the 6.25 Call is worth zero.

Step 4 Calculate the profit or loss of each option and add the results together.

Total loss of .10
(the 6.00 Call: -0- value minus .20 purchase price   = .20 loss
the 6.25 Call: .10 sales price minus -0- value   = .10 profit
net: .20 loss on 6.00 Call plus .10 profit on 6.25 Call = .10 loss)

Step 5 Chart the net profit or loss.

Figure 2–11A shows a dot indicating a loss of .10 at 6.00.

Step 6 Repeat steps 3, 4, and 5 until the profit and loss diagram is completed.

Profit and loss results over a range of futures prices from 5.90 to 6.40 are presented in Table 2–11. Figure 2–11B shows a second dot indicating a profit of .15 at 6.25. Figure 2–11C shows a third dot and a fourth dot indicating a loss of .10 at 5.90 and a profit of .15 at 6.35, respectively. Figure 2–11D shows the completed profit and loss diagram.

Observations About the Bull Call Spread

Break-even point:	6.10. This is calculated by adding the net premium paid to the strike price of the long call. In this case, 6.00 + .10 = 6.10.
Maximum risk:	Limited to the net premium paid. The most that can be lost in this example is .10. If the futures price is at or below the lower strike price, 6.00 in this example, both options expire worthless.
Profit potential:	This is limited to the difference between the strike prices less the net premium paid. In this example, the difference between the strike prices is .25 and the net premium paid is .10. Therefore, the maximum profit potential at expiration is .15 (.25 − .10).
Position created if option is in-the-money:	There are two possibilities. If the futures price at expiration is between the strikes, the long call is exercised and the short call expires. The result is a long futures position. Alternatively, if the futures price is above the higher strike at expiration, the long call is exercised and the short call is assigned. The result is no futures position, but the maximum profit potential is achieved.
Trade-off:	The positive aspect is that risk is limited to the net premium paid. This is positive relative to a long futures, which has the theoretical risk of the futures price falling to zero. It is also positive relative to an outright long, lower-strike call that would cost more. The negative aspect is that the profit potential is limited.
Desired price action:	Bullish. This strategy profits if the futures price rises above the break-even point, 6.10 at expiration, in this example.

Strategy: Bear Call Spread

Strategy defined: Sell a call and simultaneously buy another call with the same underlying and the same expiration date but with a higher strike price.

Example: Sell one 6.00 Call at .20 and buy one 6.25 Call at .10

Step 1 Describe the opening transaction completely.
Sell one 6.00 Call at .20 and buy one 6.25 Call at .10.

Step 2 Start a grid and a profit and loss table.
Adjust the grid shown in Figure 2–9 so that two strike prices, 6.00 and 6.25, are centered on the horizontal axis. Use a three-column table like Table 2–9.

Step 3 Select a futures price and calculate each strategy's value at expiration.
With the futures price at 6.00 at expiration, the 6.00 Call is worth zero and the 6.25 Call is worth zero.

Step 4 Calculate the profit or loss of each option and add the results together.

Total profit of .10
(the 6.00 Call: .20 sales price minus value of -0- = .20 profit
the 6.25 Call: -0- value minus .10 purchase price = .10 loss
net: .20 profit on 6.00 Call minus .10 loss on 6.25 Call = .10 profit)

Step 5 Chart the net profit or loss.
Figure 2–12A shows a dot indicating a profit of .10 at 6.00.

Step 6 Repeat steps 3, 4, and 5 until the profit and loss diagram is completed.
Profit and loss results over a range of futures prices from 5.90 to 6.40 are presented in Table 2–12. Figure 2–12B shows a second dot indicating a loss of .15 at 6.25. Figure 2–11C shows a third dot and a fourth dot indicating a profit of .10 at 5.90 and a loss of .15 at 6.35, respectively. Figure 2–12D shows the completed profit and loss diagram.

Figure 2–12 Bear Call Spread at .10

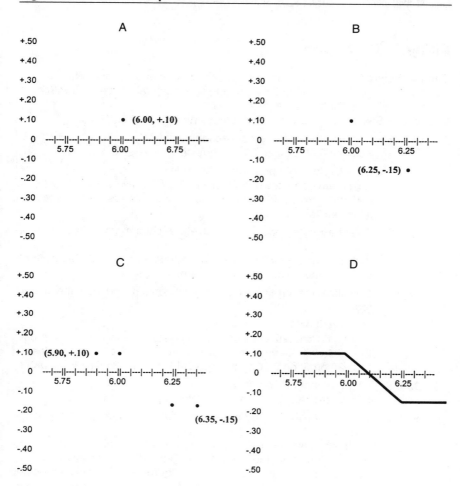

Observations About the Bear Call Spread

Break-even point: 6.10. This is calculated by adding the net premium received to the strike price of the short call. In this case, 6.00 + .10 = 6.10.

Maximum risk: Limited to the difference between the strike prices less the net premium received. The most that can be lost in this example is .15. If the futures price is above 6.25, in this example, the short 6.00 Call is assigned and the long 6.25 Call is exercised. The result is that a futures contract is sold at 6.00 and repurchased at 6.25 for a

Table 2–12 Bear Call Spread: Profit and Loss Calculations

Futures Price at Expiration	Short 6.00 Call at .20 Profit / (Loss)	Long 6.25 Call at .10 Profit / (Loss)	Combined Profit / (Loss)
6.40	− .20	+ .05	− .15
6.35	− .15	.00	− .15
6.30	− .10	− .05	− .15
6.25	− .05	− .10	− .15
6.20	.00	− .10	− .10
6.15	+ .05	− .10	− .05
6.10	+ .10	− .10	.00
6.05	+ .15	− .10	+ .05
6.00	+ .20	− .10	+ .10
5.95	+ .20	− .10	+ .10
5.90	+ .20	− .10	+ .10

loss of .25. However, .10 was the net premium received for establishing the initial position, so the net result is a loss of .15.

Profit potential:	This is limited to the net premium received, .10 in this example.
Position created if option is in-the-money:	There are two possibilities. If the futures price at expiration is between the strikes, the short call is assigned and the long call expires. The result is a short futures position. Alternatively, if the futures price is above the higher strike at expiration, then the short call is assigned, and the long call is exercised. The result is no futures position, but the maximum potential loss is realized.
Trade-off:	The positive aspect is that risk is limited. There are two negative aspects. First, profit potential is limited. Second, the profit potential is less than that of an outright short, lower-strike call portion.
Desired price action:	Neutral/bearish. This strategy profits if the futures price remains at or below the strike price of the short call, 6.00 in this example.

SUMMARY

The ability to draw expiration profit and loss diagrams is an important skill that enables hedgers and traders to understand the potential profits and risks of using futures and options. These diagrams are created by following a six-step process: describing the opening transaction completely, starting a grid and a profit and loss table, selecting a futures price and calculating the value of each option at expiration, calculating the profit or loss, charting the profit or loss, and repeating steps 3, 4, and 5 over a range of futures prices until the profit and loss diagram is completed. The six basic strategies are long and short futures, long and short call, and long and short put. These basic strategies can be combined to form more complicated strategies.

Once a profit and loss diagram has been completed, you should make these observations about the strategy: the profit potential, which may be limited or unlimited; the maximum risk, which also may be limited or unlimited; the break-even point at expiration; the futures position created if the option is in-the-money at the expiration date; and the trade-off the strategy provides. The concept of a trade-off is that there is some relatively positive aspect and some other relatively negative aspect. Understanding the trade-offs of each individual strategy will lead to strategy comparisons that will aid in the decision-making process.

The examples presented in this chapter are only a few of the many strategies that futures and options make possible. The workbook *Teach Yourself Option Strategies* can help you develop your diagram-drawing abilities. This workbook contains 34 exercises, with answers, covering basic through advanced strategies.

To order a copy of *Teach Yourself Option Strategies*, send $5.00 (to cover mailing and handling) to:

Op-Eval
Suite 200
2501 N. Lincoln Ave.
Chicago, IL 60614

Please make checks payable to *Op-Eval.*

Allow 3 to 4 weeks for delivery.

Three

Diagrams of Basic Hedging Strategies

This chapter presents the next level of profit and loss diagrams: those for hedging strategies. Diagrams of hedging strategies may at first seem similar to diagrams of trading strategies, but there are some important differences. This chapter defines what a hedging strategy is and how it differs from a trading strategy. Next, the unique aspects of diagrams of hedging strategies are explained. Finally, profit and loss diagrams of four basic hedging strategies—two for long hedgers and two for short hedgers—are presented. An expanded discussion of these and other hedging strategies appears in Chapters 8, 9, and 10.

HEDGING STRATEGY DEFINED

When used in conjunction with futures and options strategies, the word hedge means to protect or to limit risk. Consequently, a *hedging strategy is the use of futures and/or futures options that protects the purchase price or sale price of some commodity.* An example of a hedger is a farmer who has crops growing in the field or has them in storage. Farmers use hedging strategies to protect the sale price of their crops. Users of commodities, by contrast, such as cereal manufacturers that use wheat or corn, employ hedging strategies to protect the purchase price of the commodities they buy.

UNIQUE ASPECTS OF PROFIT AND LOSS DIAGRAMS OF HEDGING STRATEGIES

As was noted above, there are several differences between profit and loss (P/L) diagrams of hedging strategies and profit and loss diagrams of basic trading strategies. The first difference is that hedgers have an interest in the underlying commodity; this interest must be included on the profit and loss diagram. The second difference is that hedging strategies always have at least two parts, one of which is the interest in the underlying commodity.

51

Diagramming hedging strategies involves combining the parts. The third difference is the goal. Hedging strategies are used to attain the "best price" for the underlying commodity, and this means that profit and loss grids for hedging strategies are constructed differently than are grids for trading strategies. Each of these differences will be explained in turn.

The Interest in the Underlying Commodity

Hedgers fall into two broad categories: producers and users. Producers are "inherently long," and users are "inherently short." An *inherent position* is the fundamental ownership of or need for some commodity. *Inherently long means that a commodity is either in the process of being produced or is owned.* Farmers, for example, are inherently long, because their crops either are growing in the field or are in storage. *Inherently short means that a commodity needs to be purchased.* Flour manufacturers, for example, are in constant need of wheat to keep their facilities operating.

Some hedgers are both producers and users and therefore are both inherently long and inherently short. Feedlot operators, for example, are users of soybean meal and producers of live cattle, and so they are inherently short soybean meal and inherently long live cattle. Soybean crushers are inherently short soybeans and inherently long soybean meal and soybean oil.

Long Hedgers and Short Hedgers

A long hedger is a market participant with an inherently short position in a commodity. Long hedgers use hedging strategies that benefit from rising prices, so-called long market strategies that provide price protection for inherently short positions. A cereal manufacturer, for example, that uses wheat, corn, or rice is a long hedger because there is a constant need to buy those commodities. Some of the strategies that a cereal manufacturer might use are long wheat futures, long wheat calls, and short wheat puts. While appropriate for different market forecasts and therefore not interchangeable, each of these strategies benefits from rising prices and therefore can be used to hedge an inherently short position.

A short hedger is a market participant with an inherently long position in a commodity. Short hedgers use hedging strategies that benefit from falling prices, so-called short market strategies that provide price protection for inherently long positions. Corn, soybean, and wheat farmers are examples of long hedgers, because they own or are growing those commodities. The strategies that short hedgers use are exactly the opposite of those used by long hedgers.

Note that the interest in the underlying commodity involves a potential risk and a potential opportunity in the future. Hedgers do not necessarily want to buy or sell a commodity immediately, but they know they will need to buy it or sell it at a specific date in the future. If a hedging strategy is not used, the risk is that the future price may be "worse" than the price today. The existence of hedging strategies makes it possible for hedgers to plan for the future.

The "Best Price" Is the Goal

Although every market participant wants to "make a profit," when it comes to hedging strategies, that goal is achieved by getting the best possible price. Users of commodities want to buy at the lowest possible price, and suppliers want to sell at the highest. Generally speaking, if a user buys at a "low" price, profits will be increased. Similarly, producers who can sell at a "high" price will increase their profits. This variation on "making money" necessitates a change in the profit and loss grid, as described next.

Differences in Grid Construction

Vertical axes on grids of trading strategies are labeled "profit and loss" because this is the goal of these strategies: earning a profit at the risk of incurring a loss. Vertical axes on grids of hedging strategies, however, are labeled "final price," because a hedger's objective is to get the best price.

Horizontal axes on grids of both hedging strategies and trading strategies are labeled "futures price," because it is a higher or lower futures price that determines the success of the strategy.

CREATING DIAGRAMS FOR HEDGING STRATEGIES

The process of creating profit and loss diagrams for hedging strategies is similar to the process of creating two-part option strategies that was described in Chapter 2. The main difference is in step 3, where the "final price" is calculated rather than profit or loss. As will be explained, calculating the final price requires an extra column in the profit and loss table.

Step 1 Describe the opening transaction completely.

For hedging strategies, both the inherent position and the hedging strategy must be described. For producers, the inherent position is "long the cash market at the current price"; for users, the inherent position is "short the cash market at the current price." The "current price" is the price at which a commodity can be bought or sold in the cash market right now, and this price is needed to calculate the profit or loss from the inherent position.

Hedging strategies are described in the same way that futures and options strategies are described. "Long Soybean Futures at 5.80" and "short 250 Corn Puts at .13" are examples of complete descriptions of hedging strategies.

Step 2   Start a grid and a profit and loss table.

The horizontal axis of a profit and loss grid for a hedging strategy is labeled "Futures Price at Expiration." The term *expiration* literally means the expiration date of an option, but it could also mean the delivery date of a futures contract.

The vertical axis is labeled "Final Price." For long-hedge strategies, this is a purchase price, and for short-hedge strategies, it is a sale price. Figure 3–1 is a sample profit and loss grid for a hedging strategy.

A profit and loss table such as Table 3–1 makes calculation of the final price easy.

Column 1 indicates the range of futures prices at expiration that appear on the horizontal axis of the grid in Figure 3–1.

Figure 3–1 Sample Profit and Loss Grid for a Hedging Strategy

Final Price

   6.50

   6.40

   6.30

   6.20

   6.10

                                                 Futures Price

   6.00 ----|---|--- ‖ ---|---|---|---|--- ‖ ---|---|---|---|--- ‖ ---|---|---   at Expiration
          5.50   6.00   6.50

   5.90

   5.80

   5.70

   5.60

   5.50

Column 2 indicates the profit or loss from the inherent cash market position. An inherent long position loses money as the price of the underlying commodity falls and profits as the price rises. For inherent short positions, the situation is reversed.

Column 3 in Table 3–1 indicates the profit or loss from the hedging strategy. More complicated hedging strategies involve more than one component, and the table therefore will have more than one column devoted to the hedging strategy. Column 4 contains the combined profit or loss from the inherent position and the hedging strategy. In a completed Table 3–1, column 4 would contain the sums of the numbers that would appear in columns 2 and 3.

Column 5 in Table 3–1 contains the "Initial Cash Market Price," which is the price that a hedger would get if a transaction were made in the cash market when a hedging strategy is initiated. Column 6, the rightmost column, indicates the "Final Price." Calculation of the final price is explained in steps 3 and 4.

Steps 3 and 4   Select a futures price and calculate the final price.

The final price is calculated by combining the combined profit and loss in column 4 with the initial cash market price in column 5. For long hedgers, the final price is a purchase price, and combined profits in column 4 reduce the final purchase price below the initial cash market price. Net losses, however, increase the final purchase price above the initial cash market price.

For short hedgers the situation is reversed. The final price for short hedgers is a sale price, and combined profits in column 4 raise the final sale price above the initial cash market price. Net losses lower the final sale price for short hedgers.

Step 5   Chart the profit or loss.

This step for hedging strategies is the same as that for the trading strategies presented in Chapter 2. A dot is placed on the profit and loss grid above or below the futures price on the horizontal axis even with the final price on the vertical axis.

Step 6   Repeat steps 3, 4, and 5 until the diagram is complete.

This process is the same as the process for the strategies presented in Chapter 2. Futures prices are selected, the final price is calculated, and points are plotted on the grid. After several points are plotted, the strategy diagram is completed.

Diagrams of two long hedging strategies and then of two short hedging strategies are presented next.

Table 3–1 Sample Profit and Loss Table for a Hedging Strategy

	Col. 1	Col. 2	Col. 3	Col. 4	Col. 5	Col. 6
	Futures Price at Expiration	Inherent Position P/(L)	Hedge Strategy P/(L)	Combined P/(L) (Col. 2 + Col. 3)	Initial Cash Market Price	Final Price (combine results in Col. 4 + Col. 5)
Row 1	6.75					
Row 2	6.50					
Row 3	6.25					
Row 4	6.00					
Row 5	5.75					
Row 6	5.50					
Row 7	5.25					

Long Hedge Examples

Long hedgers are inherently short. Examples of long hedgers are cereal manufacturers, flour manufacturers, and snack food companies that are in constant need of supplies of wheat, corn, rice, or other commodities. Each step in creating a profit and loss table and a profit and loss grid will be explained below. Two basic long-hedge strategies are to buy a futures contract and to buy a call option.

Buying a Futures as a Long Hedge

Step 1   Describe the opening transaction completely.

To hedge an inherent short position in wheat, buy a wheat futures contract at 3.50.

In this example, the hedger needs a constant supply of wheat and therefore is inherently short wheat. The current market price is assumed to be 3.50 per bushel. To hedge the risk of a short cash market position, a long futures position is established. For the sake of simplicity, the futures price is assumed to be the same as the cash market price so that the complexities of basis are ignored. *Basis* is the difference between the price of the futures contract and the cash market price.

Step 2   Start a grid and a profit and loss table.

A grid similar to Figure 3–1 and a table similar to Table 3–1 will be used. The range of wheat prices in this example is from 2.25 to 4.75. Prices are stated on a "per-bushel" basis.

Steps 3 and 4   Select a futures price and calculate the final price.

Row 2 in Table 3–2 illustrates how, with a futures price of 4.00, the final purchase price is 3.50. With a futures price of 4.00 and a cash market price that is the same, column 2 shows that an inherent short cash market position at 3.50 has a loss of .50, or 50 cents. Parentheses are used in tables to indicate negative numbers, or losses. The left-upward-sloping dotted line in Figure 3–2 illustrates an inherently short position at 3.50 per bushel.

Column 3 in Table 3–2 shows that a long futures position purchased at 3.50 has a profit of .50 when the futures price is 4.00. The right-upward-sloping broken line in Figure 3–2 illustrates a long futures position at 3.50 per bushel.

Column 4 in Table 3–2 indicates a combined profit and loss of -0- with futures at a price of 4.00. And column 6 shows that when the combined profit and loss of -0- is added to the initial cash market price of 3.50 in column 5, the Final Price, which is a purchase price, is 3.50.

Table 3–2 Calculating the Final Purchase Price: Hedging an Inherent Short Position with a Long Futures

Initial cash market price: 3.50 per bushel
Hedge strategy: long futures at 3.50 per bushel

	Col. 1	Col. 2	Col. 3	Col. 4	Col. 5	Col. 6
	Futures Price at Expiration	Inherent Short at 3.50 P/(L)	Long Futures at 3.50 P/(L)	Combined P/(L) (Col. 2 + Col. 3)	Initial Cash Market Price 3.50	Final Price (Purchase Price) (Col. 5 − Col. 4)
Row 1	4.25	(.75)	+.75	-0-	3.50	3.50
Row 2	4.00	(.50)	+.50	-0-	3.50	3.50
Row 3	3.75	(.25)	+.25	-0-	3.50	3.50
Row 4	3.50	-0-	-0-	-0-	3.50	3.50
Row 5	3.25	+.25	(.25)	-0-	3.50	3.50
Row 6	3.00	+.50	(.50)	-0-	3.50	3.50
Row 7	2.75	+.75	(.75)	-0-	3.50	3.50

Final purchase price = initial cash market price minus combined profits or plus combined losses

Figure 3–2 Final Purchase Price: Hedging an Inherent Short Position with a Long Futures

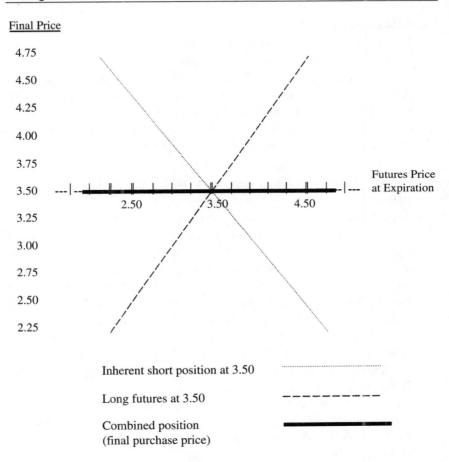

Final Price

Inherent short position at 3.50

Long futures at 3.50

Combined position
(final purchase price)

Steps 5 and 6   Chart the profit or loss and repeat the process.

Table 3–2 is a completed profit and loss table for a long futures purchased as a long hedge, and the horizontal solid line in Figure 3–2 is the completed diagram of the final purchase price. Note that the solid horizontal line is a combination of the two opposite-sloping diagonal lines.

In this example, all the prices in column 6 of Table 3–2 are the same—3.50—because the effect of hedging an inherent short position with a long futures is to lock in a purchase price. While the conclusion from Table 3–2 and Figure 3–2 may not be a revelation to experienced hedgers, this process of creating tables and diagrams is good practice for more complicated strategies involving one or more options.

Buying a Call as a Long Hedge

Step 1   Describe the opening transaction completely.

Buy a 3.50-strike Wheat Call at .25.

To hedge the risk of an inherent short cash market position, a 350 Wheat Call is purchased for .25, or 25 cents per bushel. This means that a long call position is established. The cash market price is assumed to be 3.50 per bushel, and again, the futures price is assumed to be the same so that the complexities of basis are ignored.

Step 2   Start a grid and a profit and loss table.

A grid similar to Figure 3–2 and a table similar to Table 3–2 will be used.

Steps 3 and 4   Select a futures price and calculate the final price.

Row 2 in Table 3–3 illustrates how, with a futures price of 4.00 at expiration, the final purchase price is 3.75. With a futures price of 4.00 and a cash market price that is the same, column 2 shows that an inherent short cash market position at 3.50 has a loss of .50, or 50 cents per bushel. The left-upward-sloping dotted line in Figure 3–3 illustrates an inherently short cash market position at 3.50 per bushel.

Column 3 in Table 3–3 shows that a long 350 Call, that is purchased at .25, has a profit of .25 when the futures price is 4.00 at expiration. The broken line in Figure 3–3 illustrates a long 350 Call purchased for .25, or 25 cents per bushel.

Column 4 in Table 3–3 indicates a combined loss of .25 with futures at 4.00 at expiration. And column 6 shows that when the combined loss of .25 is added to the initial cash market price of 3.50 in column 5, the final price, which is a purchase price, is 3.75.

Steps 5 and 6   Chart the profit or loss and repeat the process.

Table 3–3 is a completed profit and loss table for a long call purchased as a long hedge, and the solid line in Figure 3–3 is the completed diagram of the final purchase price. Note that the solid line is the combination of the dotted and broken lines.

In this example, there is a maximum purchase price of 3.75. At any futures price above 3.50 at expiration, the long call gives the long hedger the right to buy wheat at 3.50 per bushel. Since the 25-cent cost of the call must be added, the final purchase price is 3.75. Below a futures price of 3.50 at expiration, the call expires worthless, and wheat can be purchased at the lower price in the cash market. If the cash market price is below 3.25 at expiration, this strategy has lowered the final purchase price.

The effect of hedging an inherent short position with a long call is to lock in a maximum purchase price while leaving intact the opportunity to benefit from declining cash market prices.

Short Hedge Examples

Short hedgers are inherently long. Examples of short hedgers are farmers who are inherently long the crops they grow. Two basic short-hedge strategies are to sell a futures contract and to buy a put option.

Selling a Futures as a Short Hedge

Step 1   Describe the opening transaction completely.

Sell a Wheat futures contract at 3.50.

In this example, the hedger has wheat growing in the field and therefore is inherently long wheat at the current cash market price, which is assumed to be 3.50 per bushel. To hedge the risk of a long cash market position, a short futures position is established. Again, the futures price is assumed to be the same as the cash market price so that the complexities of basis are ignored.

Step 2   Start a grid and a profit and loss table.

A grid similar to Figure 3–2 and a table similar to Table 3–2 will be used.

Steps 3 and 4   Select a futures price and calculate the Final Price.

Row 6 in Table 3–4 illustrates how, with a futures price of 3.00 at expiration, the final sale price is 3.50. With a futures price of 3.00 and a cash market price that is the same, column 2 shows that an inherent long cash market position at 3.50 has a loss of .50, or 50 cents per bushel. The right-upward sloping dotted line in Figure 3–4 illustrates an inherently long position at 3.50 per bushel.

Column 3 in Table 3–4 shows that a short futures position that is sold at 3.50 has a profit of .50 at a price of 3.00. The left-upward slopping broken line in Figure 3–4 illustrates a short futures position at 3.50 per bushel.

Table 3–3 Calculating the Final Purchase Price: Hedging an Inherent Short Position with a Long Call

Initial cash market price: 3.50 per bushel
Hedge strategy: long 350 Call at .25 per bushel

	Col. 1 Futures Price at Expiration	Col. 2 Inherent Short at 3.50 P/(L)	Col. 3 Long 350 Call at .25 P/(L)	Col. 4 Combined P/(L) (Col. 2 + Col. 3)	Col. 5 Initial Cash Market Price 3.50	Col. 6 Final Price (Purchase Price) (Col. 5 – Col. 4)
Row 1	4.25	(.75)	+.50	(.25)	3.50	3.75
Row 2	4.00	(.50)	+.25	(.25)	3.50	3.75
Row 3	3.75	(.25)	-0-	(.25)	3.50	3.75
Row 4	3.50	-0-	(.25)	(.25)	3.50	3.75
Row 5	3.25	+.25	(.25)	-0-	3.50	3.50
Row 6	3.00	+.50	(.25)	+.25	3.50	3.25
Row 7	2.75	+.75	(.25)	+.50	3.50	3.00

Final purchase price = initial cash market price minus combined profits or plus combined losses

62

Figure 3–3 Final Purchase Price: Hedging an Inherent Short Position with a Long Call

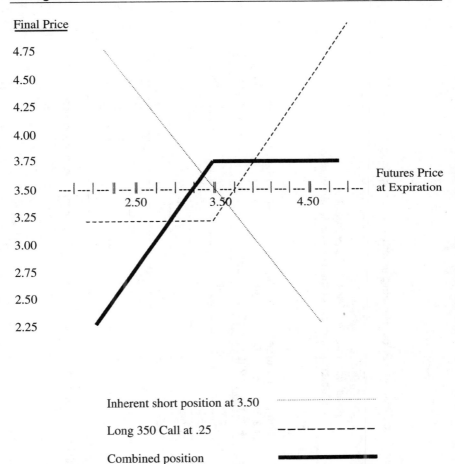

Final Price

Inherent short position at 3.50

Long 350 Call at .25

Combined position
(final purchase price)

Column 4 in Table 3–4 indicates a combined profit/loss of -0- at a futures price of 3.00. And column 6 shows that when the combined profit/loss of -0- is subtracted from the initial cash market price of 3.50 in column 5, the final price, which is a sale price, is 3.50.

Steps 5 and 6   Chart the profit or loss and repeat the process.

Table 3–4 is a completed profit and loss table for a short futures sold as a short hedge, and the horizontal solid line in Figure 3–4 is the

Table 3–4 Calculating the Final Sale Price: Hedging an Inherent Long Position with a Short Futures

Initial cash market price: 3.50 per bushel
Hedge strategy: short futures at 3.50 per bushel

	Col. 1	Col. 2	Col. 3	Col. 4	Col. 5	Col. 6
	Futures Price at Expiration	Inherent Long at 3.50 P/(L)	Short Futures at 3.50 P/(L)	Combined P/(L) (Col. 2 + Col. 3)	Initial Cash Market Price 3.50	Final Price (Sale Price) (Col. 5 + Col. 4)
Row 1	4.25	+.75	(.75)	-0-	3.50	3.50
Row 2	4.00	+.50	(.50)	-0-	3.50	3.50
Row 3	3.75	+.25	(.25)	-0-	3.50	3.50
Row 4	3.50	-0-	-0-	-0-	3.50	3.50
Row 5	3.25	(.25)	+.25	-0-	3.50	3.50
Row 6	3.00	(.50)	+.50	-0-	3.50	3.50
Row 7	2.75	(.75)	+.75	-0-	3.50	3.50

Final sale price = initial cash market price plus combined profits or minus combined losses

64

Figure 3–4 Final Sale Price: Hedging an Inherent Long Position with Short Futures

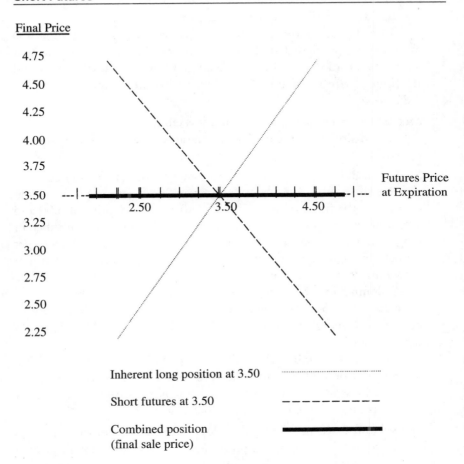

Final Price

Inherent long position at 3.50 ....

Short futures at 3.50 — — — — — — — —

Combined position
(final sale price) ▬▬▬▬▬▬▬▬▬

completed diagram of the final sale price. Note that the solid horizontal line is the combination of the two opposite-sloping diagonal lines.

In this example, all the prices in column 6 of Table 3–4 are the same—3.50—because the effect of hedging an inherent long position with a short futures is to lock in a sale price. Remember that this process of creating tables and diagrams is good practice for more complicated strategies involving one or more options.

Buying a Put as a Short Hedge

Step 1   Describe the opening transaction completely.

Buy a 3.50-strike Wheat Put at .25.

To hedge the risk of an inherent long cash market position, a 350 Wheat Put is purchased at .25, or 25 cents per bushel. This means that a long put position is established. Again, both the cash market price and the futures price are assumed to be 3.50 so that the complexities of basis are ignored.

Step 2   Start a grid and a profit and loss table.

A grid similar to Figure 3–2 and a table similar to Table 3–2 will be used.

Steps 3 and 4   Select a futures price and calculate the final price.

Row 6 in Table 3–5 illustrates how, with a futures price of 3.00 at expiration, the final sale price is 3.25. With a futures price of 3.00 and a cash market price that is the same, column 2 shows that an inherent long cash market position at 3.50 has a loss of .50, or 50 cents per bushel. The right-upward sloping line in Figure 3–5 illustrates an inherently long cash market position at 3.50 per bushel.

Column 3 in Table 3–5 shows that a long 350 Put, purchased at .25, has a profit of .25 when the futures price is 3.00 at expiration. The broken line in Figure 3–5 illustrates a long 350 Put purchased for .25, or 25 cents per bushel.

Column 4 in Table 3–5 indicates a combined loss of .25 with a futures price of 3.00 at expiration. And column 6 shows that when the combined loss of .25 is subtracted from the initial cash market price of 3.50 in column 5, the final price, which is a sale price, is 3.25.

Steps 5 and 6   Chart the profit or loss and repeat the process.

Table 3–5 is a completed profit and loss table for a long put purchased as a short hedge, and the solid line in Figure 3–5 is the completed diagram of the final sale price. Note that the solid line is the combination of the dotted and broken lines.

In this example, there is a minimum sale price of 3.25. At any futures price below 3.50 at expiration, the long put gives the short hedger the right to sell wheat at 3.50 per bushel. Since the 25-cent cost of the put must be subtracted, the final sale price is 3.25. Above a futures price of 3.50 at expiration, the put expires worthless, and the wheat can be sold at the higher price in the cash market. If the cash market price is above 3.75 at expiration, this strategy has raised the final sale price.

Table 3–5 Calculating the Final Sale Price: Hedging an Inherent Long Position with a Long Put

Initial cash market price: 3.50 per bushel
Hedge strategy: long 350 Put at .25 per bushel

	Col. 1	Col. 2	Col. 3	Col. 4	Col. 5	Col. 6
	Futures Price at Expiration	Inherent Long at 3.50 P/(L)	Long 350 Put at .25 P/(L)	Combined P/(L) (Col. 2 + Col. 3)	Initial Cash Market Price 3.50	Final Price (Sale Price) (Col. 5 + Col. 4)
Row 1	4.25	+.75	(.25)	+.50	3.50	4.00
Row 2	4.00	+.50	(.25)	+.25	3.50	3.75
Row 3	3.75	+.25	(.25)	-0-	3.50	3.50
Row 4	3.50	-0-	(.25)	(.25)	3.50	3.25
Row 5	3.25	(.25)	-0-	(.25)	3.50	3.25
Row 6	3.00	(.50)	+.25	(.25)	3.50	3.25
Row 7	2.75	(.75)	+.50	(.25)	3.50	3.25

Final sale price = initial cash market price plus combined profits or minus combined losses

Figure 3–5 Final Sale Price: Hedging an Inherent Long Position with a Long Put

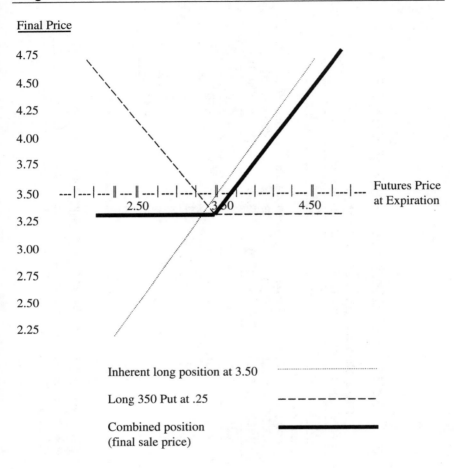

Final Price

Inherent long position at 3.50

Long 350 Put at .25

Combined position
(final sale price)

The effect of hedging an inherent long position with a long put is to lock in a minimum sale price while leaving intact the opportunity to benefit from rising cash market prices.

SUMMARY

Although there are some similarities, diagrams of hedging strategies are different from diagrams of trading strategies. First, hedgers have an inherent position in the underlying commodity, and that position must be included on the diagram. Second, hedging strategies have at least two parts and sometimes more. The third difference is that the goal of hedging strategies is to get the "best price." As a result, the vertical axis of profit and loss grids for hedging strategies is labeled "Final Price."

Four

Why Futures and Options Have Value

T heoretically, futures contracts have value for a different reason than options do. This chapter will explain the difference. The discussion will involve some elementary arithmetic, but the presentation will be conceptual in nature. After the rationale for futures and option prices is presented, options will be compared to another financial product. Finally, a brief discussion of volatility will introduce an important concept. The subject of volatility, of course, will be expanded on in several chapters in this book.

FUTURES CONTRACTS: AN EXPLANATION OF VALUE

As was stated in Chapter 1, futures contracts involve obligations for both parties. Assuming that a contract has not been closed before the delivery day, the buyer of a futures contract (the "long") is required to buy the underlying commodity, and the seller of that contract (the "short") is required to deliver. This means there is certainty that a futures contract will become a physical commodity on a known date. Consequently, given the price at which the commodity can be purchased today and given storage and delivery costs, an exact value of a futures contract can be calculated. Conceptually, the price of a futures contract is determined by the formula given in Table 4–1.

As an example, assume one year to delivery, carrying costs of 10 percent, and a cash market price, or "spot price," of soybeans of 6.00 per bushel. Given these factors, the theoretical value of a one-year soybean futures contract is 6.60, which is calculated as follows:

Table 4–1 Theoretical Value of a Futures Contract

| Spot price of underlying | + | cost of carry | = | theoretical value of futures contract |

Underlying:	the commodity and the unit of measure to be delivered as set forth in the futures contract. For example, prices of soybean futures contracts are quoted in cents per bushel, and 5,000 bushels is the underlying for one contract.
Spot price:	the price at which a commodity can be purchased today.
Cost of carry	the expense of delivering a commodity in accordance with the specifications of a futures contract. Typical expenses included in the cost of carry are storage, interest, insurance, and transportation.

Spot price + (10% per year) $\times$ (1 year) = theoretical value
of soybeans   of 1-year soybean
                                                      futures contract

$$6.00 \quad + (0.10 \times 6.00) \times 1 \quad = \quad 6.60$$

Why is this the "theoretical value"? And how can anyone be sure that a futures contract will trade in the marketplace at a price near this value? To answer these questions, consider how participants in the market for futures contracts and in the spot market for the underlying commodity will act in two different scenarios.

In the first scenario, assume that the price of the soybean futures contract is above the theoretical value of 6.60, at 7.00, for example. With soybean futures trading at 7.00, spot soybeans trading at 6.00, and a cost of carry of 60 cents, it would be profitable to purchase soybeans in the spot market for 6.00 and sell a one-year futures contract for 7.00. The cash market soybeans purchased for 6.00 per bushel could be stored, insured, and delivered for 60 cents. On the delivery date, they could be delivered at an effective price of 7.00. The result would be a profit of 40 cents per bushel.

Profit-seeking participants in a competitive market would not let such a situation exist. There would be buying pressure in the spot market and selling pressure in the futures market, and the two prices would be pushed toward each other until only the most efficient participants could make a profit. Market participants who engage in this profit-oriented activity are known as arbitrageurs. While the personal goal of every arbitrageur is to make a profit, the economic function arbitrage serves is to keep prices of related instruments "in line" with each other. This creates competition in the supply of products to all market participants, and arbitrage, from an overall perspective, thus lowers costs.

In the second scenario, assume that the price of the soybean futures contract is below the theoretical value of 6.60, at 6.00, for example. In this case, it would be more profitable for a user of soybeans in one year to buy a one-year futures contract than it would be to buy soybeans in the spot market and pay the carrying costs. The total cost of spot soybeans is 6.60 in this scenario, and so buying futures at 6.00 would reduce costs by 60 cents per bushel. Such a futures price would be so enticing that holders of soybeans for use in one year would sell their soybeans in the cash market and purchase one-year futures contracts. Such selling in the spot market and buying in the futures market would push prices together until the relationship between spot market prices and futures prices was in line with carrying costs.

In either scenario, whether futures prices are above or below theoretical value, there are market forces that tend to push those prices back "in line." The conclusion is that futures prices are based on a *cost of carry model.* Option prices, however, are based on a different model.

OPTION CONTRACTS: AN EXPLANATION OF VALUE

Prices of options depend on five variables: the underlying futures price; the expected range of futures prices, also called volatility; the strike price; the number of days to expiration; and interest rates. Each of these factors is discussed below.

It may seem obvious that option prices are related to futures prices, because option prices change as futures prices change. What is less obvious, however, is that there are two aspects of futures prices that affect option prices. First, there is the absolute futures price. The higher the futures price, the higher the price of an option, assuming that other factors are equal. For example, if futures contract A is trading at 10.00 and futures contract B is trading at 5.00, it is reasonable to expect that a 90-day 10.00-strike call on futures contract A will trade at a higher price than will a 5.00-strike call on futures contract B.

The second aspect of futures prices that affects option prices is the expected range of futures prices between the present time and expiration. Consider an extremely simplified scenario in which a futures contract, that currently is trading at 10.00 has a 50 percent chance of rising to 11.00 and a 50 percent chance of falling to 9.00 at expiration. Also, assume that interest rates are zero so that time becomes unimportant. This situation is depicted in Figure 4–1. Given these assumptions, the question is: What is the "expected value" of the 10.00-strike call?

As presented in Figure 4–2, the "expected value" of the 10.00-strike call is calculated in two steps, and the result may be surprising to some readers. First, the "expected value of each outcome" is calculated by multiplying the probability of each outcome by the value of each outcome. Second, the expected values of the individual outcomes are added together to get the "total expected value." In options, the total expected value is known as the *theoretical value.*

The value of each outcome is the intrinsic value of the option at expiration. For example, if the futures price rises to 11.00, the 10.00-strike call will have an intrinsic value of 1.00. If the futures price falls to 9.00, the 10.00-strike call will have an intrinsic value of zero and expire worthless.

The next step is to multiply each value by its probability. Since there is a 50 percent chance that the 10.00-strike call will be worth 1.00, the

Figure 4–1 Simplified Range of Outcomes

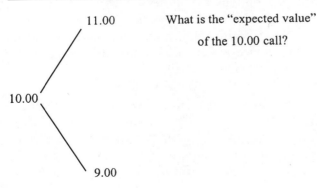

11.00   What is the "expected value"

of the 10.00 call?

10.00

9.00

Figure 4–2 Theoretical Value of a Call Option

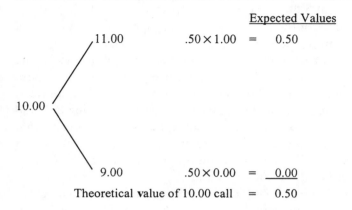

Expected Values

11.00   .50 × 1.00   =   0.50

10.00

9.00   .50 × 0.00   =   0.00

Theoretical value of 10.00 call   =   0.50

expected value of the 11.00 outcome is 0.50. There is also a 50 percent chance that the call will be worth zero, and so the expected value of the 9.00 outcome is zero.

Finally, the expected values of the individual outcomes are added together, and the result is the total expected value, or theoretical value. Figure 4–2 shows that the theoretical value of the 10.00-strike call is 0.50 (.50 × 1.00 + .50 × 0.00).

This process is similar to what insurance actuaries go through to determine the premium they charge for an insurance policy. In its simplest form, if there were a 1 percent chance that any house might burn down, the insurance company would charge an annual insurance premium of 1 percent of value to all homeowners, plus a markup to cover expenses and a profit margin. In fact, options on futures (as well as options on other instruments) are just like insurance policies! Consider the components that go into an insurance policy: asset value, deductible, time, interest rates, and risk.

> **Options are similar to insurance policies**

The value of the insured asset directly affects the price of an insurance policy. All things being equal, the more expensive the asset being insured, the higher the premium. The amount of the deductible, however, inversely affects the policy premium; the larger the deductible, the lower the premium. Time affects insurance premiums directly: the longer the time, the greater the cost of insurance. Interest rates are a factor, because insurance companies invest the premiums received. In theory, premiums will decrease if interest rates rise, because the increased income will be returned to policyholders in the form of lower insurance rates. Interest rates therefore affect insurance premiums inversely. The last factor affecting insurance premiums is risk. Risk has a direct impact on insurance premiums: the higher the risk, the higher the premium of the policy.

The components of an option's value correspond directly to the factors that determine insurance premiums, and Table 4–2 summarizes the analogy between insurance premiums and option prices. The price of the underlying futures contract corresponds to asset value. All things being equal, the more expensive an asset is, the more expensive it is to insure. Similarly, the higher the price of a futures contract, the higher the price of an option on that contract.

> **Futures price corresponds to asset value**

An option's strike price corresponds to the deductible of an insurance policy. Policies with low or no deductibles are more expensive than policies with higher deductibles. An at-the-money option is like an insurance policy with no deductible. An option with an out-of-the-money strike is like an insurance policy with a deductible: the first portion of loss is borne by the insured party. When a loss exceeds the deductible, the insurance policy pays the difference. In the case of options, the payment in excess of the

> **Strike price corresponds to deductible**

Table 4–2 Components of Price: Options Compared to Insurance Policies

Insurance Policy	Option
Asset value	Futures price
Deductible	Strike price
Time	Time
Interest rates	Interest rates
Risk	Volatility
Premium	Premium

deductible is the option's intrinsic value, and intrinsic value increases as the futures price moves beyond an option's strike price.

> **Time to expiration corresponds to length of policy**

> **Volatility corresponds to risk**

Time has a direct impact on option prices just as it has on insurance policies: the longer the period to expiration, the higher the option value. Interest rates are a factor in option prices because of the time value of money. Although the impact is small, the market does adjust option prices as interest rates change.

The word for *risk* in the options market is *volatility*. In the normal course of trading, futures prices fluctuate. The larger the fluctuation, the greater the risk; as a result, the options will be more expensive.

"VALUE" IS DIFFERENT FROM "PRICE"

It is easy to fall into a nit-picking argument over the meaning of value and price. One could argue, after all, that "they are the same." If two people agree on a price, and one buys and one sells, is it not obvious that the price of the item is its value? Despite this practical logic, however, the word value typically refers to the results of some independent analysis. A real estate appraiser, for example, might analyze market conditions to estimate the value of a property, but that property might sell at a higher or lower price. Similarly, the "blue book value" of an automobile is a guide, but it does not guarantee a price.

Throughout this book, the term *price* will refer to the market price of an option and the term *value* will refer to a computer-generated estimate of price based on certain assumptions. One aspect of hedging and trading with options is comparing the market price to a computer-generated estimate of value.

VOLATILITY INTRODUCED

Volatility is an important concept and therefore deserves additional explanation. Generally speaking, volatility means movement without regard to direction. Fluctuation is a word that is used frequently to describe the movement of futures prices, and fluctuation of futures prices can be measured in two ways. First, there is the direction of price change; second, there is the size of the change. Volatility is a measure of the size of price changes without concern about the direction. In other words, volatility is concerned with how much prices move, not whether they move up or down. In mathematical formulas that calculate option prices, volatility is expressed as a percentage, e.g., 15 percent or 20 percent, but the goal for most hedgers and traders is to develop a subjective understanding of volatility and to incorporate that understanding into hedging and trading decisions.

The Impact of Changes in Volatility

At this point it is useful to revisit the two-outcome scenario presented in Figures 4–1 and 4–2 and assume that the potential outcomes are 12.00 and 8.00. Now recalculate the expected value of the 10.00-strike call. As Figure 4–3 shows, the new theoretical value is 1.00. Since the expected range of prices has increased, the option value has increased.

Figure 4–3 demonstrates that there is a direct relationship between the range of expected outcomes and option values. Specifically, the wider the range of potential futures prices, the higher an option's value. Conceptually, this is an increase in volatility. The conclusion from Figure 4–3 is that option prices are based on an *expected volatility model.*

Figure 4–3 Increasing the Volatility

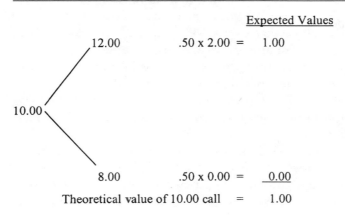

Expected Values

12.00 .50 x 2.00 = 1.00

10.00

8.00 .50 x 0.00 = 0.00

Theoretical value of 10.00 call = 1.00

In the futures markets, of course, the range of possible futures prices is infinite, but the range can be analyzed with a statistical tool commonly known as the bell-shaped curve. The percentage numbers in mathematical formulas that were referred to earlier describe the shape of this curve. Without engaging in a detailed mathematical discussion, a lower volatility percentage means less movement and lower option prices, and a higher percentage means more movement and higher option prices.

Volatility is a subject that takes time to understand and feel comfortable with. Newcomers to options should be patient and should remind themselves not to be intimidated by more experienced options traders who understand it. By identifying what is not understood and by asking questions, anyone can grasp the concept of volatility.

Insurance Analogy Concluded

What do puts insure?

What do calls insure?

This chapter has compared the components of an option's value to the factors that determine insurance premiums. It is logical to ask, If options are insurance policies, what do they insure? For newcomers, put options may be easier to understand. Puts provide protection against price declines, just as homeowner's insurance protects against a house burning down. Calls, however, protect against rising prices. If a user of corn, for example, does not own any corn or any futures contracts, the risk is that prices will rise. Calls protect users of commodities against rising prices.

When options are seen in this context – as insurancelike instruments – hedgers and traders begin to think differently about options. Suddenly there are new horizons to explore. Of course, in the housing market individuals can only buy insurance; whereas in the futures market individuals can just as easily sell insurance (sell options) or buy insurance (buy options). For individual hedgers and traders, there are valid reasons for buying insurance and for selling insurance. Which strategy is chosen depends on market opinion, hedging or trading objectives, and risk tolerance. These issues will be discussed in depth in later chapters.

Option Price Components Summarized

Table 4–3 lists the components of an option's price and summarizes how changes in the individual components change that price. Although this subject will be covered in greater depth in Chapter 7 and in Chapter 11, which explains the computer program, at this point it is sufficient to know the conceptual relationships.

SUMMARY

Futures prices are based on a cost-of-carry model. Some of the elements of cost of carry are storage charges, interest, insurance, and delivery. Market participants who engage in an activity known as arbitrage keep spot market prices and futures market prices in line with each other, and the result is an overall lowering of costs.

Option prices are based on an expected-volatility model. Option prices can best be understood when they are compared to insurance, because the components of option prices correspond directly to the components of insurance premiums. For options, the futures price corresponds to the asset value in insurance. The option strike price corresponds to the deductible component in insurance. An at-the-money option is like a no-deductible policy, and an out-of-the-money option is like a policy

Table 4–3 How Changes in Components Effect Option Prices

Component	Effect on Call Price	Effect on Put Price
Futures Price	Direct	Inverse
Strike Price	Inverse	Direct
Time	Direct	Direct
Interest Rates	Direct	Inverse
Volatility	Direct	Direct

Direct effect means: As the component increases, and other factors remain unchanged, the option price will also increase.

Inverse effect means: As the component increases, and other factors remain unchanged, the option price will decrease.

with a deductible. Time and interest rates are components of price for both options and insurance, and the factor called risk in insurance is called volatility in options.

Volatility is a measure of movement without regard to direction. While it is a statistical concept that is not easily grasped by nonmathematicians, volatility can be understood intuitively and incorporated subjectively into hedging and trading decisions.

Finally, value is different from price. Throughout this book, *price* will refer to the market price of an option and *value* will refer to a computer-generated estimate of price based on certain assumptions. One aspect of hedging and trading with options is comparing an option's price to its value.

Five

Option Price Behavior

H edgers, as opposed to traders, do not need to dwell on the information discussed in this chapter, because basic hedging strategies, as will be explained in Part 2, generally focus on strategy results on the expiration date. With some exceptions, option price behavior before expiration is primarily the realm of short-term traders. Understanding how option prices change and developing realistic expectations about the short-term behavior of option prices are the key to trading options successfully.

The value of an option, as was explained in Chapter 4, depends on five factors: futures price, strike price, time to expiration, interest rates, and volatility. In Chapter 4 those factors were explained conceptually in a static environment, but of course, in reality, they operate dynamically. This chapter first discusses the effect of a change in each component, assuming that the others remain constant. The subject of volatility will be introduced, but Chapter 6 is devoted to a discussion of this important topic. Subsequently, the discussion will cover option price changes when more than one component changes.

The following discussion gets fairly technical, and it is not necessary for hedgers to comprehend every detail. Short-term traders, however, do need to master this material. Newcomers to options may prefer to skim this chapter and come back to it when they are more familiar with the trading strategies presented in Part 3.

THE EFFECT OF FUTURES PRICE CHANGE

The impact of changing futures prices on option prices is the first subject to be investigated. The general question is: If the underlying futures price rises by one unit and other factors remain constant, by how much will the theoretical value of an option change? To take a specific example, assume a futures price of 6.00, 150 days to expiration, and a 600 Call theoretical value of approximately 23 cents. If the futures price rises 10 cents, to 6.10, and the other factors are unchanged, the theoretical value of the 600 Call will change by approximately 5 cents to 28 cents. Table 5–1 illustrates option price changes and some other important aspects of option price behavior.

Table 5–1 contains theoretical values of a 600 Call at various futures prices and various days before expiration. The theoretical values were calculated by using the OP-EVALF™ software that accompanies this text. Calculations are based on a mathematical formula known as the Black-Scholes option pricing model. This formula involves advanced calculus, and an explanation of the mathematics is beyond the scope of this book. Option values are presented in decimals rounded to the second place rather than in eighths and quarters for the sake of clarity in explaining several concepts. Table 5–1 contains 11 rows and 6 columns. The rows indicate different futures prices; the columns indicate different days before expiration.

Option prices change <u>less</u> than the change in the underlying futures price

By looking up and down the columns and across the rows of Table 5–1, one observes how changes in futures price or time to expiration or both cause changes in the option's theoretical value. For example, with a futures price of 5.80 and 90 days to expiration (column 3, row 8), the

Table 5–1 Theoretical Values of a 600 Call at Various Futures Prices and Days to Expiration (Interest Rates 5%, Volatility 15%)

		Col. 1	Col. 2	Col. 3	Col. 4	Col. 5	Col. 6
	Futures Price	150 Days	120 Days	90 Days	60 Days	30 Days	0 Days
Row 1	6.50	55.65	54.20	52.70	51.25	50.12	50.00
Row 2	6.40	47.94	46.22	44.38	42.44	40.61	40.00
Row 3	6.30	40.71	38.76	36.60	34.19	31.56	30.00
Row 4	6.20	34.03	31.90	29.48	26.68	23.27	20.00
Row 5	6.10	27.69	25.71	23.13	20.05	16.07	10.00
Row 6	6.00	22.54	20.25	17.61	14.44	10.25	0.00
Row 7	5.90	17.79	15.54	12.96	9.90	5.95	0.00
Row 8	5.80	13.73	11.60	9.20	6.43	3.10	0.00
Row 9	5.70	10.33	8.39	6.26	3.92	1.43	0.00
Row 10	5.60	7.57	5.87	4.08	2.24	0.57	0.00
Row 11	5.50	5.38	3.96	2.53	1.19	0.20	0.00

theoretical value of the 600 Call is 9.20, or 9.20 cents. If the futures price is raised by .10, the call value rises to 12.96. If the futures price is decreased by .10, the call value decreases to 6.26. In both cases, the call value changes less than does the futures price. Looking anywhere on Table 5–1, this is always true. *An option's theoretical value always changes less than one for one with a change in the futures price.*

Note also that the ratio of option price change to futures price change varies. For example, when the futures price rises by .10 from 5.60 to 5.70 at 90 days, the 600 Call rises from 4.08 to 6.26, or approximately 22 percent of the futures price change. In another situation, when the futures rises from 6.10 to 6.20 at 60 days, the call price rises from 20.05 to 26.68, or approximately 67 percent of the futures price change.

Figure 5–1 How Option Prices Change as Futures Prices Change

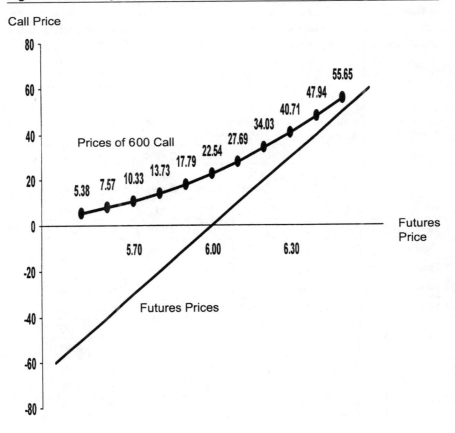

<table>
<tr><td>DELTA</td></tr>
<tr><td>Option price change per unit
of futures price change</td></tr>
</table>

Figure 5–1 is a graph showing call option price behavior relative to futures price behavior. The option values in Figure 5–1 are taken from column 1 in Table 5–1. Figure 5–1 shows graphically that option prices change less than unit for unit with price changes in the underlying futures.

DELTA

The ratio of option price change to futures price change is an important aspect of option price behavior, and it is referred to as the *delta* of an option. Specifically, *delta is the change in an option's theoretical value given a one-unit change in price of the underlying futures contract.* Table 5–2 shows the delta of the 600 Call at different futures prices and different times to expiration. The deltas in Table 5–2 correspond to the option values in Table 5–1. For example, the delta of .51 in column 1, row 6, of Table 5–2 (150 days, futures price 6.00) corresponds to the option price of 22.54 in the same cell in Table 5–1. This means the 600 Call has a theoretical value of 22.54 and a delta of .51 given the stated inputs (futures price, 6.00; strike, 6.00; days to expiration, 150; interest rates, 5 percent; volatility, 15 percent).

Table 5–2 Delta of 600 Call at Various Futures Prices and Days to Expiration (Interest Rates 5%, Volatility 15%)

		Col. 1	Col. 2	Col. 3	Col. 4	Col. 5	Col. 6
	Futures Price	**150 Days**	**120 Days**	**90 Days**	**60 Days**	**30 Days**	**0 Days**
Row 1	6.50	.79	.82	.86	.90	.97	1.00
Row 2	6.40	.75	.77	.81	.86	.93	1.00
Row 3	6.30	.70	.72	.75	.79	.87	1.00
Row 4	6.20	.64	.65	.68	.71	.78	1.00
Row 5	6.10	.58	.58	.60	.61	.66	1.00
Row 6	6.00	.51	.51	.51	.51	.51	.00
Row 7	5.90	.44	.43	.42	.40	.35	.00
Row 8	5.80	.37	.36	.33	.30	.22	.00
Row 9	5.70	.31	.29	.25	.21	.12	.00
Row 10	5.60	.25	.22	.19	.13	.06	.00
Row 11	5.50	.19	.16	.13	.08	.02	.00

The term *one unit* is used in the definition of delta because delta is the first derivative, or slope, of the curve in Figure 5–1 at one point. At each point on the curve the slope changes. Consequently, delta is dynamic: Delta changes as the futures price changes. Delta is an instantaneous measure of the rate of change in theoretical value, and delta changes as the price of the underlying changes.

Delta is used to gauge the "futures equivalency" of an option. One futures contract is the benchmark. An option with a .50 delta will have a change in theoretical value approximately equivalent to one-half of the change in price of one futures contract, assuming that all other factors are held constant.

Call deltas are positive and range from 0.00 to +1.00. Out-of-the-money call options have deltas between 0.00 and +0.50, at-the-money call options have deltas of approximately +0.50, and in-the-money call options have deltas between +0.50 and +1.00.

Put deltas are negative and range from −1.00 to 0.00. This means that the delta of a put approaches −1.00 as a futures price falls. Out-of-the-money puts have deltas between −.50 and 0.00, at-the-money puts have deltas of approximately −.50, and in-the-money puts have deltas between −1.00 and −0.50. Tables 5–3 and 5–4 show theoretical values and deltas,

Table 5–3 Theoretical Values of 600 Put at Various Futures Prices and Days to Expiration (Interest Rates 5%, Volatility 15%)

		Col. 1	Col. 2	Col. 3	Col. 4	Col. 5	Col. 6
	Futures Price	**150 Days**	**120 Days**	**90 Days**	**60 Days**	**30 Days**	**0 Days**
Row 1	6.50	6.67	5.01	3.31	1.66	0.33	0.00
Row 2	6.40	8.75	6.87	4.87	2.77	0.78	0.00
Row 3	6.30	11.32	9.25	6.97	4.44	1.69	0.00
Row 4	6.20	14.44	12.22	9.73	6.84	3.35	0.00
Row 5	6.10	18.17	15.87	13.25	10.13	6.11	0.00
Row 6	6.00	22.54	20.25	17.61	14.44	10.25	0.00
Row 7	5.90	27.59	25.38	22.85	19.82	15.91	10.00
Row 8	5.80	33.32	31.27	28.95	26.26	23.02	20.00
Row 9	5.70	39.72	37.90	35.90	33.68	31.30	30.00
Row 10	5.60	46.76	45.22	43.59	41.91	40.41	40.00
Row 11	5.50	54.37	53.14	51.92	50.78	50.00	50.00

Table 5–4 Delta of 600 Put at Various Futures Prices and Days to Expiration (Interest Rates 5%, Volatility 15%)

		Col. 1	Col. 2	Col. 3	Col. 4	Col. 5	Col. 6
	Futures Price	150 Days	120 Days	90 Days	60 Days	30 Days	0 Days
Row 1	6.50	−.19	−.16	−.13	−.09	−.03	−.00
Row 2	6.40	−.23	−.21	−.18	−.14	−.06	−.00
Row 3	6.30	−.28	−.27	−.24	−.20	−.12	−.00
Row 4	6.20	−.34	−.33	−.31	−.28	−.22	−.00
Row 5	6.10	−.40	−.40	−.39	−.38	−.34	−.00
Row 6	6.00	−.47	−.48	−.48	−.48	−.49	−.00
Row 7	5.90	−.54	−.55	−.57	−.59	−.64	−1.00
Row 8	5.80	−.61	−.63	−.65	−.70	−.78	−1.00
Row 9	5.70	−.67	−.70	−.73	−.79	−.88	−1.00
Row 10	5.60	−.73	−.76	−.80	−.86	−.94	−1.00
Row 11	5.50	−.79	−.82	−.86	−.91	−.97	−1.00

respectively, of a 600 Put option at various futures prices and days before expiration.

Call Values Relative to Put Values

For options on futures, the time value of a call is approximately equal to the time value of a put with the same underlying, the same strike price, and the same expiration date. This relationship between call and put prices holds because of a concept known as *put-call parity*. This concept is beyond the scope of this book, but put-call parity states that futures prices, call prices, and put prices must have a certain relationship with each other or there will be arbitrage opportunities for professional traders to make nearly riskless profits. In fact, one strategy employed by professional floor traders is to look for "market inefficiencies" — situations where prices are out of line with each other — and take advantage of the arbitrage opportunity. Because of the fierce competition between professional traders, such arbitrage opportunities exist only for very short periods of time, and the "inefficiency" amounts to only ⅛ or ¼ of a point. For readers interested in exploring put-call parity in depth, a book by Sheldon Natenberg, *Option Volatility and Pricing,* covers the topic very throughly.

The Relationship of Call Deltas and Put Deltas

Although call deltas are positive numbers and put deltas are negative, one might suspect that all other things being equal, the absolute values of call and put deltas would be equal. However this is not true. A comparison of Tables 5–2 and 5–4 reveals that the sums of the absolute values of call and put deltas are approximately 1.00. This is another result of put-call parity.

An Explanation of Delta

Although an in-depth mathematical explanation of delta is too complex to be included in this book, Figure 5–2 provides a brief conceptual explanation of this important aspect of option price behavior. The notion of two outcomes in each time period that was introduced in Chapter 4 is the basis for an option pricing formula known as the binomial model. To develop

Figure 5–2 Demonstration of Delta

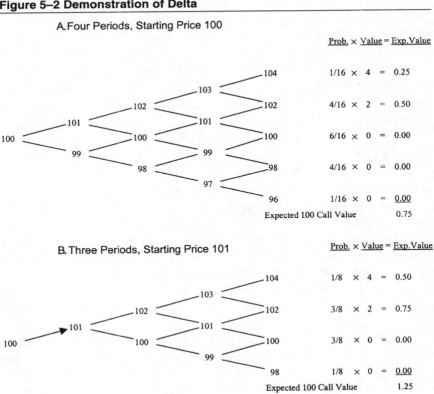

A. Four Periods, Starting Price 100

Prob. × Value = Exp.Value

104   1/16 × 4 = 0.25
103
102   102   4/16 × 2 = 0.50
101   101
100   100   100   6/16 × 0 = 0.00
99   99
98   98   4/16 × 0 = 0.00
97
96   1/16 × 0 = 0.00

Expected 1.00 Call Value   0.75

B. Three Periods, Starting Price 101

Prob. × Value = Exp.Value

104   1/8 × 4 = 0.50
103
102   102   3/8 × 2 = 0.75
101   101
100   100   100   3/8 × 0 = 0.00
99
98   1/8 × 0 = 0.00

Expected 1.00 Call Value   1.25

delta, it is necessary to expand the example in Figure 4–1 to more than one time period. The top half of Figure 5–2 illustrates a four-period binomial example. In each period, it is assumed, the futures price has a 50-50 chance of rising or falling. As the number of time periods increases to four, the range of possible outcomes expands to a high of 104 and a low of 96. The final possible outcomes, however, do not have an equal probability of occurring. The highest-probability outcomes are near the center of the range. The probabilities for each final outcome are calculated by counting the number of paths the futures price could follow to that outcome. For example, there is only one path from 100 to 104, but there are four paths from 100 to 102. The total number of paths is 16, and so there are 1 in 16 chances of ending at 104 and 4 in 16 chances of ending at 102.

In Figure 5–2A, the probability of each final outcome is shown along with the expected-value calculations. The expected, or theoretical, value of the 100 Call is 0.75.

To demonstrate delta, it is assumed the futures price rises one unit, to 101, in the first period. After this move, as shown in Figure 5–2B, there are three periods remaining until expiration. The range of possible final outcomes has narrowed to a high of 104 and a low of 98, and there are new probabilities for each remaining possible final outcome. The 1.00 Call has a new expected value of 1.25. In this case, the futures price has moved up by one unit, to 101, and the 100 Call theoretical value has moved up by .50 — equal to a delta of .50. This conclusion is consistent with the theoretical values presented in Tables 5–1 through 5–4.

THE EFFECT OF TIME

It is well known that options decrease in value with the passage of time, assuming that other factors remain constant. There are two ways to illustrate this graphically. Figure 5–3 shows option price behavior at three different times before expiration. The values used to create the four lines in Figure 5–3 are taken from columns 1, 3, 5, and 6 in Table 5–1, which are 150 days from expiration, 90 days from expiration, 30 days from expiration, and at expiration, respectively. Figure 5–3 shows how, as time passes, the graph of call option values approaches the shape of the call option expiration profit and loss diagram in Chapter 2.

The values in Table 5–1 are presented differently in Figure 5–4 to illustrate how call prices change as time passes toward expiration, assuming a constant futures price. Consider row 6 in Table 5–1, a futures price at 6.00. The 600 Call declines in value from 22.54 at 150 days, to 20.25 at 120 days, to 17.61 at

Figure 5–3 Illustration of Time Decay I

Theoretical Values of 600 Call over a Range of Futures Prices
at 150 Days, 90 Days, 30 Days, and Expiration

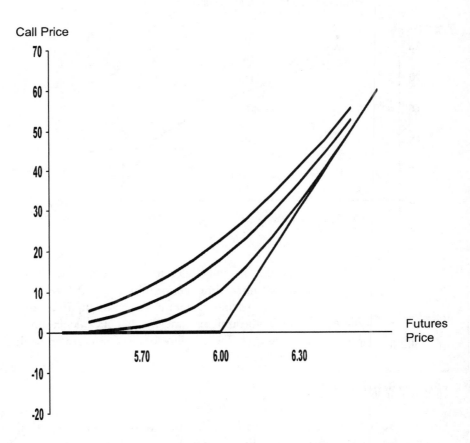

90 days, etc. The important observation is that time decay affects at-the-money options relatively little initially and relatively more as expiration approaches. Table 5–1 shows that when one-half of the time to expiration elapses, from 120 days to 60 days, approximately one-third of the 600 Call value erodes, from 20.25 to 14.44. A similar price/time relationship exists from 60 days to 30 days when the 600 Call declines from 14.44 to 10.25. Figure 5–4 illustrates time decay graphically for a 6.00 Call with the futures price held constant at 6.00.

The name for time decay in options is *theta. Theta is the change in an option's theoretical value given a one-unit change in time.* The term *one unit* is not

Figure 5–4 Illustration of Time Decay II

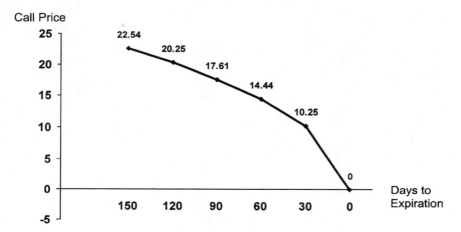

Time Decay of an At-the-Money Call

Theoretical Values of 600 Call
with Futures Price Held Constant at 6.00

<table>
<tr><td>

THETA

**Option price change per
unit of time**

</td><td>

specific; it could refer to one day, one week, or some other time period. In the OP-EVALF™ option-pricing program that accompanies this book, the unit of time for a theta calculation is seven days. Theta will be discussed in greater detail in Chapter 7.

</td></tr>
</table>

TIME DECAY VARIES

Unfortunately for newcomers to options, the effect of time decay on option values is not as simple as it may first appear. While time decay for at-the-money options is low initially and increases per unit of time as expiration approaches, time decay for in-the-money and out-of-the-money options is different. Remember, it is only the time value portion of an option that decays. Consequently, with a futures price of 6.00, 150 days to expiration, and an in-the-money 575 Call value of 36.44, time decay will affect only 11.44 of the value. Time decay during the 30-day period from 150 days to 120 days is 1.94 and is slightly higher (2.18) during the 120-to-90-day period. During the last 30 days before expiration, however, the option decreases in value by only 2.04. The conclusion is that time decay of in-the-money options is more linear, or even, than it is for at-the-money options.

A similar, more linear rate of time decay occurs for out-of-the-money options. With futures at 6.00, the value of a 625 Call decreases by 2.16 from 12.80 at 150 days to 10.65 at 120 days and then by 2.39 from 120 days to 90 days. But time decay is only 2.40, just .01 higher, from 30 days to expiration. Figure 5–5 illustrates time decay for the 625 Call (out-of-the-money) and the 575 Call (in-the-money) when the futures price is 6.00. Time decay for these options occurs at a more linear rate than it does for at-the-money options. Compare Figure 5–4 with Figure 5–5.

An Explanation of Time Decay

The binomial approach also illustrates the nonlinear nature of time decay for at-the-money options. Figure 5–6 has six time periods and demonstrates the theoretical value of the 100 Call after time periods 2, 4, and 6. Although these time periods are equal in length, the theoretical value of the option does not change in equal amounts. This conclusion is consistent with the values presented in Tables 5–1 and 5–3.

Figure 5–5 Illustration of Time Decay III

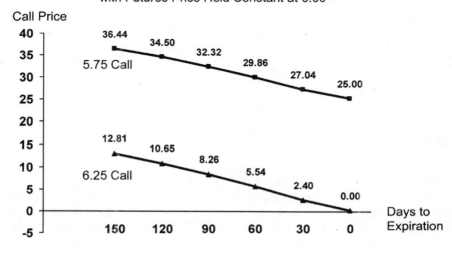

Time Decay of Out-of-the-Money and In-the-Money Calls

Theoretical Values of 575 Call and 625 Call
with Futures Price Held Constant at 6.00

Figure 5–6 Illustration of Time Decay IV

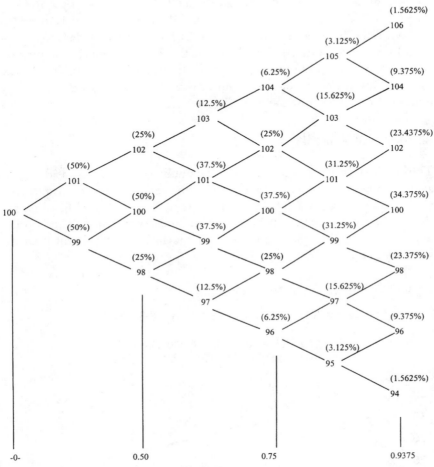

Expansion of Binomial Model to Demonstrate Option Time Decay

Theoretical Values at the Beginning of Different Time Periods

THE EFFECT OF INTEREST RATES

Among all inputs changes in interest rates have the smallest impact on option prices. In fact, for all practical purposes, the impact is insignificant, and so changes in interest rates will not be addressed in this book. After reading Chapter 11, which explains the OP-EVALF™ software, you can experiment on your own and see how option prices change as interest rates change.

The conclusion is that very large increases in interest rates decrease the prices of options on futures, but only slightly.

THE EFFECT OF VOLATILITY

> **VOLATILITY**
> A statistical measure of price change without regard to direction

As was explained in Chapter 4, volatility is a measure of movement without regard to direction. The greater the volatility, the higher the option price. Volatility is stated in percentage terms. For example, the past price action of a particular underlying security is said to "trade at 25 percent volatility," or an option theoretical value is said to be calculated "using a 30 percent volatility." Figure 5–7 illustrates how the theoretical value of a 600 Call changes as volatility changes. It is assumed that the futures price is 6.00, there are 90 days to expiration, and interest rates are 5 percent.

The direct relationship between volatility and option values illustrated in Figure 5–7 is only one of several important observations. Three more observations about volatility are as follows: (1) Volatility is a statistical measure of price movement without regard to direction, (2) each futures contract has its own volatility characteristics, and (3) the volatility characteristics of individual futures can change and in fact do change frequently. Each of these three points and many more will be explained in detail in the next chapter. Since volatility is such an important topic in any discussion of options, an entire chapter is devoted to it.

Although discussions of volatility can get complicated, do not lose track of the main goal. Hedgers and traders must learn to understand volatility conceptually as part of the subjective decision-making process. With practice and experience, any option user can master the topic of volatility.

DYNAMIC MARKETS

The discussion to this point has assumed that one component of value changes while the rest stay constant. In the real world, of course, more than one component changes at a time. Market forecasts do not call for the price of a futures contract to move up or down on the same day while volatility remains unchanged. Rather, futures prices and volatility commonly change over a period of time, and all these factors affect option prices. A forecast therefore must take all three factors into account. Referring back to Table 5–1, if a prediction called for the futures price to rise from 5.80 at 90 days

Figure 5–7 The Impact of Volatility on Option Prices

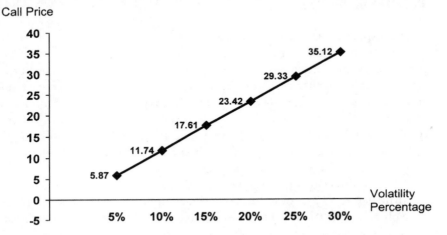

Theoretical Values of 600 Call at Various Levels of Volatility with Futures Price, 6.00; Days to Expiration, 90 Days; and Interest Rates, 5 percent

to 6.20 at 30 days, the call price might be expected to rise from 9.20 cents to 23.27 cents, assuming that interest rates and volatility do not change. If either or both of these factors change, the result will be a different option price.

Traders therefore must take into account the dynamic nature of markets. Creating tables of theoretical values such as the ones presented in this chapter help traders develop realistic expectations about option price behavior. The computer program that accompanies this book was used to create these tables, and using the program will be explained in Chapter 11. The benefit of the program is that, given a realistic expectation for option prices, traders can more easily select a strategy that matches the market forecast. With practice, any trader can master this process.

SUMMARY

Short-term option price behavior is the realm of the trader rather than the hedger, who, as will be explained in Part 2, generally focuses on strategy results at expiration. Option prices, prior to expiration, always change less than one for one with changes in futures prices. Delta is the name for the expected option price change given a one-unit futures price change. The passage of time causes option prices to decrease, all other things being equal. At-the-money options decrease with the passage of time in a non-linear manner, less initially and more as expiration nears. The time decay of in-the-money and out-of-the-money options, however, is more linear. Interest rates have a minor effect on option prices.

Volatility has a direct impact on option prices: The higher the volatility, the higher both put and call prices. Volatility is a measure of movement without regard to direction. While it is a statistical concept that is not easily grasped by nonmathematicians, volatility can be understood intuitively and incorporated subjectively into trading decisions.

Markets are dynamic, not static. Having an understanding of option price behavior and having realistic expectations about it are necessary for the successful use of options as either hedging or trading instruments.

Six

Volatility

Option traders need a conceptual understanding of volatility and how it affects trading decisions; detailed knowledge of mathematical formulas is not required. While volatility simply means movement, there are four ways of describing movement, and this can create confusion. Nevertheless, spending the time needed to understand volatility is a worthwhile endeavor, because the goal is to make better-informed trading decisions.

This chapter first defines historic volatility, and two examples of calculating historic volatility are presented. Second, future volatility, expected volatility, and implied volatility are defined. Third, an example of how two traders might evaluate the implied volatility level of an option is presented. Finally, the concept of volatility skews is introduced. The topics at the end of this chapter get quite involved, and newcomers to options may want to read Part 3, "Trading Strategies," first and then come back to this material.

VOLATILITY DEFINED

With regard to futures contracts and the prices of those contracts, *volatility* means changes in price that are measured in percentage terms without regard to direction. This means that a rise from 6.00 to 6.06 is equal in terms of volatility to a rise from 3.00 to 3.03, because both changes are 1 percent. Also, a 1 percent price rise is equal in volatility terms to a 1 percent price decline.

One difficulty in grasping the concept of volatility is that traders tend to think in terms of direction and in terms of "good" and "bad." A trader with a bullish position, for example, thinks of a price rise as good and a price decline as bad. A trader with a bearish position thinks the opposite.

If one has always thought this way, it can be difficult to think in terms of movement rather than direction.

VOLATILITY I: HISTORIC VOLATILITY

Historic volatility is a measure of actual price changes in the past. Mathematically, historic volatility is the annualized standard deviation of daily returns during a specific period. Do not let this definition intimidate you, because the following discussion is conceptual, not mathematical.

Price observations can be made over 30 days, 90 days, or some other defined period, but, in discussing historic volatility, the exact time period over which prices are observed must be specified. Daily closing prices typically are used, but daily opening prices or weekly closing prices or some other consistent method of observation could also be used.

While it seems simple to compare one specific price change to another, it is difficult to compare two series of price changes. Figure 6–1, for example, contains graphs of daily closing prices of two futures contracts. The question is: Which futures contract is more volatile? Take a moment to reflect on this question. Which futures contract do you think is more volatile? As you read on, you can compare your answer, which is based on your own subjective, visual evaluation, to the technical answer that is presented. In the process, you will learn about several aspects of volatility. A calculation of the historic volatility of Futures Contract 1 will be presented first. The process will be repeated quickly for Futures Contract 2, and then the volatilities of the two futures contracts will be compared.

The historic volatility of Futures Contract 1 is calculated from the information in Table 6–1. The leftmost column simply assigns a number to each closing price. In the real world this would be a date. The middle column contains the 23 closing prices that are graphed in Figure 6–1.

The third column in Table 6–1 contains percentage changes in price from the previous price, and these percentages are known as *daily returns*. Assuming two price observations in row A and row B, a percentage price change, or daily return, is calculated by subtracting the closing price in row A from the closing price in row B and then dividing the difference by the price in row A. Consider the number –1.0% in the day 1 row. Subtracting the closing price on day 0, 250, from the closing price on day 1, 247½, yields a difference of minus 2½. This difference is then divided by the closing price on day 0, 250, and the result is –0.01, or –1.0 percent. There is no price change for day 0, because this is the first price observation, and so the previous price is unknown.

Figure 6–1 Which Futures Contract Is More Volatile?

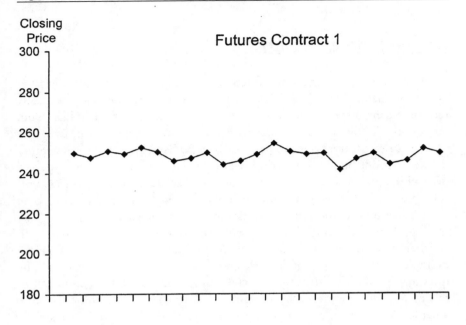

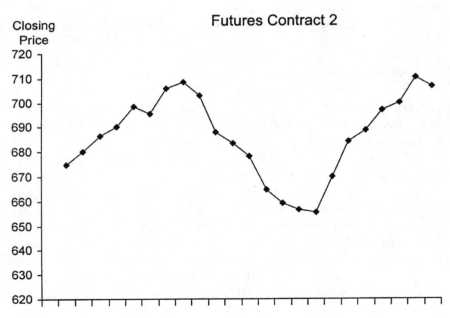

Table 6–1 Futures Contract 1: Calculation of Historic Volatility

Day	Closing Price	Daily Return (Day2−Day1)/Day1
0	250	—
1	247½	−1.0%
2	250¾	+1.3%
3	249¼	−0.6%
4	252½	+1.3%
5	250½	−0.8%
6	245¾	−0.2%
7	247¼	+0.6%
8	249¾	+1.0%
9	244¼	−2.2%
10	246	+0.7%
11	248¾	+1.1%
12	254¼	+2.2%
13	250¼	−1.6%
14	249	−0.5%
15	249½	+0.2%
16	241½	−3.3%
17	246¾	+0.2%
18	249¼	+1.0%
19	244¼	−2.0%
20	246	+0.7%
21	251¾	+2.3%
22	249½	−0.9%

Historic volatility = annualized standard deviation of daily returns = 24.8%

Historic volatility is the annualized standardized deviation of the numbers in the third column, and the result, 24.8 percent, appears at the bottom of Table 6–1. Although the mathematics of standard deviations is beyond the scope of this book, this calculation is a standard spreadsheet function, and so it is relatively easy for the mathematically inclined to do their own research.

At this point, those who are not mathematically inclined may have some questions, such as, What does "24.8 percent volatility" mean? What is a standard deviation? Is it necessary to learn math to trade options?

No, it is not necessary to learn math to trade options! The standard deviation and "24.8 percent volatility" can best be explained by comparing the price action of Futures Contract 1 to the price action of Futures Contract 2. Table 6–2 contains the first of two methods of comparison.

Table 6–2 lists daily closing prices and percentage changes for Futures Contract 2 on the same row as the corresponding information for Futures Contract 1. From observation 0 to observation 1, for example, the –1.0 percent price change in Futures Contract 1 corresponds to the +0.8 percent price change in Futures Price 2. Look down Table 6–2, and you will observe that the absolute value of every percentage change in Futures Contract 1 is larger than the corresponding percentage change in Futures Contract 2. This is the first indication that the volatility of Futures Contract 1 is higher than the volatility of Futures Contract 2.

Some may find this result surprising since Futures Contract 2 rose 30 points, fell 50 points, and then rose 50 points, while Futures Contract 1 traded within a 10-point range. But remember that volatility is a measure of percentage price changes, not direction. Futures Contract 2 had several smaller percentage changes in the same direction relative to Futures Contract 1. When one is discussing volatility, "several smaller percentage changes" is the operative term.

In the real world, of course, it is unlikely that every percentage change in one futures contract will be larger or smaller than every corresponding percentage change in another futures contract. Therefore, Table 6–3 presents another method of comparing the volatilities: The absolute values of the percentage changes are listed in order by size from smallest to largest.

Table 6–3 is a conceptual presentation of a statistical concept. Statisticians compare subgroups of observations. Fifteen observations, for example, is 68 percent, or approximately two-thirds, of the 22 price-change observations. Table 6–3 shows that the smallest 15 percentage price changes for Futures Contract 2 are less than 1.2 percent and average 0.6 percent. In contrast, the smallest 15 percentage price changes for Futures Contract 1 are less than 1.6 percent and average 0.9 percent. The comparison in this subgroup indicates that Futures Contract 1 has a higher volatility than does Futures Contract 2.

Table 6–3 also compares the smallest 21 observations, or approximately 95 percent of the total observations. Again, the measures for Futures

Table 6-2 Comparison of Daily Price Changes of Two Futures Contracts

Day	Futures Price 1 Closing Price	Futures Price 1 Daily Return (Day2 – Day1)/Day1	Price 2 Closing Price	Futures Price 2 Daily Return (Day2 – Day1)/Day1
0	250	—	675	—
1	247½	−1.0%	680¼	+0.8
2	250¾	+1.3%	686¾	+0.9
3	249¼	−0.6%	690	+0.5
4	252½	+1.3%	698½	+1.2
5	250½	−0.8%	695¼	-0.5
6	245¾	−0.2%	705¾	+0.1
7	247¼	+0.6%	708½	+0.4
8	249¾	+1.0%	703	−0.8
9	244¼	−2.2%	687¾	−0.2
10	246	+0.7%	683¼	−0.6
11	248¾	+1.1%	678¼	−0.7
12	254¼	+2.2%	664¾	−2.0
13	250¼	−1.6%	659¼	−0.8
14	249	−0.5%	656¾	−0.4
15	249½	+0.2%	655½	−0.2
16	241½	−3.3%	670	+2.2
17	246¾	+2.2%	684¼	+2.1
18	249¼	+1.0%	688½	+0.6
19	244¼	−2.0%	697	+1.2
20	246	+0.7%	699¾	+0.4
21	251¾	+2.3%	710¼	+1.5
22	249½	−0.9%	706¾	−0.5

Annualized standard deviation of daily returns = 24.8%

Annualized standard deviation of daily returns = 18.9%

Contract 1 are greater than those for Futures Contract 2. The absolute values of 21 percentage changes were less than 2.3 percent for Futures Contract 1 but were less than 2.2 percent for Futures Contract 2. Also, the average of these changes was 1.3 percent for Futures Contract 1 and 1.0 percent for Futures Contract 2. The conclusion, therefore, is that statistically, Futures Contract 1 was more volatile than Futures Contract 2 during the historic period observed.

Table 6–3 Ranking of Percentage Price Changes: Comparison of Historic Volatilities of Two Futures Contracts

Futures Price 1			Futures Price 2		
Day	I%I	Breakdown	Day	I%I	Breakdown
15	0.2	⎞ ⎞	15	0.2	⎞ ⎞
14	0.5	│ │	14	0.4	│ │
3	0.6	│ │	7	0.4	│ │
7	0.6	│ │	20	0.4	│ │
10	0.7	│ │	5	0.5	│ │
20	0.7	│ │	3	0.5	│68% │
5	0.8	│ │	22	0.5	│less │
22	0.9	│ │	18	0.6	│than │
1	1.0	│68% │	10	0.7	│1.2% │
8	1.0	│less │	11	0.7	│Avg. │95%
18	1.0	│than │	1	0.8	│0.6% │less
11	1.1	│1.6% │	8	0.8	│ │than
4	1.3	│Avg. │	13	0.8	│ │2.2%
2	1.3	│0.9% │	2	1.0	│ │Avg.
13	1.6	⎠ │95%	4	1.2	⎠ │1.0%
6	1.9	│less	19	1.2	│
19	2.0	│than	21	1.5	│
17	2.2	│2.3%	6	1.5	│
12	2.2	│Avg.	12	2.0	│
9	2.2	│1.3%	17	2.1	│
21	2.3	⎠	16	2.2	⎠
16	3.2		9	2.2	

Now that historic volatility has been introduced, future volatility, expected volatility, and implied volatility will be defined.

VOLATILITY 2: FUTURE VOLATILITY

Future volatility means the annualized standard deviation of daily returns during some future period, typically between the present time and an option expiration. And it is future volatility that option pricing formulas need as an input in order to calculate the theoretical value of an option. Unfortunately, future volatility is known only after it has become historic volatility. Consequently, the volatility numbers used in option pricing formulas are only *estimates* of future volatility. This may be a shock to those who place their faith in theoretical values, because it raises questions about those values. If the volatility number in a formula is only an estimate of future volatility, the calculated value must only be an estimate of theoretical value. And that is correct! So-called theoretical values are only estimates, and as with any estimate, they must be interpreted very carefully.

VOLATILITY 3: EXPECTED VOLATILITY

Option traders study market conditions and historic price action to forecast volatility just as agricultural analysts research supply-demand relationships, carryover levels, weather patterns, and the like, to make commodity price predictions. *Expected volatility* is an estimate of future volatility used by a trader in an option pricing formula to estimate an option's theoretical value. Since forecasts vary, there is no specific number on which everyone can agree as expected volatility.

Consider a situation in which two experienced option traders, Sharon and Ken, disagree on their estimates of the future volatility of Futures Contract 3. Assume that 10 weeks ago the most recent 30 closing levels of Futures Contract 3 indicated a historic volatility of 22 percent. Assume also that 6 weeks ago, 3 weeks ago, and yesterday, the same calculation using the then most recent 30 closing futures prices indicated historic volatilities of 21 percent, 19 percent, and 18 percent, respectively. Sharon and Ken cannot dispute these historic volatility percentages, because they are the results of mathematical calculations.

Sharon and Ken can, however, make different forecasts. Sharon, for example, may believe that the downward trend in volatility will continue, and she might expect that in one week, the 30-day historic volatility will be

17 percent. Consequently, Sharon may use 17 percent volatility in her option pricing formula. Ken, however, may believe that the downward trend is about to reverse and that historic volatility will be higher in 1 week. He therefore, may predict that in 7 days, the 30-day historic volatility will be 20 percent. Consequently, he may use 20 percent in his option pricing formula. Just as research analysts have differing opinions on the outlook for commodity prices, option traders differ on their expected volatilities.

Volatility 4: Implied Volatility

Implied volatility is the volatility percentage that explains the current market price of an option. This concept is best illustrated with an example. Consider a situation in which Frank, an experienced soybean option trader, uses OP-EVALF™ to estimate the theoretical value of the November Soybean 650 Call.

Figure 6–2 is a Call/Put Pricer page from OP-EVAL™ created by Frank. He input the current November Soybean Futures price of 6.42, inter-

Figure 6–2 Frank's Initial Call/Put Pricer Page

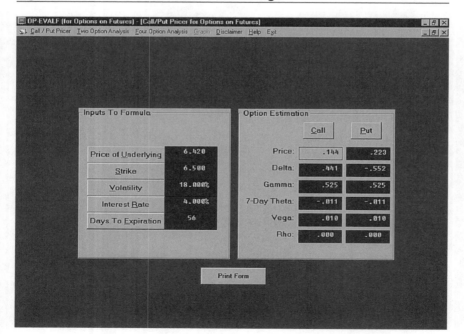

est rates of 4 percent, and days to November expiration of 56. Frank chose a volatility of 18 percent because this was the historic volatility based on the 30 most recent daily closing futures prices. Given Frank's inputs, OP-EVALF™ calculates a value of .144, or 14.4 cents, for the November Soybean 650 Call.

Frank now calls his broker and discovers that the November 650 Call is trading at 21! What is going on? Did Frank do something wrong? Or could the market be assuming something different from what Frank is assuming?

Could the market be assuming a different futures price? No. The futures price is known to be 6.42. Could the market be assuming a different strike price or time to expiration? Again the answer is no, because these are observable factors. Could the market be assuming a different interest rate? The answer here is also no. While interest rates may not be exactly observable, Chapter 4 explained that differences in interest rates have only a minor impact on option values. Thus, even if the market were assuming an interest rate 1 percent higher or lower than the one Frank is assuming, the difference in option value would not be more than 6 cents, which is the difference between the market price of the November 650 Call and the value calculated by Frank.

What, then, can account for the difference? The only remaining factor is volatility. It must be that the market is assuming a different volatility.

What volatility is the market assuming? Figure 6–3 is a Call/Put Pricer page from OP-EVALF™ in which the price of .210 has been entered in the Call rectangle and the Enter key has been pressed. The result is that OP-EVALF™ has calculated a volatility figure of 24.702 percent. This is the volatility percentage that explains the market price of the November 650 Call in this example, and this is the implied volatility of this option.

The Role of Supply and Demand

The forces of supply and demand determine option prices, just as they determine all prices in free markets. Since future volatility is the only variable in an option pricing formula that cannot be observed, it is the volatility percentage that must be adjusted to explain the market price of an option. As was explained above, implied volatility is the volatility percentage which, if used in the formula, produces the option's market price as the theoretical value. In the example above of Frank's 650 Call, 24.702 percent is the volatility percentage that made the formula's calculated value equal the option's market price.

Figure 6–3 Calculation of Implied Volatility

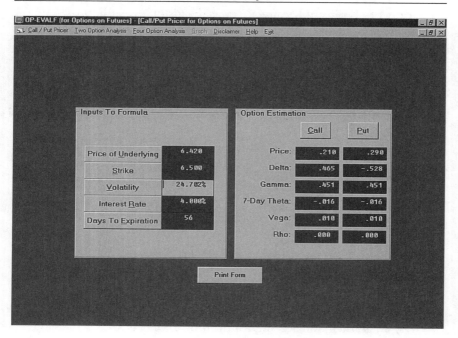

Implied volatility makes it possible to track market conditions. It is common parlance to describe Frank's soybean call as "trading at 24.702 percent volatility," and such information makes comparisons possible. This call, for example, at some previous time, may have been trading at a higher or lower implied volatility. If all other factors are equal, an option trading at a lower implied volatility is a relatively better purchase and an option trading at a higher implied volatility is a relatively better sale. But rarely, if ever, are all other factors equal, and so the level of implied volatility is not in and of itself an indication to buy or sell an option. Implied volatility is, however, important information for a trader to incorporate into the subjective decision-making process.

Changes in Implied Volatility

The implied volatility of futures options is important information because implied volatility changes frequently, and these changes can have a dramatic effect on the results of hedging and trading strategies. It is therefore important to understand why implied volatility changes and how it affects trading decisions.

One explanation of why implied volatility changes is based on the analogy between options and insurance presented in Chapter 4. In that analogy, volatility was compared to the risk factor in insurance, and the level of insurance premiums, it was explained, depends partly on the level of risk.

If an insurance company had records, for example, that 1 out of 100 homes is destroyed by fire, then in theory, fire insurance would cost 1 percent of the value of a home plus a profit margin. But if the insurance company perceives that fire will destroy a greater percentage of homes in the future than it did in the past, it will raise its premiums. Similarly, if the company perceives that fire will destroy fewer homes, premiums will be lowered. However, insurance companies live in a competitive environment, and some premiums are set to "meet the competition." This means that premiums sometimes are raised above the calculated level and sometimes are lowered below that level.

Historic volatility is like the insurance company's records of actual experience, expected volatility is like a particular insurance company's perception of future risk, and implied volatility is like the competitive premium level in the market. In options, many market participants compete, just as many insurance companies compete. It is the perception of the marketplace, through the forces of supply and demand, which determines implied volatility. Since perceptions change, implied volatility changes.

An example of when implied volatility might rise occurs when a weather forecaster announces the possibility of a drought. Before the announcement, it may have been reasonable to believe that the future volatility of the futures prices would be the same as historic volatility. Consequently, the implied volatility of option prices might have been close to historic volatility. The announcement, however, is likely to change expectations.

After the announcement there is reason to believe that prices could rise or fall dramatically next week, depending on developing weather conditions. Such a change in expectations would mean that buyers of options would be willing to pay higher prices, and sellers of options would want to receive higher prices. This change in consensus means that implied volatility has increased.

An example of when implied volatility might decline is after the possibility of a drought disappears. If developing weather patterns make it evident that there will not be a drought, there probably will be a reduction of anxiety about future price changes. If such developments occur, option sellers will be willing to receive lower prices and option buyers will only be willing to pay lower prices. Consequently, implied volatility will decrease.

Option traders use the implied volatility of an option to make a subjective judgement about an option's relative value. This concept is important and will be explained next.

Implied Volatility Is a Common Denominator

The price-earning ratio is a "common denominator" in stock market analysis that allows comparison across a range of variables, such as the number of shares outstanding, the value of company assets, and total sales, to name just a few. If the p/e ratio of Company A is 15, it is trading at a relatively lower value per share than Company B, whose p/e ratio is 20. This is true even if Company A has $6 billion in sales and a stock price of $100 and Company B has $1 billion in sales and a stock price of $50. Other common denominators are book value per share, sales per share, and percentage growth of earnings. The "per-share" amount of these variables provides insight for making judgments about the value of a particular stock.

Implied volatility does a thing for option prices similar to what p/e ratios do for stock prices. Implied volatility is a common denominator that makes it possible to compare options. Prices of options on two different futures contracts can be compared, and prices of the same option at different times can be compared.

Consider a 90-day 220 Corn Call trading at 30 cents. Without knowing the implied volatility, it is impossible to compare the price of this call to a 45-day 3.30 Wheat Call trading at 20 cents. However, if it is known that the implied volatility of the Corn Call is 18 percent and that the implied volatility of the Wheat Call is 28 percent there is a basis for describing the relative values of these two options.

Implied volatility also makes it possible to compare the same option at two different times when the price of the underlying and the time to expiration have changed. Assume that day 1 is 85 days to expiration, December Wheat is 3.18, the 320 Call is trading at 14¾ cents, and the implied volatility of this call is 20 percent. Also assume that day 2 is 65 days to expiration, the futures price is 3.33, the price of the 320 Call is 21½ cents, and the implied volatility is 20 percent. Given this information, it can be said that on day 2, this option is a "better relative value in volatility terms" than it is on day 1. It can also be said that its total price is higher and that it has less time to expiration. There are three variables that describe an option.

Implied volatility is information that can be used as part of the subjective decision-making process, but implied volatility alone does not give a specific recommendation to buy or sell.

Is 50 percent implied volatility high? Is 15 percent low? There are no absolute answers to such questions. There are only relative answers. By keeping track of implied volatility, a trader can gain historical perspective. As a result, better-informed predictions can be made. This does not guarantee that the predictions will be accurate, but generally speaking, predictions based on more information are better.

"Overvalued" and "Undervalued"

Now that the four types of volatility have been defined, the discussion will focus on the concept of value. There is perhaps no greater misconception in the options business than the one involving the meaning of the terms *overvalued* and *undervalued*. Novice traders misconstrue these terms to mean that "easy money" can be made by purchasing options "below theoretical value" or selling options "above theoretical value." Nothing could be further from reality.

An option will appear overvalued or undervalued at one particular moment only because an option pricing formula, at that moment, calculates a "value" different from the market price. If a "value" of 7 is calculated but the option is trading at 6, for example, that option appears to be undervalued. A trader who purchases this option will profit only if the option returns to the "theoretical value" and *all other factors remain constant*. But other factors remaining constant means that the futures price and the time to expiration remain constant and only the volatility changes. Is such a scenario likely or even possible? Definitely not!

Reflect for a moment on the difference between the calculated theoretical value of 7 and the market price of 6 in the previous paragraph. What is the *conceptual difference* between 6 and 7? Is it the underlying futures price level? No. Is it the strike price, the time to expiration, or interest rates? Again, no. The difference is the volatility percentage. The volatility percentage used in the formula is the trader's expected volatility, and the volatility percentage that explains the market price is the implied volatility. Therefore, this option appears undervalued because the trader's expected volatility is higher than the implied volatility. When an option appears overvalued, it is because a trader's expected volatility is lower than the implied volatility.

This is an important concept. "Undervalued" and "overvalued" depend on the relationship of expected volatility to implied volatility.

Implied volatility can be objectively observed, because market prices can be observed but expected volatility depends on the judgment of a trader. Therefore "overvalued" and "undervalued" depend on the same judgment.

The subjective nature of the terms *overvalued* and *undervalued* raises questions about the concept of theoretical value. The term *theoretical value* sounds impressive and authoritative, but theoretical value depends on future volatility, and future volatility is unknown. This means that any price presented as the theoretical value of an option is actually only an estimate, an educated guess. This may be a startling notion to new option traders, but everything depends on judgment in trading, including the determination of value.

Two Traders, Two Opinions About Value

Consider two experienced wheat option traders and how they might arrive at different conclusions about the "value" of a particular option. Tom is an engineer in Boston who "day-trades" wheat options when he is not swamped at work. Susan is a marketing analyst in Atlanta who has a different trading style. She charts wheat futures and looks for patterns that, in her opinion, predict a 5- to 10-day move of 10 to 20 cents.

On the day in question, July wheat futures are trading at 2.95, it is 45 days to the expiration of July options, and the July Wheat 300 Call is trading at 5¼ cents. In this example we assume that interest rates are 4.50 percent. Tom predicts that July Wheat futures will rise 5 cents to 3.00 today, and he is considering the purchase of the July 300 Call at 5¼.

Tom has observed that both the historic volatility of wheat futures and the implied volatility of wheat options have been declining. Tom calculates a 15 percent 30-day historic volatility of the wheat futures price and an implied volatility of 18 percent for the July 300 Call. Tom believes that the implied volatility of this call will drop to 15 percent by the end of today, and he creates Table 6–4 to estimate how the July 300 Call will change in price if his forecast is realized.

As Table 6–4 indicates, if July Wheat futures rise to 3.00 today and implied volatility falls to 15 percent, the July 300 Call will rise from 5¼(row 3, column 1) to 6¼ (row 8, column 2) for a profit of 1 cent. Table 6–4 also shows that if implied volatility remains at 18 percent, the 300 Call will rise from 5¼ to 7½ (row 8, column 1). If Tom's futures price forecast is wrong, and July Wheat futures are unchanged or decline 1 cent and if implied volatility decreases to 15 percent, Table 6–4 shows that the July 300 Call will decline to 4⅛ or to 3¾.

Table 6–4 Tom's Analysis of the July Wheat 300 Call
(Days to Expiration, 45; Interest rates, 4.5%)

	Futures Price	Col. 1 18% Volatility	Col. 2 15% Volatility
Row 1	293	4½	3⅜
Row 2	294	4⅞	3¾
Row 3	295	5¼	4⅛
Row 4	296	5⅝	4½
Row 5	297	6	4⅞
Row 6	298	6½	5¼
Row 7	299	7	5¾
Row 8	300	7½	6¼
Row 9	301	8	6¾

To Tom, the risk/reward of this trade does not seem justified. A 1-cent profit if his forecast is exactly correct is not worth the risk of a 1⅛ -cent or 1½-cent loss if futures are unchanged or decline 1 cent. To Tom, this call appears "overvalued." Tom does not purchase the July 300 Call and looks for another trade.

The second trader, Susan, analyzes the same situation and arrives at a different conclusion. Susan is considering buying the July 300 Call, because she forecasts a 20-cent rise in July Wheat futures in 7 days and a rise in implied volatility to 22 percent. Susan creates Table 6–5 to estimate the results of her forecast.

If Susan's forecast is realized, July Wheat Futures will be 3.15 at 38 days to expiration, and Table 6–5 estimates that the price of the July 300 Call will be 18 cents (row 6, column 2). Purchasing the 300 Call for 5¼ and selling it at 18 results in a profit of 12¾ cents, not including commissions. Table 6–5 also estimates that if implied volatility remains constant at 18 percent, the price of the 300 Call will be 16⅞ cents (row 6, column 1). Purchasing the 300 Call at 5¼ and selling it a 16⅞ yields a profit of 11⅝ cents, not including commissions. The rise in implied volatility accounts for 1⅛ cents of Susan's estimated 12¾-cent profit, but she still estimates a profit if volatility is unchanged.

If July Wheat futures decline to 290, Susan's forecast for the futures price will be wrong. If, however, her forecasts for time and implied volatility are correct, Table 6–5 estimates that the price of the 300 Call will be 4¼ (row 1, column 2). Of course, if the implied volatility remains unchanged at 18 percent, Table 6–5 indicates that the price of the 300 Call will be 3 cents (row 1, column 1), a loss of 2¼ cents, not including commissions, from a purchase price of 5¼. To Susan, this analysis indicates that the July 300 Call appears undervalued, because she profits if all three parts of her forecast are accurate. She also profits if her futures price level and time forecasts are accurate but implied volatility is unchanged. She anticipates only a 1-cent loss before commissions if her time and volatility forecasts are accurate but the futures price declines 5 cents. Confident about her forecast and willing to assume a loss if all three parts of her forecast are wrong, Susan instructs her broker to purchase the July Wheat 300 Call at 5¼ cents.

Tom and Susan agreed that the 300 Call is trading at an implied volatility of 18 percent. However, they disagreed on whether it was overvalued or undervalued, because they have different trading styles and, in this case, have different expected volatilities.

The general conclusion is that value, like beauty, is in the eye of the beholder. The only variable in the market price of an option that cannot be observed objectively is implied volatility, and the only variable in the calculation of an option's theoretical value is expected volatility. Therefore, a judgment that the market price of an option is above or below theoretical value is actually a judgment about the relationship of the implied volatility to the expected volatility.

Table 6–5 Susan's Analysis of the July Wheat 300 Call
(Days to Expiration, 38; Interest rates, 4.5%)

		Col. 1	Col. 2
	Futures Price	**18% Volatility**	**22% Volatility**
Row 1	290	3	4¼
Row 2	295	4⅝	6⅛
Row 3	300	6⅛	8½
Row 4	305	9¼	11¼
Row 5	310	13⅜	14½
Row 6	315	16⅞	18

VOLATILITY SKEWS

The term *volatility skew* describes a market condition in which options with the same underlying and the same expiration but with different strike prices trade at different implied volatilities. This is a common occurrence in markets for options on futures contracts.

Table 6–6 contains prices and implied volatilities of August Live Cattle options. There are calls and puts with 11 strike prices. The August Live Cattle futures price is 65.20, interest rates are 4.50 percent, and it is 58 days to expiration. Note that the implied volatility of the at-the-money 65 Call and 65 Put is 30.0 percent (row 6). Note also that the implied volatilities of the other options increase as strike prices increase or decrease. The implied volatility of the 64 Call and 64 Put, for example, is 30.80 percent.

Figure 6-4 presents the information in Table 6–6 in graphical form. Note that the line above 65 is not symmetrical with the line below 65. Also note that neither line is perfectly straight. Although this information is not real data on a real futures contract, Table 6–6 and Figure 6-4 are illustrative of the varying levels of implied volatility of options on futures. In hectic market environments, the overall level of implied volatility and the slopes of implied volatility skews change frequently. Option traders must be aware of these potential changes and prepare themselves accordingly.

Table 6–6 Volatility Skews
(August Live Cattle, 65.20; Interest Rates, 4.5%; Days to Expiration, 58)

	Call Price	Strike Price	Put Price	Implied Volatility
Row 1	6.58	60	1.43	34.40%
Row 2	5.83	61	1.65	33.40%
Row 3	5.10	62	1.93	32.60%
Row 4	4.40	63	2.23	31.70%
Row 5	3.78	64	2.58	30.80%
Row 6	3.18	65	2.98	30.00%
Row 7	2.75	66	3.55	30.40%
Row 8	2.40	67	4.18	30.90%
Row 9	2.08	68	4.85	31.30%
Row 10	1.80	69	5.58	31.70%
Row 11	1.55	70	6.33	32.20%

Figure 6–4 Graph of Volatility Skew

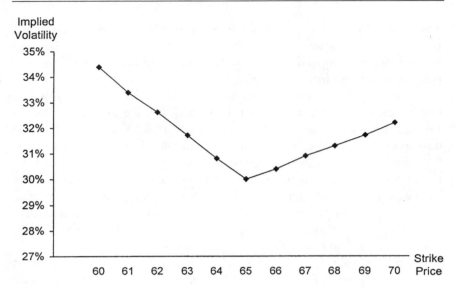

Why Skews Exist

It seems illogical that one underlying instrument could have more than one volatility, and to date, no theoretical reason for the existence of volatility skews has been presented. One practical explanation, however, has been suggested. Since option prices are determined by supply and demand, it is possible that there are different forces of supply and demand for different options. Since options are analogous to insurance policies and strike prices are analogous to deductibles, it is possible that there are different elements of supply and demand for the different protection, i.e., insurance, offered by options with different strike prices. It is possible that there is more demand for "cheap insurance policies," i.e., policies with a low absolute price.

To meet this increased demand, the logic goes, sellers of low-cost insurance policies require a "high-risk premium." In options terminology, this means a high implied volatility, not a high absolute price.

How Volatility Skews Affect Trading Decisions

Traders must consider the existence of volatility skews when making forecasts. Assume, for example, that out-of-the-money option Strike O is trading at a higher implied volatility than at-the-money option Strike A. As the futures price moves from Strike A to Strike O, there may be a tendency for the implied volatility of the call and put with Strike O to decrease and for the implied volatility of the call and put with Strike A to increase.

Consider the forecasting problem being addressed by Brian, an experienced live cattle option trader. Brian is studying the purchase of an August Live Cattle 61 Put. For this example, assume an August Live Cattle futures price of 65.20 and the option prices and market conditions in Table 6–6, i.e., 58 days to expiration, interest rates of 4.50 percent, and the implied volatilities indicated. Brian must first state his forecasts for the futures price, the time to expiration, and the implied volatility of the August 61 Put.

Brian is bearish, predicting that the August Live Cattle futures will decline to 61 cents in 2 weeks. He also believes that implied volatility will remain constant. Brian's volatility forecast, however, raises a question.

What does "implied volatility will remain constant" mean when there is a volatility skew? What implied volatility level should Brian use when estimating the value of the 61 Put? If the futures price declines to 61 cents in 2 weeks, as Brian predicts, the 61 Put will have moved from 4.20 cents out-of-the-money to at-the-money. If the "implied volatility level remains constant," as Brian predicts, the implied volatility of the 61 Put will decline to 30.00 percent from 33.40 percent. Table 6–7 shows the implications of this change.

Column 1 of Table 6–7 shows the initial market conditions in which the futures price level is 65.20, there are 58 days to expiration, the implied volatility is 33.40 percent, and the 61 Put is 1.65. Column 2 estimates a price of 2.80 for the 61 Put assuming a futures price of 61.00 and 44 days to expiration, and the implied volatility of the 61 Put remains at 33.40%. Column 3 estimates a price of 2.50 for the 61 Put, assuming the same conditions as column 2 except that implied volatility of the 61 Put declines to 30.00 percent. This difference means that Brian will make 0.85 per option instead of 1.15 per option. Whether this difference is sufficient to dissuade Brian from making this trade is a subjective decision that only he can make. Nevertheless, even if Brian is confident about his forecasts for the futures price and time, the existence of the volatility skew has an impact on his decision.

The conclusion from Brian's example is that if other factors remain constant, the existence of implied volatility skews tends to be a disadvantage for buyers of out-of-the-money options. Other factors, of course, rarely, if ever, remain constant. There could be a change in the overall level of implied volatility, or there could be a change in the slope of the volatility skew. Changes in either or both of these market conditions could change in favor of or against a particular option strategy. Consequently, option traders must consider the existence of volatility skews and the overall level of implied volatility.

Table 6–7 Brian Analyzes the Impact of the Volatility Skew

	Col. 1	Col. 2			Col. 3		
	Initial Inputs	Futures Price and Days Changed; Volatility Unchanged			Futures Price, Days, and Volatility Changed		
Inputs							
Futures price	65.20	→	61.00		→	61.00	
Strike price	61						
Volatility	33.40%	→	33.40%		→	30.00%	
Interest rates	4.5%						
Days to expiration	58	→	44		→	44	
Outputs							
61 Put price	1.65	→	2.80		→	2.50	
Estimated profit			1.15			0.85	

SUMMARY

Volatility means changes in price without regard to direction. Historic volatility is a measure of actual price changes during a specific time period in the past. Expected volatility is a trader's forecast of volatility used in an option pricing formula to estimate the theoretical value of an option. Implied volatility is the volatility percentage that explains the current market price of an option.

Implied volatility is the common denominator of option prices. Similar to the way in which p/e ratios allow comparisons of stock prices over a range of variables such as total earnings and number of shares outstanding, implied volatility allows a comparison of prices of options on different futures contracts and a comparison of prices of the same option at different times.

The theoretical value of an option is a statistical concept, and traders should focus on relative value, not absolute value. The terms overvalued and undervalued describe a relationship between implied volatility and expected volatility. Two traders can different their opinion of the relative value of the same option if they have different market forecasts and different trading styles.

Volatility skews describe a market condition in which options with the same underlying and same expiration date but with different strike prices trade at different implied volatilities. Traders must consider both volatility skews and the overall level of implied volatility when making forecasts.

Seven

Option Price Behavior II: The Greeks

This chapter explains the five option "estimators," delta, gamma, theta, vega, and rho, which are frequently referred to as "the Greeks." Each is an estimate of the change in option value caused by a change in one of the inputs to an option pricing formula, assuming that other factors remain constant. Used in conjunction with a specific market forecast, these tools are helpful in estimating the potential profit or loss of a particular strategy, and they help hedgers and traders choose between a number of strategies that are appropriate for a specific market forecast.

This chapter defines the Greeks and explains why they are positively or negatively correlated to option values. Second, it discusses how each of the Greeks changes with changes in futures price and time to expiration. Third, position Greeks are explained. It is important to understand that position Greeks are different from Greeks of option values.

The discussion in this chapter gets fairly technical. Consequently, readers with less experience may want to skim this chapter or skip it for now and come back to it after reading Part 3, "Trading Strategies." Reading Part 3 first will raise questions about how and why option prices behave the way they do. After one reads through the examples in that section, some of the detailed information in this chapter may seem more relevant to the decision-making process.

DELTA

As discussed in Chapter 5, the price of the underlying instrument is an important factor in the determination of option values. *Delta is an estimate of the change in option value given a one-unit change in the price of the underlying instrument, assuming that other factors remain constant.* Delta answers this question: If the underlying futures price rises or falls by one point, how much should I make or lose?

117

The tables in this chapter were created using the software OP-EVALF™, which is explained in detail in Chapter 11. Table 7–1 assumes the default parameters in OP-EVALF™: a futures price of 600, a strike price of 600, volatility of 15 percent, interest rates of 5 percent, and 30 days to expiration. Given these inputs, four of the outputs on the Call/Put Pricer page are a 600 Call value of 10.251, a 600 Call delta of +.506, a 600 Put value of 10.251, and a 600 Put delta of –.489.

In Table 7–1, the delta of the 600 Call estimates that if the futures price rises by 1 cent to 6.01 and other factors remain constant, the 600 Call value will rise by .506 to 10.757. The delta of the 600 Put estimates that under the same circumstances, the 600 Put value will fall by .489 to 9.762. These deltas closely estimate the change in call and put values, but not exactly, as the values to the right of the arrows in Table 7–1 show. Raising the futures price to 601 while leaving the other factors unchanged causes the 600 Call value to increase to 10.765, a change of +.514, slightly more than the delta. The 600 Put value decreases to 9.769, a change slightly less than the absolute value of the put's delta. The differences between the estimated changes and the actual changes will be explained in the section entitled "Gamma." First, however, there are some observations to be made about delta.

Mathematically, the delta of an option is the first derivative of option value with respect to change in the price of the underlying. While this technical definition may be helpful to some, it is undoubtedly confusing to

Table 7–1 Illustration of Delta

	Initial Inputs		Inputs with Changed Futures Price
Inputs:			
Futures price	6.00	→	6.01
Strike price	6.00		
Volatility	15%		
Interest rates	5%		
Days to Expiration	30		

	Initial Outputs		New Outputs
Outputs:			
600 Call price	10.251	→	10.765
600 Call delta	+0.506		
600 Put price	10.251	→	9.769
600 Put delta	−0.489		

lothers. It is not important to know the mathematics, but it is important to understand the concept that delta is an estimate of the change in option value given a one-unit change in the price of the underlying with other factors remaining constant. As will be shown later, a one-unit change in the price of the underlying causes relatively bigger changes in the values of in-the-money options, relatively smaller changes in the values of at-the-money options, and even smaller changes in the values of out-of-the-money options.

> **DELTA**
> Estimated change in option value resulting from a one-unit change in the price of the underlying futures

Call Values Have Positive Deltas

The plus sign (+) associated with the delta of the 600 Call in Table 7–1 indicates a positive, or direct, relationship between the change in price of the underlying instrument and the change in the theoretical value of the call. As Table 7–1 illustrates, when only the underlying futures price rises, the theoretical value of the 600 Call also rises. It should be noted that a plus or minus sign associated with an *option value* may be different from the sign of an *option position*. The subject of position deltas will be discussed later.

Put Values Have Negative Deltas

The minus sign (–) associated with the delta of the 600 Put indicates a negative, or opposite, relationship between the change in the price of the underlying instrument and the change in the value of the put. In Table 7–1, a rise in the futures price caused the put value to decline.

Finding Deltas in OP-EVALF™

Delta appears in the OP-EVALF™ program on three pages in two different forms. On the Call/Put Pricer page, deltas appear under the respective call and put values. On the Two Option Analysis and the Four Option Analysis pages, deltas appear in two places. Deltas of individual options appear in the Delta row, and a spread delta appears in the rectangle labeled as such. The *spread delta* is the sum of the deltas of individual options in a position. How traders might use a spread delta is explained in Chapter 14, "Trading Vertical Spreads."

GAMMA

Refer back to Table 7–1 and note that the delta of +.506 does not exactly predict the 600 Call value after a one-point increase in the underlying futures price. Why? This difference between the estimated change in value and the actual change in value occurs because the delta changes when the price of the underlying changes. *Gamma is an estimate of the change in delta for a one-unit change in the price of the underlying instrument, assuming other factors remain constant.* Mathematically, gamma is the second derivative of the option pricing formula with respect to change in the price of the underlying. Gamma answers this question: How much does my exposure to the market change when the underlying futures price changes; i.e., how much does my delta change? Gamma also makes it possible to estimate more accurately the change in option value when the underlying futures price changes.

Table 7–2 illustrates the concept of gamma by starting with the information in Table 7–1 and adding the new call and put deltas and the call and put gammas before and after the change in the futures price. When the futures price rises from 6.00 to 6.01, Table 7–2 shows that the delta of the 600 Call increases from +.506 to +.522, a rise of .016, a change almost exactly equal to the gamma. The difference is due to rounding.

Table 7–2 Illustration of Gamma (1)

	Initial Inputs		Inputs with Changed Futures Price
Inputs:			
Futures price	6.00	→	6.01
Strike price	6.00		
Volatility	15%		
Interest rates	5%		
Days to expiration	30		

	Initial Outputs		New Outputs
Outputs:			
600 Call price	10.251	→	10.765
600 Call delta	+0.506	→	+0.522
600 Call gamma	+0.015	→	+0.015
600 Put price	10.251	→	9.769
600 Put delta	−0.489	→	−0.474
600 Put gamma	+0.015	→	+0.015

Similarly, the delta of the 600 Put *increases* by .015 from −.489 to −.474. That's right! This is an *increase* in the put delta. For readers comfortable with math, this may seem obvious. Others should take note: It is important to keep track of plus signs and minus signs and increases and decreases in value.

While the gammas of the both the 600 Call and the 600 Put remain constant when the futures price rises in Table 7–2, this will not always be the case. Also, as is the case in Table 7–2, the change in call and put deltas will not always exactly equal the gammas. There will frequently be small differences resulting from rounding and changing gammas. Nothing is constant in the options business!

> **GAMMA**
> Estimated change in option delta resulting from a change in the price of the underlying

Gammas of Option Values Are Positive

Plus signs are associated with gammas of both calls and puts, because a change in delta is positively correlated to a change in the price of the underlying. Table 7–2 illustrates that an increase in the futures price causes an increase in the deltas of both the 600 Call and the 600 Put. Table 7–3 shows

Table 7–3 Illustration of Gamma (2)

	Initial Inputs		Inputs with Changed Futures Price
Inputs:			
Futures price	6.00	→	5.99
Strike price	6.00		
Volatility	15%		
Interest rates	5%		
Days to expiration	30		

	Initial Outputs		New Outputs
Outputs:			
600 Call price	10.251	→	9.752
600 Call delta	+0.506	→	+0.491
600 Call gamma	+0.015	→	+0.015
600 Put price	10.251	→	10.748
600 Put delta	−0.489	→	−0.505
600 Put gamma	+0.015	→	+0.015

that a decrease in the futures price causes a decrease in the deltas of both options. As the futures price decreases from 6.00 to 5.99 and other factors remain constant, the 600 Call delta decreases from +.506 to +.491. The 600 Put delta also decreases, from -.489 to -.505. This is a positive correlation: futures price up, delta up; futures price down, delta down.

Another observation is that the gammas of calls and puts with the same underlying, same strike price, and same expiration date are equal. This is always true because of a technical concept known as call-put parity. According to this concept, if the call and the put have the same underlying, the same strike price, and the same expiration date, if the delta of the call increases, the absolute value of the put delta must decrease by an equal amount. Consequently, since the deltas of the call and the put change by the same amount, their gammas must be equal, because gamma is the change in delta. An in-depth discussion of call-put parity is beyond the scope of this book, but readers interested in this topic can refer to a book by Sheldon Natenberg, *Option Volatility and Pricing.*

Vega

> **VEGA**
> **Estimated change in option value resulting from a 1 percent change in volatility**

Vega is the change in option value that results from a 1 percent change in the volatility assumption, assuming that other factors remain constant. Mathematically, vega is the first derivative of option price with respect to change in volatility. Since first derivatives are theoretically "instantaneous rates of change" and since vega estimates the impact of a "1 percent change," there will frequently be rounding errors. Vega answers this question: If volatility changes by 1 percent, how much do I make or lose?

Table 7–4 illustrates how both the at-the-money 600 Call and 600 Put values change from 10.251 to 10.934 when the volatility assumption is increased from 15 percent to 16 percent.

Vegas of Option Values Are Positive

Vegas of both call values and put values are positive, because option values are positively correlated to changes in volatility, i.e., volatility up, option value up; volatility down, option value down.

Another result of the call-put parity concept mentioned above is that vegas of calls and puts with the same underlying, the same strike price, and the same expiration date are equal. According to call-put parity, there is

Table 7–4 Illustration of Vega

	Initial Inputs		Inputs with Changed Volatility
Inputs:			
Futures price	6.00		
Strike price	6.00		
Volatility	15%	→	16%
Interest rates	5%		
Days to expiration	30		

	Initial Outputs		New Outputs
Outputs:			
600 Call price	10.251	→	10.934
600 Call vega	+0.683		
600 Put price	10.251	→	10.934
600 Put vega	+0.683		

a quantifiable relationship between the price of the underlying instrument and the prices of calls and puts with the same strike and the same expiration. For the call-put parity relationship to be maintained, when the call or put value increases, the corresponding put or call value must rise by an identical amount. Thus, vegas of calls and puts with the same underlying, strike, and expiration must be equal.

Readers familiar with the Greek alphabet may note that vega is not a Greek letter. It is not clear how the use of this term evolved, but it is employed commonly in the options industry. One belief is that option traders wanted a short word beginning with a *V* and sounding like delta, gamma, and theta. But exactly who coined the term and when it was first used are not known. Some mathematicians and writers use another Greek letter, such as kappa or lambda, instead of vega. Why there is no uniform terminology for such a widely discussed topic as volatility is one of the quirks of the options business. It is just another indication of how flexible options traders must be!

THETA

Theta is an estimate of the change in option value given a one-unit change in time to expiration, assuming that other factors remain constant. Theta answers this question: If time passes, how much do I make or lose? Table 7–5 illustrates what happens to at-the-money call and put values when days to expiration are

THETA
Estimated change in
option value resulting
from a "one-unit" change
in the time to expiration

lowered from 30 to 23. The call values of the 600 Call and 600 Put decrease from 10.251 to 8.984, a change of –1.267, almost exactly equal to the theta of –1.266. Slight differences between the theta and the change in option value are due to rounding and the fact that thetas change.

The definition of theta raises an important question: What is "one unit of time"? Mathematically, theta is the first derivative of option value with respect to change in time to expiration. This means, theoretically, that "one unit of time" is instantaneous. Such a concept, however, is not helpful to traders who need a tool they can use to estimate the impact of time decay on a strategy. While many professional traders use a "1-day theta," individual traders generally have a different time frame, perhaps 2 to 3 days or 2 to 3 weeks or some other time frame. Consequently, there is no "right" definition of what "one unit of time" is.

OP-EVALF™ calculates a "7-day theta" when days to expiration is greater than 10 and a "1-day theta" when days to expiration is 10 or less. These theta calculations are the result of subtracting the value in 7 days (or 1 day) from the current value and were chosen because they are thought to

Table 7-5 Illustration of Theta

Inputs	Initial Inputs		Inputs with Changed Days to Expiration
Inputs			
Futures price	6.00		
Strike price	6.00		
Volatility	15%		
Interest rates	5%		
Days to expiration	30	→	23

	Initial Outputs		New Outputs
Outputs			
600 Call price	10.251	→	8.984
600 Call theta (7-day)	-1.266		
600 Put price	10.251	→	8.984
600 Put theta (7-day)	−1.266		

be typical time frames for individual, nonprofessional traders. Different programs, of course, define the term *unit of time* differently, and so it is important to know how a theta is defined before attempting to use any program to estimate option price behavior.

Thetas of Option Values Are Negative

The minus sign associated with theta is sometimes a source of confusion to new option traders. Option values themselves are directly correlated to changes in the days to expiration: the more time to expiration, the higher an option's value, and the less time, the lower the value, assuming that other factors are constant. Consequently, one might think that thetas should be preceded by plus signs. But they are preceded by minus signs! Why?

It is standard practice to have a minus sign in front of thetas because options decrease in value the longer they are held, other factors remaining constant. The minus sign associated with thetas assumes that the option is owned and decays, or loses money, as expiration approaches.

Experienced option traders may be aware that there is one exception to the rule about thetas being preceded by negative signs. Although an in-depth discussion of this topic is beyond the scope of this book, it is possible for the theoretical value of a deep in-the-money European-style option to be less than intrinsic value. This can occur because European-style options cannot be exercised early. When such a situation exists, the option has a positive theta that indicates that its theoretical value increases to intrinsic value as expiration approaches. Options on futures in the United States, however, are American-style, and so negative signs always precede thetas of these options.

RHO

Rho is an estimate of the change in option value given a 1 percent change in interest rates, assuming other factors remain constant. Rho answers this question: If interest rates change by 1 percent, how much do I make or lose? Table 7–6 illustrates how the 600 Call and 600 Put values change when the interest rate is increased from 5 percent to 6 percent. The values of the at-the-money 600 Call and 600 Put decrease from 10.251 to 10.242, a change almost exactly equal to the rho of –0.008.

> **RHO**
> Estimated change in option value resulting from a 1 percent change in interest rates

Table 7-6 Illustration of Rho

	Initial Inputs	Inputs with Changed Interest Rate
Inputs:		
Futures price	6.00	
Strike price	6.00	
Volatility	15%	
Interest rates	5% →	6%
Days to expiration	30	

	Initial Outputs	New Outputs
Outputs:		
600 Call price	10.251 →	10.242
600 Call rho	−0.008	
600 Put price	10.251 →	10.242
600 Put rho	−0.008	

Rhos of options on futures are negative because of cost-of-carry considerations. Conceptually, as interest rates rise, the cost of owning an option increases. Therefore, in a relative sense, options become less valuable. A detailed discussion of interest rates and option prices is beyond the scope of this book. Fortunately, the impact of changes in interest rates on short-term option values is small. Traders of short-term futures options therefore do not need to be as concerned with rho as they should be with the other Greeks. Consequently, the impact of interest rates and rho will not be discussed in this book.

HOW THE GREEKS CHANGE

It is difficult to measure something when the measure itself changes, and the task of estimating changes in option values is complicated by the fact that the Greeks change when market conditions change. To illustrate this concept, Table 7–7 presents a grid of 600 Call values, 600 Put values, and corresponding Greeks at various futures prices and days to expiration, assuming volatility of 15 percent and interest rates of 5 percent. A study of this table reveals how delta, gamma, vega, and theta change as market conditions change. The concepts in Table 7–7 are important for option traders who must consider the impact of changing market conditions on their strategies.

How Deltas Change

Delta estimates how much an option value changes when the underlying futures price changes and other factors remain constant. There are four general rules about how deltas change. Because calls have positive deltas and puts have negative deltas, the four rules will be stated by using the absolute values of the deltas.

The first rule relates to deltas of in-the-money, at-the-money, and out-of-the-money options. In-the-money options have deltas with absolute values greater than +.500, at-the-money options have deltas with absolute values of approximately +.500, and out-of-the-money options have deltas with absolute values less than +.500.

Table 7–7 verifies these rules. With a futures price of 625, the 600 Call is in-the-money and the 600 Put is out-of-the-money. Row A shows that the absolute value of the delta of the 600 Call is always above +.500 and that the absolute value of the delta of the 600 Put is always below +.500. With a futures price of 5.75, the situation is reversed. The 600 Call is out-of-the-money, the 600 Put is in-the-money, and the absolute values of their deltas are also reversed.

With the futures price at 6.00, both the 600 Call and the 600 Put are at-the-money, and the absolute values of their deltas are approximately +.500. They are not exactly +.500 because of the log-normal distribution assumption in the Black-Scholes option pricing model. In a log-normal distribution, prices can rise indefinitely, but they can fall only to zero. Consequently, there is a slight upward skew. The mathematics of this concept is beyond the scope of this book, but it is explained in *Futures, Options and Other Derivative Securities* by John Hull.

The second general rule relates to how deltas change as expiration approaches. The absolute values of deltas of in-the-money options increase toward +1.00 as expiration approaches, the absolute values of deltas of at-the-money options remain near +.500, and the absolute values of deltas of out-of-the-money options decrease toward zero as expiration approaches.

The third rule relates to how deltas change as the underlying futures price changes. Both call and put deltas increase as the underlying instrument rises in price and decrease as the underlying falls in price. Column 1 in Table 7–7 shows that, as the futures price rises, the 600 Call delta rises from +.185 (row E) to +.507 (row C) to +.813 (row A) and the 600 Put delta rises from −.810 (row F) to −.488 (row D) to −.183 (row B). Remember to keep increases and decreases straight when minus signs are involved! The same concept — deltas rising with a rising futures price and falling with a falling futures price — holds true for any column in Table 7–7.

Table 7-7 Delta, Gamma, Vega, and Theta for In-the-Money, At-the-Money, and Out-of-the-Money Options

		Col. 1 35 Days	Col. 2 28 Days	Col. 3 21 Days	Col. 4 14 Days	Col. 5 7 Days	Col. 6 EXP.
Row	Call/Put			Futures Price 6.25			
A	**600 Call**	**27.835**	**27.086**	**26.335**	**25.626**	**25.094**	**25.000**
	Delta	.813	.839	.873	.918	.975	1.000
	Gamma	.009	.009	.009	.008	.004	.000
	Vega	.524	.429	.320	.193	.055	.000
	Theta (7-day)	−.748	−.751	−.710	−.531	−.043*	.000
B	**600 Put**	**2.954**	**2.182**	**1.407**	**.674**	**.118**	**0.000**
	Delta	−.183	−.157	−.124	−.080	−.024	0.000
	Gamma	.009	.009	.009	.008	.004	.000
	Vega	.524	.429	.320	.193	.055	.000
	Theta (7-day)	−.772	−.775	−.734	−.555	−.037*	.000
				Futures Price 6.00			
C	**600 Call**	**11.064**	**9.906**	**8.587**	**7.018**	**4.968**	**0.000**
	Delta	.507	.506	.506	.505	.504	.000
	Gamma	.014	.016	.018	.023	.032	.000
	Vega	.737	.660	.572	.468	.331	.000
	Theta (7-day)	−1.158	−1.319	−1.569	−2.051	−.368*	.000

D

600 Put	11.064	9.906	8.587	7.018	4.968	0.000
Delta	−.488	−.490	−.491	−.493	−.495	.000
Gamma	.014	.016	.018	.023	.032	.000
Vega	.737	.660	.572	.468	.331	.000
Theta (7-day)	−1.158	−1.319	−1.569	−2.051	−.368*	.000

Futures Price 5.75

E

600 Call	2.646	1.933	1.224	.567	0.091	0.000
Delta	.185	.157	.122	.076	.021	.000
Gamma	.010	.010	.010	.009	.005	.000
Vega	.487	.395	.291	.171	.045	.000
Theta (7-day)	−.714	−.708	−.658	−.476	−.038	.000

F

600 Put	27.527	26.834	26.152	25.519	25.067	25.000
Delta	−.810	−.838	−.875	−.922	−.978	−1.000
Gamma	.010	.010	.010	.009	.005	.000
Vega	.487	.395	.291	.171	.045	.000
Theta (7-day)	−.690	−.685	−.634	−.452	−.034	.000

* 1-day theta.

The fourth general rule is that the sum of the absolute values of the call delta and put delta is approximately +1.00. With the futures price at 5.75 at 35 days to expiration, for example, the delta of the 600 Call is +.185 and the delta of the 600 Put is −.810. The sum of the absolute values of these numbers, +.995, does not exactly equal 1.000 because of cost-of-carry considerations. This relationship is another result of the call-put relationship, and this is true at any point in Table 7–7.

How Gammas Change

Table 7–7 shows that gammas are biggest when options are at-the-money and increase for at-the-money options as expiration approaches. For in-the-money and out-of-the-money options, gammas increase for a while and then decrease. How gammas change is significant to option traders, because it explains the way option prices behave as an underlying futures price changes and as options change from being out-of-the-money to being at-the-money and then in-the-money. Out-of-the-money options, with low deltas and smaller gammas, do not respond dramatically to small changes in the underlying futures price. However, as the futures price approaches the strike price, the newly at-the-money option seems to "explode," moving noticeably more than its delta. Such option price behavior can bring tears of joy to option owners and screams of horror to option writers.

Consider the case of Floyd, who bought a 600 Call for 2⅜, or approximately 2.646, when soybean futures were 5.75 at 35 days to expiration (Table 7–7, column 1, row E). If the futures price rises to 6.25 at 14 days to expiration, Floyd's call rises to 25⅝, or approximately 25.626 (column 4, row A). This amounts to an unrealized profit of 23 cents, or $1,150, per option on the 50-cent rise in the futures price in 28 days. However, if the futures price then falls 25 cents in the next week, his call will decline to 5, or approximately 4.968 (column 5, row C). Thus, in only one-quarter of the time and with 50 percent of the futures price change, nearly all of Floyd's profit is lost. It is the delta of .918, up from .185 initially, that explains the potential for loss. If Floyd is aware of the new sensitivities to market changes, he may be inclined to take his profit more quickly if the market starts to move down.

How Vegas Change

Table 7–7 shows that vegas, the change in option value from a 1 percent change in volatility, are biggest when options are at-the-money and that they decrease as expiration approaches. In any column, vegas are biggest in rows

C and D, when the 600 Call and 600 Put are at-the-money. Vegas are biggest for at-the-money options, because a change in price of the underlying futures contract of any size has the biggest impact on these options.

Looking across any row from column 1 to column 6, the vegas get smaller. Vegas decrease as expiration approaches because the potential for movement is less when there is less time to expiration.

How Thetas Change

It is important to understand how thetas change, because the impact of time erosion on option prices is frequently misunderstood, oversimplified, or both. A word of warning: Thetas are preceded by minus signs. Therefore, discussions of "biggest" and "smallest" can be confusing. Read this section carefully!

Option thetas are smallest (highest absolute value) when options are at-the-money. In any column in Table 7–7, the thetas are largest in rows C and D, when the 600 Call and 600 Put are at-the-money. At-the-money options have larger time values than do in-the-money or out-of-the-money options, and it is the time value portion of an option's price that erodes. Therefore, given the same amount of time to expiration, at-the-money options lose more value per unit of time than do in-the-money or out-of-the-money options.

Thetas of at-the-money options decrease (increase in absolute value) as expiration approaches, and they are smallest (highest absolute value) during the last unit of time before expiration.

Thetas of in-the-money and out-of-the-money options behave differently than do thetas of at-the-money options. They get smaller (absolute value increases) for a while, but then they get larger (absolute value decreases) as expiration approaches. In row A, with a futures price of 625, the 600 Call is in-the-money and its theta decreases from –0.748 in column 1 to –0.7?1 incolumn 2. It then increases to –0.710 in column 3 and to –0.531 i? umn 4. With a futures price of 6.25, the 600 Put is out-of-the-mone? row B illustrates that its theta changes in a similar fashion, decreasin? column 1 to column 2 and then increasing in columns 3 and 4. Traders be careful about making generalizations about the impact of time decay option values.

How does a trader use theta? Theta estimates how much a position will make or lose over some period of time. Knowing this, a trader buying options can compare delta and theta to estimate how much the underlying must move in a specific time period in order for the delta effect (price movement of the underlying) to make more than the theta effect (time decay).

POSITION GREEKS

The term position *refers to whether an option is purchased (long) or written (short).* For example, if Frank buys 10 250 Corn Calls, his "position" is "long 10." If Michelle buys 15 340 Wheat Puts and sells 15 320 Wheat Puts, her position is "long 15 340 Puts and short 15 320 Puts."

What Frank and Michelle and all traders need is a method of estimating how their positions will perform if market conditions change, i.e., if one or more of the inputs to the option pricing formula changes. *With the exception of a position's gamma, position Greeks indicate whether a position will profit or lose when a particular input to the option pricing formula is changed. Position gammas estimate how the delta of the position changes as the price of the underlying futures contract changes.*

How position Greeks are calculated and interpreted will be explained after the following discussion of the use of positive and negative signs. As will be explained, plus and minus signs can have three different meanings.

"Plus" and "Minus" Have Three Different Meanings

When associated with a *quantity of options* in a position such as "+6 210 May Corn Puts at 9½" or "−20 650 November Soybean Calls at 29¼," the plus sign means "long" and the minus sign means "short." These positions should be read as "long 6 2.10-strike May Corn Puts at 9½ cents each" and "short 20 6.50-strike November Soybean Calls at 29¼ cents each."

When associated with the *Greek of an option value*, such as "the call has a vega of +0.32," the plus sign means that the option value is positively correlated to changes in the factor associated with that Greek, i.e., volatility up, call price up. An example of a minus sign being associated with a Greek of an option value is "the put has a delta of −0.35." This means the option price is negatively correlated to price changes in the underlying, i.e., underlying price up, put price down.

Finally, when associated with a *Greek of an option position*, plus and minus signs, with one exception, indicate whether a position will profit from or lose from an increase in the corresponding factor. If, for example, in "the vega of Felecia's three long calls is +2.733," the plus sign means that Felecia's position will profit by 2.733 points if volatility rises 1 percent and other factors remain constant. In "the theta of Dione's four long puts is −3.644," the minus sign means that Dione's position will lose 3.644 points if time changes by one unit and other factors remain constant.

Although the three different meanings may be hard to remember without some practice, keep this in mind: (1) long or short, (2) positively or negatively correlated, (3) profit or loss. During the following discussion of position Greeks, keep in mind that plus and minus signs can mean any of these things depending on usage.

Position Deltas

A position with a positive delta will profit if the price of the underlying rises and will lose if it declines, assuming that other factors remain constant. Long call positions and short put positions have positive deltas, and Table 7–8 shows an example of each. Position 1 is long four 575 July Soybean Calls at 9¼ cents each. It is important to keep track of the plus and minus signs because, as later examples will illustrate, some long option positions have negative Greeks and some short option positions have positive Greeks.

In position 1 in Table 7–8, the position delta of +1.032 is the product of the quantity of long calls (+4) and the option delta (+0.258). The position delta estimates that if the underlying futures contract, July Soybeans in this case, rises by 1 cent and other factors remain constant, the position of these four long calls will profit by 1.032 cents, or approximately $50 (1 cent per bushel on 5,000 bushels), not including transaction costs. The position delta also estimates that this amount will be lost if the July Soybean futures contract falls by 1 cent.

Position 2 in Table 7–8 is short six 320 December Wheat Puts at 12½ cents each. The position delta of +2.742 estimates that these six short puts will make (or lose) 2.742 cents, or approximately $137.50, if December Wheat futures rise (or fall) by 1 cent and other factors remain constant.

Table 7–8 Positions with Positive Deltas

Position Described	Option Position	×	Option Delta	=	Position Delta
1. Long 4 July Soybean 575 Calls at 9¼ each	+4	×	+0.258	=	+1.032
2. Short 6 December Wheat 320 Puts at 12½ each	−6	×	−0.457	=	+2.742

Positions with positive deltas profit when the underlying futures price rises and other factors remain constant and lose when the underlying futures price declines.

Table 7–9 shows that short call positions and long put positions have negative deltas. A position with a negative delta will lose money if the price of the underlying futures contract rises and profit if it declines, assuming that other factors remain constant. Position 1 in Table 7–9 is short nine 180 May Soybean Meal Calls at 12.50 each. The position has a delta of –3.033, which means that it will lose 3.033, or $303.30, if futures rise by one dollar and make that amount if the futures price declines by one dollar.

Position 2 in Table 7–9 is long three 19.50 September Soybean Oil Puts at 0.55 each. The position delta is –1.875. These are obviously in-the-money puts, because the delta of each put is –0.652.

Position Gammas

Gammas of positions do not indicate profit or loss. They indicate how the position delta will change when the price of the underlying changes. *A positive position gamma indicates that the position delta will change in the same direction as the change in price of the underlying. A negative gamma indicates that the position delta will change in the opposite direction as the change in price of the underlying.*

Table 7–10 shows that long call positions and long put positions have positive gammas. Position 1 in Table 7–10 is long 15 August 66 Live Cattle Calls at 2.20 each. This call position has a gamma of +0.210. This means that as the August Live Cattle Futures rise 1 cent and other factors remain constant, the position delta will rise by +0.210. Also, if the futures price falls by 1 cent, the position delta will fall by this amount. Positive gamma means this: futures up, position delta up; futures down, position delta down.

With a positive gamma, the change in delta works to the advantage of the position. Referring back to Table 7–2, as the underlying futures price increases from 6.00 to 6.01, the delta of the 600 Call increases from +0.506

Table 7–9 Positions with Negative Delta

Position Described	Option Position	×	Option Delta	=	Position Delta
1. Short 9 May Soybean Meal 180 Calls at 12.50 each	−9	×	+0.337	=	−3.033
2. Long 3 September Soybean Oil 19.50 Puts at 0.55 each	+3	×	−0.652	=	−1.875

Positions with negative deltas profit when the underlying futures price declines and other factors remain constant and profit when the underlying futures price declines.

Table 7–10 Positions with Positive Gamma

Position Described	Option Position	×	Option Gamma	=	Position Gamma
1. Long 15 August Live Cattle 66 Calls at 2.20 each	+15	×	+0.014	=	+0.210
2. Long 10 January Orange Juice 80.00 Puts at 6.55 each	+10	×	+0.012	=	+0.120

"Positive gamma" means that the delta of a position changes in the same direction as the change in the price of the underlying futures contract, i.e., futures up, delta up; futures down, delta down.

to +0.522. Underlying price up,delta up! This benifits the call owner,because of the   market exposure, i.e., delta, is changing in the call owner's favor. Initially, the call owner's exposure to the market was a delta of +0.506, which means that for every one-point increase in the underlying, with other factors constant, the call owner participates by approximately 50 percent. After a one-cent price rise in the futures price, however, the call owner's exposure has increased to approximately 52 percent. And as the market continues to rise, the call owner makes more and more per unit of price change in the underlying futures, because the delta of the position is increasing toward +1.00.

What about a price decline? Look back at Table 7–3. As the price of the underlying declines and other factors remain constant, the call owner loses less than the amount estimated by the initial delta. This happens because the delta decreases from +0.506 to +0.491. With a futures price decline to 5.99, the 600 Call declines from 10.251 to 9.752, a decline of 0.499, which is less than the initial delta of +0.506. Losing less than the amount estimated by the original delta is a benefit to the call owner.

Now consider a long put position. Position 2 in Table 7–10 is long 10 January Orange Juice 80.00 Puts at 6.55 each. The position gamma is +0.120, which means that as the futures price declines by 1 cent, the delta of this position will decrease by 0.120. Futures price down, delta down! When the market declines, a trader wants as low a delta as possible (or a negative delta with a high absolute value). It is important to remember that a delta of −5.120 is lower and "more short" than a delta of −5.000.

A decline in the position delta as the market declines is the result of the position's positive gamma, and it is a beneficial change in market exposure for a put owner. As the market continues to fall, the put owner's exposure decreases toward −1.00 per long put, or −10.00 in the case of 10 long puts.

A positive position gamma also has a beneficial impact on a long put position when the market rises. A positive position gamma means that the delta of the long put increases as the futures price rises. Consequently, less is lost than was estimated by the original delta.

Negative Gamma   Table 7–11 shows that short call positions and short put positions have negative gammas. Negative gamma means that the delta of a position will change in the opposite direction as the price change of the underlying, i.e., futures up, position delta down; futures down, position delta up.

Position 1 in Table 7–11 is short 2 March Coffee 75.00 Calls at 8.40 cents each. The position gamma of −0.018 indicates that as the price of March Coffee futures rises by 1 cent and other factors remain constant, the position delta will decrease by 0.018. Also, if the futures price falls by 1 cent, the position delta will rise by this amount.

Position 2 in Table 7–11 is short 11 December Wheat 320 Puts at 4⅜ cents each. The position gamma of −1.210 estimates that the position delta will decrease by this amount if the futures price rises 1 cent and will increase by this amount if the futures price falls by 1 cent and other factors remain constant.

When a position has a negative gamma, the change in delta works to the disadvantage of the position. Assume that the 600 Call in Table 7–2 is sold, and so the initial delta of the short call position is −0.506 and the position gamma is −0.015. This position gamma estimates that an increase in the futures price from 6.00 to 6.01 causes the position delta to decrease by 0.015 from −0.506 to −0.512 (actually, the new delta is −0.522). Underlying price up, delta down! This hurts the short call position, because the loss of 0.514 as the short call rises in price from 10.251 to 10.765 is greater than the loss which was estimated by the initial delta of -0.506. As the market

Table 7–11 Positions with Negative Gamma

Position Described	Option Position	×	Option Gamma	=	Position Gamma
1. Short 2 March Coffee 75.00 Calls at 8.40 each	−2	x	+0.009	=	−0.018
2. Short 11 December Wheat 320 Puts at 4⅜ each	−11	x	-0.010	=	−1.210

"Negative gamma" means that the delta of a position changes in the opposite direction as the change in the price of the underlying futures contract, i.e., futures up, delta down; futures down, delta up.

continues to rise, the position loses more and more per unit of futures price rise as the exposure to the market of the short call position continues to decline toward −1.00 per short call.

Table 7–3 shows that when the futures price declines, the change in delta of a position with a negative gamma also works to the disadvantage of the short call position. Assuming that the 600 Call in Table 7–3 is sold, the initial delta is −0.506. As the futures price declines from 6.00 to 5.99, the short call position profits less than the amount estimated by the delta of −0.506. The profit is less because the delta of the short call position is increasing from −0.506 to −0.491. Making less than the amount estimated by the original delta is a disadvantage for the call writer.

Now consider a short put position. Assuming the 600 Put in Table 7–3 is sold, a decrease in the futures price from 6.00 to 5.99 causes the put to rise in price from 10.251 to 10.748, a change in value of 0.497, which is a loss for the put seller. The loss for the put seller is greater than that estimated by the initial delta of −0.489, because the delta of the short put position increased from +0.489 to +0.505. This change in market exposure is a disadvantage for the put seller, because more is lost than was estimated by the original delta. As the market continues to fall, the put seller's market exposure increases toward +1.00 per short put.

When a futures price rises, the delta of a short put position decreases. This works to the disadvantage of put sellers, because less is made than was estimated by the initial delta. This occurs because the short put position has a negative gamma, which means that the delta changes in the direction opposite to the change in the price of the underlying futures. Futures up, delta of short put down!

Position Vegas

A position with a positive vega will profit if volatility rises and other factors remain constant. Since option values rise when volatility rises, option owners profit when volatility increases and other factors remain constant. Table 7–12 shows that long call and long put positions have positive vegas. The vega of +1.375 of position 1 in Table 7–12 means that if volatility rises by 1 percent and other factors remain constant, the position of long five January Sugar 900 Calls will profit by 1.375, or $137.50

A position with a negative vega will lose if volatility rises and profit if volatility declines, assuming that other factors remain constant. Table 7–13 shows that short call and short put positions have negative vegas. Position 1 in Table 7–13 is short 20 December Soybean Meal 170 Calls at 4.50 each.

Table 7–12 Positions with Positive Vega

Position Described	Option Position	×	Option Vega	=	Position Vega
1. Long 5 January Sugar 900 Calls at .069 each	+ 5	x	+0.275	=	+1.375
2. Long 20 December Wheat 240 Puts at 16½ each	+20	x	+0.194	=	+3.880

Positions with positive vega profit when volatility rises and lose when volatility declines.

The position vega of –4.460 means that if volatility rises by 1 percent and other factors are the same, this position will lose 4.460, or $440.60. The vega also estimates that if volatility falls by 1 percent, the position will profit by $440.60.

Position Thetas

The theta of a position estimates whether that position will profit or lose as time passes toward expiration and other factors remain constant. Since option values decay over time, short call and short put positions profit if factors other than time are unchanged, and so those positions have positive thetas. Position 1 in Table 7–14 is short five September Soybean Oil 22.00 Calls at .65 each. The position theta of 0.60 estimates that the position will profit by $360 (.01 = $6) if the time to expiration is reduced by "one unit" and other factors remain constant.

Position 2 in Table 7–14 is short 20 500 Soybean Puts at 16½ cents each. This position has a positive theta of +22.540, which estimates that the position will profit by $1,127 if "one unit of time" passes and other factors are unchanged. The OP-EVALF™ program defines one unit of time as 7 calendar days.

A position with a negative theta will incur a loss if only the time to expiration changes. Long option positions have negative thetas. Table 7–15 shows two long option positions: long 15 May Cotton 65 Calls at 1.60 each and long 8 December Corn 1.90 Puts at 8½ cents each. The theta of position 1 of –1.95 means that if only time to expiration is reduced by "one unit," the position will lose 1.95. The theta of –4.16 of position 2 means that 4.16 cents, or $208, will be lost if "one unit of time" passes and other factors remain constant.

Table 7–13 Positions with Negative Vega

Position Described	Option Position	×	Option Vega	=	Position Vega
1. Short 20 December Soybean Meal 170 Calls at 065 each	−20	x	+0.223	=	−4.460
2. Short 6 July Corn 210 Puts at 6½ each	−6	x	+0.293	=	+1.758

Positions with negative vega profit when volatility declines and profit when volatility rises.

Table 7–14 Positions with Positive Theta

Position Described	Option Position	×	Option Theta	=	Position Theta
1. Short 5 September Soybean Oil 22.00 Calls at 0.65 each	−5	x	−0.120	=	+ 0.600
2. Short 20 November Soybean 500 Puts at 16½ each	−20	x	−1.127	=	+22.540

Positions with positive theta profit as time passes toward expiration.

Position Greeks Summarized

Table 7–16 matches long and short options with positive and negative position Greeks. Long calls have positive deltas, positive gammas, positive vegas, and negative thetas. Short calls have negative deltas, gammas, and vegas and positive thetas. Long puts have negative deltas and thetas and positive gammas and vegas. Short puts have positive deltas and thetas and negative gammas and vegas. No two rows in Table 7–16 are the same. Each option position has its own unique sensitivities to changes in price of the underlying, volatility, and time to expiration. Although this is confusing at first, with a little practice, an understanding of position Greeks can help option traders select appropriate strategies for particular market forecasts.

SUMMARY

The Greeks are tools used by option traders to estimate the profit or loss impact of changes in market conditions on option positions. Delta is an estimate of the change in option theoretical value given a one-point change in the price of the underlying instrument. Gamma is an estimate of change in delta for a one-point change in the price of the underlying. Vega is an estimate of

Table 7–15 Positions with Negative Theta

Position Described	Option Position	×	Option Theta	=	Position Theta
1. Long 15 May Cotton 65 Calls at 1.60 each	+15	×	−0.130	=	−1.950
2. Long 8 December Corn 190 Puts at 8½ each	+ 8	×	−0.520	=	−4.160

Positions with negative theta lose as time passes toward expiration.

Table 7–16 Summary of Position Greeks

Position	Change in Price of Underlying	Change in Delta	Change in Volatility	Change in Time to Expiration
	Delta	Gamma	Vega	Theta
Long call	+	+	+	−
Short call	−	−	−	+
Long put	−	+	+	−
Short put	+	−	−	+

+ indicate that a position will profit, or benefit, from an increase in an input and incur a loss from, or be hurt by, a decrease, assuming that other inputs remain constant.
- indicate that a position will incur a loss from, or be hurt by, an increase in an input and profit, or benefit, from a decrease, assuming that other inputs remain constant.

the change in option value resulting from a 1 percent change in volatility, and theta is an estimate of the change in option value resulting from a one-unit change in time to expiration. Traders who use computer programs should be sure to know the definition of "unit of time" used by the program.

The Greeks change as market conditions change, and this complicates the job of estimating how option prices will behave as market conditions change. The absolute values of deltas of in-the-money options are greater than +.50 initially and increase toward +1.00 as expiration approaches. The absolute value of deltas of at-the-money options remain near +.50 as expiration approaches, and the absolute value of deltas of out-of-the-money options are initially less than +.50 and decrease toward zero as expiration approaches. Gammas are biggest for at-the-money options, and they tend to increase as expiration approaches. Vegas are biggest for at-the-money options, and they decrease as expiration approaches. Thetas are smallest (largest absolute value) for at-the-money options. The behavior of thetas as expiration approaches differs for at-the-money options versus in-the-money or out-of-the-money options.

Plus and minus signs indicate "long" or "short" when used in conjunction with a quantity of options in a position. They indicate a positive or negative correlation when used in conjunction with option values, and they indicate profit or loss when used in conjunction with option positions.

Positions with positive deltas are long calls and short puts. If other factors remain constant, these positions profit with a rise in the price of the underlying instrument and lose with a decline. Short calls and long puts are positions with negative deltas.

The delta of a position with a positive gamma changes in the same direction as the change in price of the underlying: futures price up, delta up; futures price down, delta down. Long calls and long puts are positions with positive gammas. Negative gamma means that the delta of a position changes in the opposite direction as the change in price of the underlying: futures price up, delta down; futures price down, delta up. Short calls and short puts are positions that have negative gammas.

Positive vega means that a position will profit if volatility rises and lose if volatility declines, assuming that other factors remain constant. Long calls and long puts are positions with a positive vega. Negative vega means that a position will lose if volatility rises and profit if volatility declines. Short calls and short puts are positions that have negative vegas.

Long calls and long puts are positions with a negative theta, because they lose money as time passes toward expiration and other factors remain constant. Short calls and short puts are positions with a positive theta. They profit as time passes toward expiration and other factors remain constant.

With a little practice, any trader can learn to interpret the Greeks. This skill is valuable in anticipating how strategies will perform with changes in market conditions.

Part 2

Hedging Strategies

Eight

Strategies for Long Hedgers

L ong hedgers are market participants who have "inherently short" positions. They need to acquire supplies.

There are four basic ways in which long hedgers can use futures and options to protect themselves against price risk. They can (1) buy futures contracts, (2) buy call options, (3) sell put options, and (4) combine buying calls and selling puts to create a strategy known as the bullish collar.

The discussion of each of these strategies will be presented in five parts. First, the theory of the strategy will be explained. Second, a practical example with both rising price and declining price scenarios will be presented. Third, potential opportunities and risks will be summarized. Fourth, the forecast that justifies using the strategy will be discussed. Fifth, the psychology for using the strategy will be explained.

Before the strategies are discussed, some introductory comments are warranted.

"I Want the Best Strategy"

It is important to recognize that there is no "best" strategy. If a best strategy existed, everyone would use it and there would be no need for other strategies. Each strategy offers a unique set of advantages and disadvantages; this is what is meant by the term *trade-offs*. Some hedging strategies lock in the current market price and eliminate the opportunity to benefit if prices improve. This is good if prices move in the right direction, but it is bad if they move the wrong way.

Other hedging strategies lock in a price and leave open the opportunity to benefit if prices improve. The opportunity to benefit from improving prices is the advantage of these strategies, but the disadvantage is that "locked-in price" is less favorable than the current market price. Consequently, prices have to improve by an amount greater than the cost of the strategy to make the strategy worthwhile.

The challenge for hedgers is to match the needs of a specific situation with the trade-offs of a particular strategy. If processing margins are relatively narrow, the cost of being able to benefit from improved prices may be prohibitive. In other cases, where margins permit paying for the ability to benefit from improved prices, the market forecast may call for worse prices. In such cases, the strategy of choice may be to lock in the current price rather than pay for the opportunity to benefit from improved prices.

LONG FUTURES AS A LONG HEDGE

The Theory

Buying futures contracts as a long hedge was discussed briefly in Chapter 3. When a forecast indicates rising price action, buying futures is the hedging strategy of choice, because the current market price is locked in without any additional costs. Table 8–1 and Figure 8–1 illustrate the theory of buying a futures contract as a long hedge.

Table 8–1 has six columns. Column 1 contains a range of futures prices. Column 2 shows the profit or loss from the inherent short cash market position. Remember that a long hedger, by definition, needs to acquire supplies and therefore is inherently short the commodity in question. In Table 8–1, the cash market price is assumed to be the same as the futures price because in row 4 the starting price of $3.00 per bushel is also the starting price, or break-even price, of the inherent short position. In the practical example that follows, the cash market price and the futures price are assumed to be different.

Column 3 shows the profit or loss from the long futures position. In this example, it is assumed that a futures contract is purchased at $3.00 per bushel. Column 4 contains the combined profit or loss of the long futures and the inherent short market position. The final purchase price in column 6 is calculated by combining the combined profit in column 4 with the initial cash market price in column 5. A combined profit is subtracted from the initial cash market price, because hedging profits decrease the final purchase price relative to the initial cash market price. A combined loss is added to the

Table 8-1 Calculating the Final Purchase Price: Hedging an Inherent Short Position with a Long Futures

Initial cash market price: 3.00 per bushel
Hedge strategy: long futures at 3.00 per bushel

	Col. 1 Futures Price at Expiration	Col. 2 Inherent Short Position P/(L)	Col. 3 Long Futures at 3.00 P/(L)	Col. 4 Combined P/(L) (Col. 2 + Col. 3)	Col. 5 Initial Cash Market Price 3.00	Col. 6 Final Price (Purchase Price) (Col. 5 – Col. 4)
Row 1	3.75	(.75)	+.75	-0-	3.00	3.00
Row 2	3.50	(.50)	+.50	-0-	3.00	3.00
Row 3	3.25	(.25)	+.25	-0-	3.00	3.00
Row 4	3.00	-0-	-0-	-0-	3.00	3.00
Row 5	2.75	+.25	(.25)	-0-	3.00	3.00
Row 6	2.50	+.50	(.50)	-0-	3.00	3.00
Row 7	2.25	+.75	(.75)	-0-	3.00	3.00

Final purchase price = Initial cash market price minus combined profits or plus combined losses

initial cash market price, because hedging losses increase the final purchase price relative to the initial cash market price.

The conclusion from Table 8–1 is that a long futures contract locks in the current market price as the final purchase price. On the one hand, it is impossible in theory to do worse than the current price, no matter how high prices may rise. On the other hand, it is also impossible to do better, because the futures contract will decline in price along with a decline in cash market prices. This conclusion is presented graphically Figure 8–1. The long futures contract is represented by the right-upward-sloping broken line, and

Figure 8–1 Final Purchase Price: Hedging an Inherent Short Position with a Long Futures

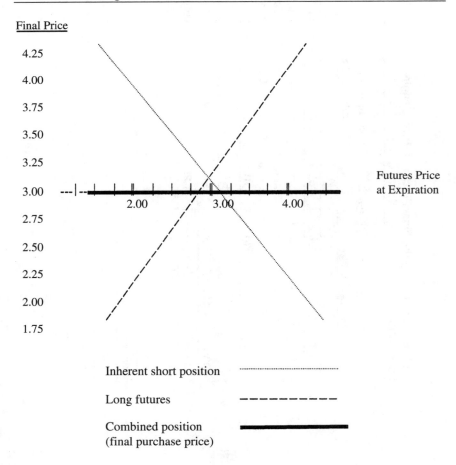

the inherent short cash market position is represented by the left-upward-sloping dotted line. The solid horizontal line represents the final purchase price and corresponds to column 6 in Table 8–1.

A Practical Example

Consider the case of Flour Manufacturing Co. (FMCO), which wants to hedge its purchasing needs for wheat in November. To estimate a purchase price, FMCO needs to know the current price of the appropriate futures contract and the basis. Typically, the futures contract with a delivery date closest to but not before the anticipated need is the appropriate contract to use for hedging purposes.

Basis is the difference between the cash price of the commodity in question and the futures price. Basis is defined as the cash price minus the futures price. In the case of wheat, corn, and soybeans, basis is quoted in cents per bushel. Basis can range from positive (cash price higher than futures) to negative (cash price lower than futures). If a local cash market price is 10 cents higher than the futures price, the basis is described as "10 over." If the cash price is 10 cents lower than the futures price, the basis is "10 under."

The term *strengthens* refers to a changing market condition in which the cash market price increases relative to the futures price; the difference therefore becomes more positive or less negative. The term *weakens* refers to the opposite situation, in which cash prices decrease relative to futures prices. The difference then becomes less positive or more negative.

Since there are a number of locations where cash markets for grain exist, the most useful basis is calculated by using a cash market price as close to the source of supply as possible. For this example, assume that FMCO uses Moline, Illinois, as its supply point.

Estimating Purchasing Costs

Assume a December Wheat futures price of $3.00 and a Moline cash price of $3.10. Given these prices, the basis is "10 over" ($3.10 – $3.00). Assuming no change in prices and no change in the basis, Table 8–1A shows how FMCO can estimate its cost of wheat at $3.10 per bushel.

Prices are not likely to remain unchanged, however, so consider the impact on purchasing costs if prices rise, as FMCO expects, and if prices decline.

Table 8–1A Long Futures as a Long Hedge: Estimating a Purchase Price

Futures Price	+	Expected Basis	=	Expected Purchase Price
$3.00	+	$0.10	=	$3.10

Prices Rise. Fast-forward to late November, when FMCO is ready to buy wheat. Assume that the price of December Wheat futures has risen to $3.50 and that Moline cash prices have risen to $3.55. Note that the basis has "weakened," because the Moline cash price is now only "5 over" the price of December Wheat futures. In this scenario, FMCO can buy wheat in the Moline cash market at $3.55 and sell its December Wheat futures contract at $3.50. As Table 8–1B shows, FMCO will calculate its actual cost of wheat as $3.05, 5 cents better than originally estimated.

In this example, gains from the long futures position offset the higher cost of wheat in the cash market, but the basis changed. As a result, FMCO's actual costs were different from its estimated cost. In this example, the basis changed in FMCO's favor, because the Moline cash price declined from 10 cents over the futures price to 5 cents over it. It is the "weakening basis" that accounted for the fact that the net purchase price was 5 cents lower than the original estimate of $3.10. If the basis had strengthened, actual costs would have been higher than originally estimated.

Prices Decline. In this scenario, assume that the price of December Wheat futures falls to $2.50 and that the Moline cash price falls to $2.65. Given these changes, if FMCO buys wheat in the Moline cash market at $2.65 and sells its December Wheat futures contract at $2.50, its actual cost of wheat is $3.15, 5 cents more than originally estimated. Table 8–1C shows these calculations.

Opportunities and Risks

Buying a futures contract as a long hedge provides the opportunity to lock in a purchase price today even if prices rise before the delivery date in the future. The risk is that if prices decline, the "locked-in price" will be higher than the

Table 8–1B Long Futures as a Long Hedge: Prices Rise and Basis Weakens

	Moline Cash Market	December Futures	Basis
June 1	$3.10	$3.00	$0.10
November 22	$3.55	$3.50	$0.05

Calculation of actual cost:	Cash purchase price	$3.55
	Minus profit on futures contract	−0.50
	Net purchase price	$3.05

Table 8–1C Long Futures as a Long Hedge: Prices Decline and Basis Strengthens

	Moline Cash Market	December Futures	Basis
June 1	$3.10	$3.00	$0.10
November 22	$2.65	$2.50	$0.15

Calculation of actual cost:	Cash purchase price	$2.65
	Plus loss on futures contract	+0.50
	Net purchase price	$3.15

potentially lower price if no hedge had been implemented. Another risk is that a futures position does not protect against adverse changes in basis.

Forecast Justifying a Long Futures Hedge

Long hedgers who buy futures contracts must be forecasting rising prices, or they must be unwilling to assume the risk of rising prices. If prices decline, the forecast was wrong, because in hindsight, a better purchase price could have been achieved by not hedging.

Psychology for Hedging with Long Futures

No one is always right in forecasting market prices, and so hedgers must learn to live with some wrong forecasts. For many people this is a hard adjustment. Rather than focus on one "right" or "wrong" forecast, however, long hedgers should remember that they are in the business of buying supplies at "cost-effective" prices so that business profits can be made from processing. This means that hedging decisions should be made in such a way that one right decision or one wrong decision does not "make or break" a business. Hedgers must think in terms of "average costs," and they must not make "all or nothing" hedges. Generally speaking, hedgers are better off if they spread their hedging activities over a year or a growing season.

LONG CALLS AS A LONG HEDGE

The Theory

Table 8–2 and Figure 8–2 illustrate the theory of buying calls as a long hedge. Table 8–2 has six columns that are similar to those in Table 8–1. Column 1 contains a range of futures prices. Column 2 shows the profit or loss from the inherent short cash market position, and column 3 shows the profit or loss from the long call position. In this example, it is assumed that a 300 Call is purchased for 25 cents per bushel. Column 4 contains the combined profit or loss of the long call and the inherent short market position. The final purchase price in column 6 is calculated in the same way as it was in Table 8–1. Combined profits in column 4 are subtracted from the initial cash market price in column 5, because hedging profits decrease the final purchase price relative to the initial cash market price. Combined losses in column 4 are added to the initial cash market price in column 5, because hedging losses increase the final purchase price relative to the initial cash market price.

The conclusion from Table 8–2 is that buying call options offers a different set of trade-offs than that which results from buying futures contracts. There are two positive aspects of buying calls and one negative aspect. Buying calls locks in a known, maximum purchase price, assuming that the basis is unchanged. Buying calls also makes it possible for a long hedger to benefit, by getting a lower purchase price, if prices decline. The disadvantage is that calls have a cost, and this cost raises the price that is locked in. The locked-in, or maximum, price is above the current market price. This conclusion is presented graphically Figure 8–2. The horizontal and right-upward-sloping broken line represents the long call, and the left-upward-sloping dotted line represents the inherent short cash market position. The horizontal and left-downward-sloping solid line represents the final purchase price and corresponds to column 6 in Table 8–2.

Table 8–2 Calculating the Final Purchase Price: Hedging an Inherent Short Position with a Long Call

	Col. 1	Col. 2	Col. 3	Col. 4	Col. 5	Col. 6
		Initial cash market price: Hedge strategy:		300 per bushel long 300 Call at .25 per bushel		
	Futures Price at Expiration	Inherent Short Position P/(L)	Long 300 Call At .25 P/(L)	Combined P/(L) (Col. 2 + Col. 3)	Initial Cash Market Price 3.00	Final Price (Purchase Price) (Col. 5 – Col. 4)
Row 1	3.75	(.75)	+.50	(.25)	3.00	3.25
Row 2	3.50	(.50)	+.25	(.25)	3.00	3.25
Row 3	3.25	(.25)	-0-	(.25)	3.00	3.25
Row 4	3.00	-0-	(.25)	(.25)	3.00	3.25
Row 5	2.75	+.25	(.25)	-0-	3.00	3.00
Row 6	2.50	+.50	(.25)	+.25	3.00	2.75
Row 7	2.25	+.75	(.25)	+.50	3.00	2.50

Final purchase price = Initial cash market price minus combined profits or plus combined losses

Figure 8–2 Final Purchase Price: Hedging an Inherent Short Position with a Long Call

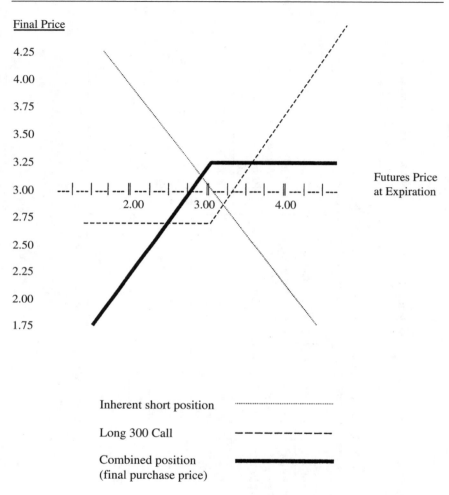

Inherent short position	⋯⋯⋯⋯⋯⋯⋯
Long 300 Call	– – – – – – – – –
Combined position (final purchase price)	▬▬▬▬▬▬▬

A Practical Example

Return to the example of Flour Manufacturing Co. and its desire to hedge its purchasing needs for wheat in November. To estimate a purchase price, FMCO needs to know the current price of the appropriate call option and the basis. Like the appropriate futures contract, the appropriate call will have an expiration date closest to but not before the anticipated need.

Estimating Purchasing Costs

As in the long futures example above, assume a December Wheat futures price of $3.00 and a Moline cash market price of $3.10. Instead of buying a December Wheat futures contract, however, FMCO buys a December Wheat 3.00 Call for 25 cents. Assuming no change in prices and no change in basis, Table 8–2A shows how FMCO can estimate its maximum cost of wheat at $3.35 per bushel.

Note that, as defined in Chapter 1, the "effective futures price for a long call" is equal to the strike price of the call plus the premium paid. In this example, the 300 Call has a strike price of $3.00, and its cost is 25 cents. Consequently, the effective futures price, if the call is exercised, is $3.25 ($3.00 + $0.25).

FMCO's estimated maximum purchase price therefore is $3.35 per bushel. Although this price is higher than the current market price of December futures by the cost of the call and the basis, the following scenarios illustrate that paying a premium for a call can have a benefit if the market behaves in a certain way. We now revisit the outcomes, one when prices rise and one when prices decline.

Prices Rise. Fast-forward again to late November, when FMCO is ready to buy wheat. If the price of December Wheat futures is $3.50, the December Wheat 300 Call will be trading for at least 50 cents. Assuming, as before, that Moline cash prices have risen to $3.55, FMCO can buy wheat in the Moline cash market and sell its 300 Call for $0.50, for a profit of 25 cents. As Table 8–2B shows, FMCO can calculate its actual cost of wheat as $3.30, 5 cents better than the original estimate.

In this example, the profit from the long call partially offsets the higher cost of wheat in the cash market. As before, the "weakening basis"

Table 8–2A Long Hedge with Long Calls: Estimating a Maximum Purchase Price

Effective Futures Price	+	Expected Basis	=	Expected Purchase Price
$3.25	+	$0.10	=	$3.35

Table 8–2B Long Hedge with Long Calls: Prices Rise and Basis Weakens

	Moline Cash Market	December Futures	Basis	300 Call
June 1	$3.10	$3.00	$0.10	$0.25
November 22	$3.55	$3.50	$0.05	$0.50

Calculation of actual cost:		
	Cash purchase price	$3.55
	Minus profit on call option	− 0.25
	Net purchase price	$3.30

accounted for why the actual cost of $3.30 was 5 cents lower than the originally estimated maximum price of $3.35. The opportunity to profit from an improvement in the basis, at the risk of losing from an adverse change, is an aspect of options just as it is an aspect of futures.

Prices Decline. As above, assume that the price of December Wheat futures falls to $2.50 and that the Moline cash price falls to $2.65. With December Wheat futures trading at $2.50 at the expiration of December options, the December 300 Call will expire worthless, and so the cost of 25 cents will be lost. By buying wheat in the Moline cash market at $2.65 and writing off as a loss the cost of the 300 Call, FMCO can calculate its actual cost of wheat at $2.90, as shown in Table 8–2C.

Opportunities and Risks

This example shows that buying calls gives long hedgers an opportunity to benefit if commodity prices fall. In this example, the losses from the call were limited to 25 cents, and so any decline beyond 25 cents was a benefit to FMCO, the wheat buyer. This example, however, also shows the risks of buying calls as a long hedge. First, the maximum purchase price locked in by the call is above the current futures price. In this example, the locked-in futures price is $3.25, which is above the initial futures price of $3.00 by the cost of the call. The second risk is that potential adverse changes in basis are not covered by long calls.

**Table 8–2C Long Hedge with Long Calls: Prices Decline
and Basis Strengthens**

	Moline Cash Market	December Futures	Basis	300 Call
June 1	$3.10	$3.00	$0.10	$0.25
November 22	$2.65	$2.50	$0.15	$0.00

Calculation of actual cost:	Cash purchase price	$2.65
	Plus loss on call option	+ 0.25
	Net purchase price	$2.90

Forecast Justifying a Long Call Hedge

Since buying calls gives long hedgers an opportunity to benefit if prices fall, the forecast must be for prices to fall. That's right! Long hedgers who buy calls must forecast that prices will decline. This idea may be a surprise to some readers, but remember, a long hedger's goal is to get the lowest possible purchasing price. It is only speculators who want to profit by buying calls at a low price and selling them at a high price. The thinking process for hedging is different from that for speculating.

Psychology for Hedging with Long Calls

Long hedgers should view call options as insurance policies. Buying calls is the long hedger's strategy of choice when the forecast is "bearish but worried." An example might be the period immediately before a crop report. If a long hedger is bearish but worried that the report will change market sentiment from bearish to bullish unexpectedly, a long call position will at least lock in a known maximum purchase price if prices start to rise.

Another time when a long hedger might be "bearish but worried" is after a long bear market. A long hedger may see no reason for the bear market to end, but experience sometimes indicates that the time when it is least expected is the time when protection from a price rise is needed. These are obviously situations that require judgment and a willingness to lose the call premium.

Another consideration is profit margins. The cost of a call must be "affordable." If the effective purchase price of the futures, assuming that the call is exercised, is prohibitive, buying calls is not a viable hedging alternative. Buying calls is not a panacea; it is another hedging alternative with a unique set of trade-offs.

SHORT PUTS AS A LONG HEDGE

The Theory

Selling puts offers long hedgers a third set of trade-offs. Table 8–3 and Figure 8–3 illustrate the theory of selling puts as a long hedge.

Table 8–3 contains six columns that are similar to those in Tables 8–1 and 8–2. Column 1 contains a range of futures prices. Column 2 shows the profit or loss from the inherent short cash market position, and column 3 shows the profit or loss from the short put. In this example, it is assumed that a 300 Put is sold for 25 cents per bushel. Column 4 contains the combined profit or loss of the short put and the inherent short market position, and the final purchase price in column 6 is calculated in the same way as it was in Tables 8–1 and 8–2. Combined profits in column 4 are subtracted from the initial cash market price in column 5, because hedging profits decrease the final purchase price relative to the initial cash market price. Combined losses in column 4 are added to the initial cash market price in column 5, because hedging losses increase the final purchase price relative to the initial cash market price.

The conclusion from Table 8–3 is that selling puts has three positive aspects and one negative aspect. The first positive aspect is that a cash payment is received when the strategy is initiated. The second positive aspect is that if the futures price is at or below the strike price at expiration, the effective purchase price is below the futures price at the time when the put was sold. The third positive aspect is that the put premium received offers some upside protection in the event that futures prices rise. The negative aspect is that no maximum purchase price is locked in, because futures prices can rise beyond the amount of the put premium received. Selling puts offers only limited protection for long hedgers. This conclusion is presented graphically in Figure 8–2. The horizontal and left-downward-sloping broken line represents the short put, and the left-upward-sloping dotted line represents the inherent short cash market position. The horizontal and right-upward-sloping solid line represents the final purchase price and corresponds to column 6 in Table 8–3.

Table 8–3 Calculating the Final Purchase Price: Hedging an Inherent Short Position with a Short Put

Initial cash market price: 3.00 per bushel
Hedge strategy: short 300 Put at .25 per bushel

	Col. 1	Col. 2	Col. 3	Col. 4	Col. 5	Col. 6
	Futures Price at Expiration	Inherent Short Position P/(L)	Short 300 Put at .25 P/(L)	Combined P/(L) (Col. 2 + Col. 3)	Initial Cash Market Price 3.00	Final Price (Purchase Price) (Col. 5 − Col. 4)
Row 1	3.75	(.75)	+.25	(.50)	3.00	3.50
Row 2	3.50	(.50)	+.25	(.25)	3.00	3.25
Row 3	3.25	(.25)	+.25	-0-	3.00	3.00
Row 4	3.00	-0-	+.25	+.25	3.00	2.75
Row 5	2.75	+.25	-0-	+.25	3.00	2.75
Row 6	2.50	+.50	(.25)	+.25	3.00	2.75
Row 7	2.25	+.75	(.50)	+.25	3.00	2.75

Final Purchase Price = initial cash market price minus combined profits or plus combined losses

159

Figure 8–3 Final Purchase Price: Hedging an Inherent Short Position with a Short Put

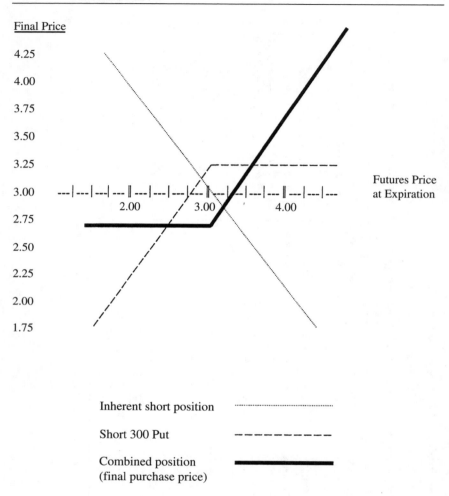

Inherent short position	....
Short 300 Put	– – – – – – – – –
Combined position (final purchase price)	▬▬▬▬▬▬

A Practical Example

Consider again the example of Flour Manufacturing Co. and its desire to hedge its purchasing needs for wheat in November. To estimate a purchase price, FMCO needs to know the current price of the appropriate put option and the basis.

Estimating Purchasing Costs

As in the previous examples, assume a December Wheat futures price of $3.00 and a Moline cash price of $3.10, so that the basis is "10 over." To hedge its inherent short position, FMCO sells a December 300 Put for 25 cents. Assuming no change in prices and no change in the basis, FMCO can estimate its purchasing cost at $2.85 per bushel as presented in Table 8–3A.

The "effective futures price" in this example is equal to the strike price of the put minus the premium received. Consequently, the effective futures price, if the put is assigned, is $2.75 ($3.00 – $0.25). Including the basis, FMCO's estimated purchase price, assuming that the put is assigned, is therefore, $2.85 per bushel. This price is lower than the current market price of December Wheat futures by the put premium net of the basis. The following two scenarios illustrate how the put premium received can benefit FMCO if the market behaves in a certain way.

Prices Rise.   In late November, when FMCO is ready to buy wheat, assume that December Wheat futures have risen to 3.50 and that the Moline cash price has risen to 3.55. With December Wheat futures trading at $3.50 at the expiration of December options, the December 300 Put will expire worthless, and so the 25-cent premium received will be kept as income. By buying wheat in the Moline cash market at $3.55 and recognizing the premium from the 300 Put as a profit, FMCO can calculate its actual cost of wheat at $3.30, as shown in Table 8–3B.

In this example, the 25-cent profit from the short put partially offset the 50-cent rise in futures prices. The actual cost of $3.30 was only 20 cents higher than the initial estimate, because the weakening basis worked to FMCO's advantage.

Prices Decline.   As previously, assume that the price of December Wheat falls to $2.50 and that the Moline cash price falls to $2.65. With December Wheat futures trading at $2.50 at the expiration of December options, the

Table 8–3A Long Hedge with Short Puts: Estimating a Purchase Price

Effective Futures Price	+	Expected Basis	=	Expected Purchase Price
$2.75	+	$0.10	=	$2.85

Table 8–3B Long Hedge with Short Puts: Prices Rise and Basis Weakens

	Moline Cash Market	December Futures	Basis	300 Put
June 1	$2.70	$2.60	$0.10	$0.25
November 22	$3.15	$3.10	$0.05	$0.00

Calculation of effective cost:	Cash purchase price	$3.55
	Minus profit on put option	– 0.25
	Net purchase price	$3.30

December 300 Put will be trading for approximately 50 cents. Therefore, there will be a loss of 25 cents on the short put position. By buying wheat in the Moline cash market at $2.65 and covering the short put at 50 cents, FMCO can calculate its actual cost of wheat at $2.90, as shown in Table 8–3C.

This example shows that selling puts makes it possible for long hedgers to benefit if commodity prices fall. In this example, the losses from the short put were 25 cents, but the put did not begin to lose until the underlying wheat futures contract declined by 25 cents, the premium received. That premium received was a benefit to FMCO, the wheat buyer. As this example also shows, the basis also played a role in the determination of the final actual purchase price. In this example, the price of wheat declined 50 cents, 20 cents of which accrued to FMCO as a lower final purchase price for wheat. There were two reasons, however, why the full 50 cents did not accrue to FMCO. First, the loss on the short put was 25 cents; second, the basis also changed 5 cents against FMCO's position.

Opportunity and Risks

The premium received from short puts creates an opportunity to lower the effective purchase price of futures contracts. In stable or declining markets, the effective purchase price is lower than the prevailing price at the time when the put is sold. There are two risks, however. First, the premium received offers only limited upside protection if futures prices rise. Second, short puts establish a minimum purchase price, and long hedgers do not benefit if prices decline below that level.

Table 8–3C Long Hedge with Short Puts: Prices Decline and Basis Strengthens

	Moline Cash Market	December Futures	Basis	300 Put
June 1	$3.10	$3.00	$0.10	$0.25
November 22	$2.65	$2.50	$0.15	$0.50

Calculation of effective cost:	Cash purchase price	$2.65
	Plus loss on put option	+ 0.25
	Net purchase price	$2.90

Forecast Justifying a Short Put Hedge

Short puts benefit long hedgers most if futures prices trade in a narrow range around the strike price of the put. Neutral price action must therefore be predicted.

Psychology for Hedging with Short Puts

This example shows that short puts have different advantages and different disadvantages than do long futures and long calls. They also benefit long hedgers in different market scenarios. Whereas long futures lock in the current futures price and long calls lock in a futures price above the current level, the effective purchase price for short puts is below the current futures price, assuming that the puts are assigned. If futures prices rise, however, the put premium offers only limited upside protection.

Since short puts offer a third set of trade-offs, it stands to reason that hedgers should use them when their forecasts are different. Long hedgers should sell puts when they are neutral on the market. Remember, long hedgers want to buy the underlying, and the put premium received reduces the effective purchase price only if futures prices do not rise or fall "too much."

An example of a time when a long hedger might be "neutral" is during the middle of a growing season when all seems to be going well, rainfall is adequate, the weather is constructive, and crop reports are in line with expectations. Therefore, little price movement is expected. A short put position will bring in some option premium that increases profit if the forecast is correct. The put premium also offers some protection if prices rise. Since there is a risk of being unhedged if prices rise "too much," long hedgers who sell puts must be ready to buy futures if prices begin to rise dramatically.

THE BULLISH COLLAR AS A LONG HEDGE

The Theory

A strategy known as the bullish collar was created with the goal of getting the advantages of the long call without its disadvantages. The act of purchasing a call with a strike price above the current futures price and simultaneously selling a put with a strike price below the current futures price creates a bullish collar. The call locks in a maximum purchase price, and the put premium received reduces the cost of the call. The short put, however, establishes a minimum purchase price. Table 8–4 and Figure 8–4 illustrate the theory of the bullish collar as a long hedge.

Table 8–4 is similar to Tables 8–1, 8–2, and 8–3 except that it has seven columns. Two columns are required to show the profit or loss from the two components of the strategy. Column 3 shows the profit or loss from the long call, and column 4 shows the profit or loss from the short put. In this example, it is assumed that a 320 Call is purchased for 15 cents per bushel and that a 280 Put is sold for 15 cents per bushel. Column 5 contains the combined profit or loss of the long call, the short put, and the inherent short market position. The final purchase price in column 7 is calculated in a way similar to previous tables, by subtracting combined profit in column 5 from the initial cash market price in column 6 or by adding the combined loss to the initial cash market price.

The conclusion from Table 8–4 is that the bullish collar offers a fourth set of trade-offs. There are three positive aspects and two negative aspects. The bullish collar requires little or no initial cash payment. It leaves open the possibility for long hedgers to reduce purchasing costs if prices decline, and it locks in a known, maximum purchase price, assuming that the basis is unchanged. The negative aspects are that the possibility of reducing purchasing costs is limited and that the maximum price locked in is above the current price. This conclusion is presented graphically Figure 8–4. The three lighter lines in that figure represent the components of the strategy: the inherent short position, the long call, and the short put. The heavy solid line represents the final purchase price and corresponds to column 7 in Table 8–4.

Table 8–4 Calculating the Final Purchase Price: Hedging an Inherent Short Position with a Bullish Collar

Initial cash market price: 3.00 per bushel

Hedge strategy: long a 320 Call at .15 and short a 280 Put at .15

	Col. 1 Futures Price at Expiration	Col. 2 Inherent Short Position P/(L)	Col. 3 Long 320 Call at .15 P/(L)	Col. 4 Short 280 Put at .15 P/(L)	Col. 5 Combined P/(L) (Col. 2 + Col. 3)	Col. 6 Initial Cash Market Price 3.00	Col. 7 Final Price (Purchase Price) (Col. 5–Col. 4)
Row 1	3.50	(.50)	+.15	+.15	(.20)	3.00	3.20
Row 2	3.40	(.40)	+.05	+.15	(.20)	3.00	3.20
Row 3	3.30	(.30)	(.05)	+.15	(.20)	3.00	3.20
Row 4	3.20	(.20)	(.15)	+.15	(.20)	3.00	3.20
Row 5	3.10	(.10)	(.15)	+.15	(.10)	3.00	3.10
Row 6	3.00	0.00	(.15)	+.15	0.00	3.00	3.00
Row 7	2.90	+.10	(.15)	+.15	+.10	3.00	2.90
Row 8	2.80	+.20	(.15)	+.15	+.20	3.00	2.80
Row 9	2.70	+.30	(.15)	+.05	+.20	3.00	2.80
Row 10	2.60	+.40	(.15)	(.05)	+.20	3.00	2.80
Row 11	2.50	+.50	(.15)	(.15)	+.20	3.00	2.80

Final purchase price = Initial cash market price minus combined profits or plus combined losses

Figure 8–4 Final Purchase Price: Hedging an Inherent Short Position with a Bullish Collar

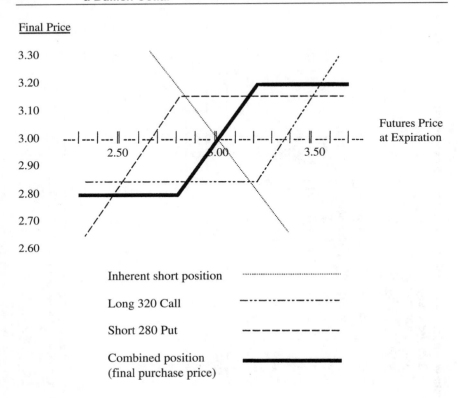

Inherent short position	··
Long 320 Call	— · — · · — · · — · —
Short 280 Put	— — — — — — — —
Combined position (final purchase price)	▬▬▬▬▬▬▬

A Practical Example

Consider again the case of Flour Manufacturing Co. and its desire to hedge its purchasing needs for wheat in November. To estimate a purchase price, FMCO needs to know the current prices of the appropriate call and put and the basis.

Estimating Purchase Costs

As in the examples above, assume a December Wheat futures price of $3.00 and a Moline cash price of $3.10, so that the basis is "10 over." Assume also that FMCO creates a bullish collar by buying a December 320 Call for 15 cents and simultaneously selling a December 280 Put for 15 cents. Given these assumptions, FMCO can estimate its purchasing costs as presented in Table 8–4A.

The effective futures price is equal to the current futures price plus the net premium paid or minus the net premium received. Since the futures price is 3.00 and the net cost of the bullish collar is zero in this example, the effective purchase price of the futures is $3.00 ($3.00 + $0.15 – $0.15). The following scenarios illustrate how the bullish collar can benefit long hedgers if the market behaves in a certain way.

Prices Rise. Fast-forward one last time to late November, when FMCO is ready to buy wheat. Assume that the price of December Wheat futures prices has risen to $3.50 and that the Moline cash price has risen to $3.55.

In this scenario, the December 320 Call will be trading for at least 30 cents, and the December 280 Put will expire worthless. FMCO can buy wheat in the Moline cash market at $3.55, sell its 3.20 Call for 30 cents, and realize the 15-cent profit on its short 280 Put. As Table 8–4B shows, FMCO will calculate its actual cost of wheat as $3.25, 15 cents worse than initially estimated.

Table 8–4A The Bullish Collar as a Long Hedge: Estimating a Purchase Price

Effective Futures Price	+	Expected Basis	=	Expected Purchase Price
$3.00	+	$0.10	=	$3.10

Table 8–4B Long Hedge with Bullish Collar: Prices Rise and Basis Weakens

	Moline Cash Market	December Futures	Basis	320 Call	280 Put
June 1	$3.10	$3.00	$0.10	$0.15	$0.15
November 22	$3.55	$3.50	$0.05	$0.30	$0.00

Calculation of actual cost:	Cash purchase price	$3.55
	Minus profit on call option	– 0.15
	Minus profit on put option	– 0.15
	Net purchase price	$3.25

In this example, the total 30-cent profit from the two options partially offset the 50-cent price rise in futures prices. As in previous examples, the "weakening basis" accounted for why the actual cost of $3.25 was only 15 cents higher than initially estimated.

Prices Decline. As above, assume that the price of December Wheat futures falls to $2.50 and that the Moline cash price falls to $2.65. With December Wheat futures trading at $2.50 at the expiration of December options, the December 3.20 Call will expire worthless, and the December 2.80 Put will be trading for approximately 30 cents. By buying wheat in the Moline cash market at $2.65, covering the short 3.00 Put, and writing off as a loss the cost of the 3.20 Call, FMCO can calculate its actual cost of wheat at $2.95, as shown in Table 8–4C.

This example shows that a bullish collar makes it possible for long hedgers to benefit if commodity prices fall. In this example, the losses from the short put and long call positions were 30 cents, but losses did not begin to occur at expiration until the underlying wheat futures contract declined by 20 cents, below the strike price of the put. That decline in wheat prices was a benefit to FMCO, the wheat buyer. As this example also shows, the basis also played a role in the determination of the final actual purchase price. In this example, the price of wheat declined 50 cents, 20 cents of which accrued to FMCO as a lower final purchase price for wheat.

Table 8–4C Bullish Collar as a Long Hedge: Prices Decline and Basis Strengthens

	Moline Cash Market	December Futures	Basis	320 Call	280 Put
June 1	$3.10	$3.00	$0.10	$0.15	$0.15
November 22	$2.65	$2.50	$0.15	$0.00	$0.30

Calculation of actual cost:		
	Cash purchase price	$2.65
	Plus loss profit on call option	+ 0.15
	Plus loss on put option	+ 0.15
	Net purchase price	$2.95

Opportunities and Risks

The positive aspects of a bullish collar are that the cost is lower than simply buying a call, there is an opportunity to benefit when prices are lower, and a maximum price is locked in. The disadvantages are that the benefit from lower prices is limited to the strike price of the put and that the maximum price locked in is above the current price.

Forecast Justifying a Bullish Collar Hedge

Long hedgers must predict neutral to bearish price action to choose a bullish collar, because the actual purchase price is reduced only if prices decline. As will be explained next, the motivations for choosing a bullish collar are complex.

Psychology for Hedging with a Bullish Collar

The motivation for buying calls as a long hedge was described as "bearish but worried." While the bullish collar strategy leaves intact the opportunity to benefit from declining prices, it also limits that opportunity. There must, therefore, be an additional twist to the motivation for selecting this strategy. Long hedgers should choose bullish collars for one of two reasons.

First, if a long hedger is "bearish but worried and calls are too expensive," a bullish collar is appropriate. The "bearish" part of the forecast explains why someone wants to be unhedged in an attempt to benefit from declining prices. The "worried" part explains why someone feels the need to buy calls, and the "calls are too expensive" part explains why someone would sell puts.

The meaning of "too expensive" is subjective and will vary from hedger to hedger. The basis for making a judgment, however, is processing margins. If the margin for a soybean crusher, for example, is 15 cents per bushel, it is hard for that crusher to justify buying a call that costs 20 cents. However, if a put can be sold to reduce the cost of such a call, the purchase may be justified.

A second motivation for the bullish collar is the perceived need for "low-cost disaster insurance." Options, remember, are similar to insurance policies, and purchased calls for long hedgers act like insurance against rising prices. Remember also that an option's strike price and distance from current futures prices correspond to the deductible component of an insurance policy. The farther a strike price of a call is above the current futures price, the more like a disaster insurance policy that call is. Only if prices rise very dramatically will the call have a payoff value. Rather than "pay" for such a call, a long hedger can sell a put with a strike price equally far below the current futures price. The premium from the put can be applied toward the cost of the call, and the long hedger will have a low-cost insurance policy against unforeseen very sharp rises in prices.

SUMMARY

There are four basic strategies that long hedgers can use to protect themselves against price risk. They can buy futures, buy calls, sell puts, and combine long calls and short puts to create a bullish collar.

Long futures should be used when long hedgers are forecasting rising prices. The opportunity is that today's prices can be locked in if prices rise as forecast. The risk is that prices decline, in which case the opportunity to benefit from declining prices has been eliminated.

Long calls should be purchased when long hedgers are "bullish but worried." Purchased calls lock in a maximum purchase price and make it possible to benefit from decreasing prices, but the locked-in price is above the current price.

Selling puts is appropriate for long hedgers when neutral price action is forecast. The premium received from selling puts lowers the purchase price for futures contracts, but the upside protection of short puts is limited to the premium received.

Bullish collars can be used when long hedgers are bearish but worried and the price of calls is "too high." If processing margins are too low to justify the cost of calls, out-of-the-money puts can be sold to lower the net amount paid for calls. The advantages of bullish collars are that a maximum purchase price is established, the opportunity to benefit from lower prices exists, and the net cost of the calls is reduced. The disadvantages, are that the locked-in price is above the current price and that the potential benefit from falling prices is limited to the strike price of the put.

Nine

Strategies for Short Hedgers

Short hedgers are market participants who have "inherently long" positions. They have produce to sell.

There are four basic ways in which short hedgers can use futures and options to protect themselves against price risk. First, they can sell futures contracts. Second, they can buy put options. Third, they can sell call options. Fourth, they can combine buying puts and selling calls to create a strategy known as the bearish collar.

The discussion of each of these strategies will be presented in five parts. First, the theory of the strategy will be explained. Second, a practical example that includes scenarios with both declining prices and rising prices will be presented. Third, potential opportunities and risks will be summarized. Fourth, the forecast that justifies using the strategy will be discussed. Fifth, the psychology for using the strategy will be explained.

If you have not read Chapter 8, then it is suggested that you read the introductory comments to that chapter before beginning this one. The first point made in those comments is that there is no "best" strategy. Each strategy offers a unique set of advantages and disadvantages; this is what is meant by the term *trade-offs*. The second point is that the challenge for hedgers is to match the needs of a specific situation with the trade-offs of a particular strategy.

SHORT FUTURES AS A SHORT HEDGE

The Theory

When a forecast indicates falling price action, selling futures is the hedging strategy of choice, because the current price is locked in without any additional costs. Table 9–1 and Figure 9–1 illustrate the theory of selling a futures contract as a short hedge.

Table 9–1 has six columns. Column 1 contains a range of futures prices. Column 2 shows the profit or loss from the inherent long cash market position. Remember that a short hedger, by definition, has produce to sell and therefore is inherently long the commodity in question. In Table 9–1, the cash market price is assumed to be the same as the futures price, because, in row 4, the price of $6.00 per bushel is also the break-even price of the inherent long position. In the practical example that follows, the cash market price is assumed to be different from the futures price.

Column 3 shows the profit or loss from the short futures position. In this example, it is assumed that a futures contract is sold at $6.00 per bushel. Column 4 contains the combined profit or loss of the short futures position and the inherent long market position. The final sale price in column 6 is calculated by combining the combined profit (or loss) in column 4 with the initial cash market price in column 5. A combined profit is added to the initial cash market price, because hedging profits increase the final sale price relative to the initial cash market price. A combined loss is subtracted from the initial cash market price, because hedging losses decrease the final sale price relative to the initial cash market price.

The conclusion from Table 9–1 is that a short futures contract locks in the current market price as the final sale price. On the one hand, it is impossible in theory, to do worse than the current price, no matter how low prices may fall. On the other hand, it is also impossible to do better, because the futures contract will rise in price along with a rise in cash market prices. This conclusion is presented graphically Figure 9–1. The short futures contract is represented by the left-upward-sloping broken line, and the inherent long cash market position is represented by the right-upward-sloping dotted line. The solid horizontal line represents the final sale price, and it corresponds to column 6 in Table 9–1.

A Practical Example

Consider the case of Farmer Lee, who wants to hedge a soybean crop that will be ready to deliver in October. To estimate a sale price, Lee needs to know the current price of the appropriate futures contract and the basis. Typically, the futures contract with a delivery date closest to but not before the anticipated need is the appropriate contract to use for hedging purposes.

Table 9–1 Calculating the Final Sale Price: Hedging an Inherent Long Position with a Short Futures

Initial cash market price: 6.00 per bushel

hedge strategy: short futures at 6.00 per bushel

	Col. 1	Col. 2	Col. 3	Col. 4	Col. 5	Col. 6
	Futures Price at Expiration	Inherent Long Position P/(L)	Short Futures at 6.00 P/(L)	Combined P/(L) (Col. 2 + Col. 3)	Initial Cash Market Price 6.00	Final Price (Sale Price) (Col. 5 + Col. 4)
Row 1	6.75	+.75	(.75)	-0-	6.00	6.00
Row 2	6.50	+.50	(.50)	-0-	6.00	6.00
Row 3	6.25	+.25	(.25)	-0-	6.00	6.00
Row 4	6.00	-0-	-0-	-0-	6.00	6.00
Row 5	5.75	(.25)	+.25	-0-	6.00	6.00
Row 6	5.50	(.50)	+.50	-0-	6.00	6.00
Row 7	5.25	(.75)	+.75	-0-	6.00	6.00

Final sale price = initial cash market price plus combined profits or minus combined losses

Figure 9–1 Final Sale Price: Hedging an Inherent Long Position with a Short Futures

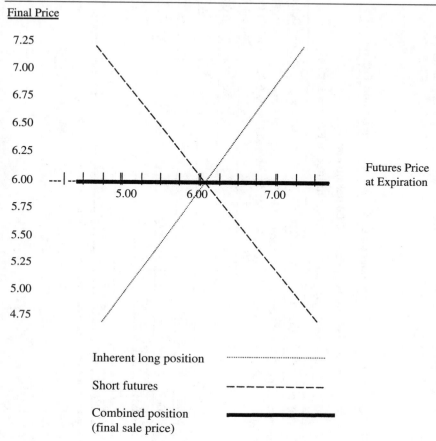

Inherent long position   ....

Short futures   — — — — — — — —

Combined position
(final sale price)   ████████████████

As was discussed in the last chapter, basis is defined as the cash price minus the futures price. Basis can range from positive (cash price higher than futures) to negative (cash price lower than futures).

Estimating a Sale Price

Assume a November Soybean futures price of $6.00 and a Davenport, Iowa, cash price of $5.85. Given these prices, the basis is "15 under" ($5.85 – $6.00). Assuming no change in prices and no change in the basis, Table 9–1A shows how Lee can estimate a sale price of soybeans at $5.85 per bushel.

Prices are not likely to remain unchanged, however, so consider the impact on the sale price if prices fall as Lee expects and if prices rise.

Prices Fall. Fast-forward to mid-October when Lee is ready to deliver soybeans. Assume that the price of November Soybean futures has fallen to $5.00 and that Davenport cash prices have fallen to $4.90. Note that the basis has "strengthened," because the Davenport cash price is now only "10 under" the price of November Soybean futures.

In this scenario, Lee can sell soybeans in the Davenport cash market at $4.90 and buy the November Soybean futures contract at $5.00. Note that buying this contract closes the existing short position. As Table 9–1B shows, Lee will calculate the actual selling price of soybeans as $5.90, 5 cents better than originally estimated.

In this example, profits from the short futures position offset the lower selling price of soybeans in the cash market, but the basis changed. As a result, Lee's actual selling price was different from the estimated selling price. In this example, the basis changed in Lee's favor, because the Davenport cash price rose from 15 cents under the futures price to 10 cents under. It is the "strengthening basis" that accounted for the fact that the final sale price was

Table 9–1 A Short Futures as a Short Hedge: Estimating a Sale Price

Futures Price	+	Expected Basis	=	Expected Sale Price
$6.00	+	($0.15)	=	$5.85

Table 9–1 B Short Futures as a Short Hedge: Prices Fall and Basis Strengthens

	Davenport Cash Market	November Futures	Basis
June 15	$5.85	$6.00	($0.15)
October 18	$4.90	$5.00	($0.10)

Calculation of actual sale price:
Cash sale price	$4.90
Plus profit on futures contract	+1.00
Final sale price	$5.90

5 cents higher than the original estimate of $5.85. If the basis had weakened, the final sale price would have been lower than originally estimated.

Prices Rise. In this scenario, assume that the price of November Soybean futures rises to $7.00 and that the Davenport cash price rises to $6.80. Given these changes, if Lee sells soybeans in the Davenport cash market at $6.80 and buys the November Soybean futures contract at $7.00, the final sale price is $5.80, 5 cents less than originally estimated. Table 9–1C shows these calculations.

Opportunities and Risks

Selling a futures contract as a short hedge provides the opportunity to lock in a sale price today even if prices decline before the delivery date in the future. The risk is that if prices rise, the "locked-in price" will be lower than the potentially higher price if no hedge had been implemented. Another risk is that a futures position does not protect against adverse changes in basis.

Forecast Justifying a Short Futures Hedge

Short hedgers who sell futures contracts must be forecasting falling prices or they must be unwilling to assume the risk of falling prices. If prices rise, the forecast was wrong, because in hindsight, a better sale price could have been achieved by not hedging.

Table 9–1C Short Futures as a Short Hedge: Prices Rise and Basis Weakens

	Davenport Cash Market	November Futures	Basis
June 15	$5.85	$6.00	($0.15)
October 18	$6.80	$7.00	($0.20)

Calculation of final sale price:	
Cash sale price	$6.80
Minus loss on futures contract	−1.00
Final sale price	$5.80

Psychology for Hedging with Short Futures

No one is always right in forecasting market prices, and so hedgers must learn to live with some wrong forecasts. For many people this is a hard adjustment. Rather than focus on one "right" or "wrong" forecast, however, short hedgers should remember that they are in the business of selling produce at "above-cost" prices so that profits can be made from farming (or from processing). This means that hedging decisions should be made in such a way that one right decision or one wrong decision does not "make or break" a business. Hedgers must think in terms of "average prices," and they must not make "all or nothing" hedges. Generally speaking, hedgers are better off if they spread their hedging activities over a year or a growing season.

LONG PUTS AS A SHORT HEDGE

The Theory

Table 9–2 and Figure 9–2 illustrate the theory of buying puts as a short hedge. Table 9–2 has six columns that are similar to those in Table 9–1. Column 1 contains a range of futures prices. Column 2 shows the profit or loss from the inherent long cash market position, and Column 3 shows the profit or loss from the long put position. In this example, it is assumed that a 6.00 Put is purchased for 25 cents per bushel. Column 4 contains the combined profit or loss of the long put and the inherent long cash market position. The final sale price in Column 6 is calculated in the same way as it was in Table 9–1. Combined profits in column 4 are added to the initial cash market price in column 5, because hedging profits raise the final sale price relative to the initial cash market price. Combined losses in column 4 are subtracted from the initial cash market price in column 5, because hedging losses decrease the final sale price relative to the initial cash market price.

The conclusion from Table 9–2 is that buying put options offers a different set of trade-offs than does selling futures contracts. There are two positive aspects and one negative aspect of buying puts. Buying a put locks in a known, minimum selling price, assuming the basis is unchanged. Buying puts also makes it possible for a short hedger to benefit, by getting a higher sale price, if prices rise. The disadvantage is that puts have a cost, and this cost lowers the price that is locked in. The locked-in, or minimum, price is below the current market price. This conclusion is presented graphically in Figure 9–2. The horizontal and left-upward-sloping broken line represents the long put, and the right-upward-slopping dotted line represents the inherent long cash

Table 9–2 Calculating the Final Sale Price: Hedging an Inherent Long Position with a Long Put

Initial cash market price: 6.00 per bushel

Hedge strategy: Long 600 Put at .25 per bushel

	Col. 1	Col. 2	Col. 3	Col. 4	Col. 5	Col. 6
	Futures Price at Expiration	Inherent Long Position P/(L)	Long 600 Put at .25 P/(L)	Combined P/(L) (Col. 2 + Col. 3)	Initial Cash Market Price 6.00	Final Price (Sale Price) (Col. 5 + Col. 4)
Row 1	6.75	+.75	(.25)	+.50	6.00	6.50
Row 2	6.50	+.50	(.25)	+.25	6.00	6.25
Row 3	6.25	+.25	(.25)	-0-	6.00	6.00
Row 4	6.00	-0-	(.25)	(.25)	6.00	5.75
Row 5	5.75	(.25)	-0-	(.25)	6.00	5.75
Row 6	5.50	(.50)	+.25	(.25)	6.00	5.75
Row 7	5.25	(.75)	+.50	(.25)	6.00	5.75

Final sale price = initial cash market price plus combined profits or minus combined losses

Figure 9–2 Final Sale Price: Hedging an Inherent Long Position with a Long Put

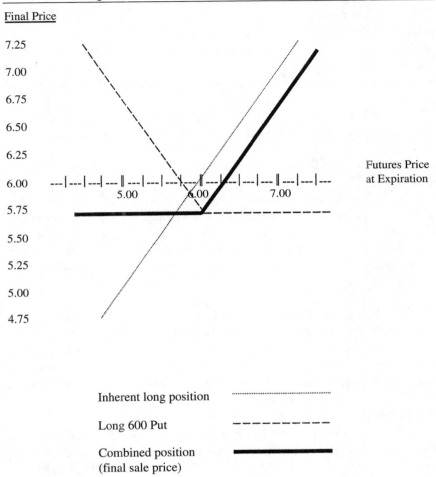

Final Price

Inherent long position ....

Long 600 Put ─ ─ ─ ─ ─ ─ ─ ─ ─

Combined position ▬▬▬▬▬▬▬▬
(final sale price)

market position. The horizontal and right-upward-sloping solid line represents the final sale price and corresponds to column 6 in Table 9–2A.

Practical Example

Return to the example of Farmer Lee, who wants to hedge a soybean crop for delivery in October. To estimate a sale price, Lee needs to know the current price of the appropriate put option and the basis. Like the appropriate futures contract, the appropriate put will have an expiration date closest to but not before the anticipated need.

Estimating a Sale Price

As in the short futures example above, assume a November Soybean futures price of $6.00 and a Davenport cash market price of $5.85. Instead of selling a November Soybean futures contract, however, Lee buys a November Soybean 600 Put for 25 cents. Assuming no change in prices and no change in basis, Table 9–2A shows how Lee can estimate the minimum sale price of soybeans at $5.60 per bushel.

Note that as defined in Chapter 1, the effective futures price for a long put is equal to the strike price of the put minus the premium paid. In this example, the 600 Put has a strike price of $6.00, and its cost is 25 cents. Consequently, the effective futures price, if the put is exercised, is $5.75 ($6.00 – $0.25).

Lee's estimated minimum sale price therefore is $5.60 per bushel. Although this price is lower than the current market price of November futures by the cost of the put and the basis, the following scenarios illustrate that paying a premium for a put can provide a benefit if the market behaves in a certain way. We now revisit the outcomes: one when prices fall and one when prices rise.

Prices Fall. Fast-forward again to mid-October, when Lee is ready to deliver soybeans. If the price of November Soybean futures is $5.00, the November Soybean 600 Put will be trading for at least $1.00. Assuming, as before, that Davenport cash prices have fallen to $4.90, Lee can sell soybeans in the Davenport cash market and sell the 600 Put for $1.00 for a profit of 75 cents. As Table 9–2B shows, Lee can calculate actual sale price of soybeans as $5.65, 5 cents better than the original minimum price estimate.

In this example, the profit from the long put partially offset the lower price of soybeans in the cash market. As before, the "strengthening basis" explained why the final sale price of $5.65 was 5 cents higher than the originally estimated minimum price of $5.60. As was mentioned in the last chapter, the opportunity to profit from an improvement in the basis, at the

Table 9–2A Long Put as a Short Hedge: Estimating a Minimum Sale Price

Effective Futures Price	+	Expected Basis	=	Expected Sale Price
$5.75	+	($0.10)	=	$5.60

Table 9–2B Long Put as a Short Hedge: Prices Fall and Basis Strengthens

	Davenport Cash Market	November Futures	Basis	600 Put
June 15	$5.85	$6.00	($0.15)	$0.25
October 18	$4.90	$5.00	($0.10)	$1.00

Calculation of actual sale price:	Cash sale price	$4.90
	Plus profit on put option	+ 0.75
	Final sale price	$5.65

risk of losing from an adverse change, is an aspect of options just as it is an aspect of futures.

Prices Rise. As above, assume that the price of November Soybean futures rises to $7.00 and that the Davenport cash price rises to $6.80. With November Soybean futures trading at $7.00 at the expiration of November options, the November 600 Put will expire worthless, and so the cost of 25 cents will be lost. By selling soybeans in the Davenport cash market at $6.80 and writing off as a loss the cost of the 600 Put, Lee can calculate the final sale price of soybeans at $6.55, as shown in Table 9–2C

Opportunities and Risks

This example shows that buying puts gives short hedgers the opportunity to benefit if commodity prices rise. In this example, the losses from the put were limited to 25 cents, and so any price rise beyond 25 cents was a benefit to Lee, the soybean seller. This example, however, also shows the risks of buying puts as a short hedge. First, the minimum sale price locked in by the put is below the current futures price. In this example, the locked-in futures price is $5.75, which is below the initial futures price of $6.00 by the cost of the put. The second risk is that potential adverse changes in basis are not covered by long puts.

Forecast Justifying a Long Put Hedge

Since buying puts gives short hedgers the opportunity to benefit if prices rise, the forecast must be for prices to rise. That's right! Short hedgers who buy puts must forecast that prices will rise. This idea may be a surprise to some, but remember, a short hedger's goal is to get the highest possible sale price. It is only speculators who want to profit by buying puts at a low price

Table 9–2C Long Put as a Short Hedge: Prices Rise and Basis Weakens

	Davenport Cash Market	November Futures	Basis	600 Put
June 15	$5.85	$6.00	($0.15)	$0.25
October 18	$6.80	$7.00	($0.10)	$0.00

Calculation of actual sale price:	Cash sale price	$6.80
	Minus loss on put option	– 0.25
	Final sale price	$6.55

and selling them at a high price. The thinking process for hedging is different from that for speculating.

Psychology for Hedging with Long Puts

Short hedgers should view put options as insurance policies. Buying puts is the short hedger's strategy of choice when the forecast is "bullish but worried." An example might be the period immediately before a crop report. If a short hedger is bullish but worried that the report will change market sentiment from bullish to bearish unexpectedly, a long put position will at least lock in a known minimum sale price if prices start to fall.

Another time when a short hedger might be "bullish but worried" is after a long bull market. A short hedger may see no reason for the bull market to end, but experience sometimes indicates that when it is least expected, protection from a price decline is needed. These are obviously situations that require judgment and a willingness to lose the put premium.

Another consideration is profit margins. The cost of a put must be "affordable." If the effective sale price of the futures, assuming that the put is exercised, is prohibitive, buying puts is not a viable hedging alternative. Buying puts is not a panacea; it is just another hedging alternative with a unique set of trade-offs.

SHORT CALLS AS A SHORT HEDGE

The Theory

Selling calls offers short hedgers a third set of trade-offs. Table 9–3 and Figure 9–3 illustrate the theory of selling calls as a short hedge.

Table 9-3 contains six columns that are similar to those in Tables 9-1 and 9-2. Column 1 contains a range of futures prices. Column 2 shows the profit or loss from the inherent long cash market position, and column

3 shows the profit or loss from the short call. In this example, it is assumed that a 600 Call is sold for 25 cents per bushel. Column 4 contains the combined profit or loss of the short call and the inherent long cash market position. The final sale price in column 6 is calculated by combining column 4 and column 5. Combined profits in column 4 are added to the initial cash market price in column 5, because hedging profits increase the final sale price relative to the initial cash market price. Combined losses in column 4 are subtracted from the initial cash market price in column 5, because hedging losses decrease the final sale price relative to the initial cash market price.

The conclusion from Table 9–3 is that selling calls has three positive aspects and one negative aspect. The first positive aspect is that a cash payment is received when the strategy is initiated. The second is that if the futures price is at or above the strike price at expiration, the effective sale price is above the futures price at the time when the call was sold. The third positive aspect is that the call premium received offers some downside protection in the event that futures prices fall. The negative aspect is that no minimum sale price is locked in, because futures prices can fall beyond the amount of the call premium received.

Selling calls offers only limited protection for short hedgers. This conclusion is presented graphically in Figure 9–3. The horizontal and right-downward-sloping broken line represents the short call, and the right-upward-sloping dotted line represents the inherent long cash market position. The horizontal and left-downward-sloping solid line represents the final sale price, and corresponds to column 6 in Table 9–3.

A Practical Example

Consider again the example of Farmer Lee, who wants to hedge a soybean crop for delivery in October. To estimate a sale price, Lee needs to know the current price of the appropriate call option and the basis.

Estimating a Sale Price

As in the previous examples, assume a November Soybean futures price of $6.00 and a Davenport cash price of $5.85, so that the basis is "15 under." To hedge the inherent long position, Lee sells a November 600 Call for 25 cents. Assuming no change in prices and no change in the basis, Lee can estimate the sale price at $6.10 per bushel as presented in Table 9–3A.

The effective futures price in this example is equal to the strike price of the call plus the premium received. Consequently, the effective futures

Table 9–3 Calculating the Final Sale Price: Hedging an Inherent Long Position with a Short Call

Initial cash market price: 6.00 per bushel
Hedge strategy: short 600 Call at .25

	Col. 1 Futures Price at Expiration	Col. 2 Inherent Long Position P/(L)	Col. 3 Short 600 Call at P/(L)	Col. 4 Combined P/(L) (Col. 2 + Col. 3)	Col. 5 Initial Cash Market Price 6.00	Col. 6 Final Price (Sale Price) (Col. 5 + Col. 4)
Row 1	6.75	+.75	(.50)	+.25	6.00	6.25
Row 2	6.50	+.50	(.25)	+.25	6.00	6.25
Row 3	6.25	+.25	-0-	+.25	6.00	6.25
Row 4	6.00	-0-	+.25	+.25	6.00	6.25
Row 5	5.75	(.25)	+.25	-0-	6.00	6.00
Row 6	5.50	(.50)	+.25	(.25)	6.00	5.75
Row 7	5.25	(.75)	+.25	(.50)	6.00	5.50

Final sale price = initial cash market price plus combined profits or minus combined losses

184

Figure 9–3   Final Sale Price: Hedging an Inherent Long Position with a Short Call

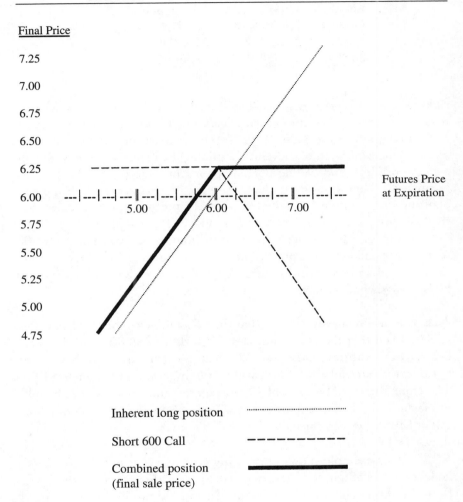

Final Price

7.25

7.00

6.75

6.50

6.25

6.00   Futures Price
at Expiration

5.00   6.00   7.00

5.75

5.50

5.25

5.00

4.75

Inherent long position	⋯⋯⋯⋯⋯⋯
Short 600 Call	– – – – – – –
Combined position (final sale price)	▬▬▬▬▬

price, if the call is assigned, is $6.25 (6.00 + 0.25). Including the basis, Lee's estimated sale price, assuming that the call is assigned, therefore is $6.10 per bushel. This price is higher than the current market price of November Soybean futures by the call premium net of the basis. The following two scenarios illustrate how the call premium received can benefit Lee if the market behaves in a certain way.

Table 9–3A Short Calls as a Short Hedge: Estimating a Sale Price

Effective Futures Price	+	Expected Basis	=	Expected Sale Price
$6.25	+	($0.15)	=	$6.10

Prices Fall. In mid-October, when Lee is ready to deliver soybeans, assume that November Soybean futures have fallen to 5.00 and that the Davenport cash price has fallen to 4.90. With November Soybean futures trading at $5.00 at the expiration of November options, the November 600 Call will expire worthless, and so the 25-cent premium received will be kept as income. By selling soybeans in the Davenport cash market at $4.90 and recognizing the premium from the 600 Call as a profit, Lee can calculate the final sale price of soybeans at $5.15 as shown in Table 9–3B.

In this example, the 25-cent profit from the short call partially offset the $1.00 fall in futures prices. The actual sale price of $5.15 was 70 cents lower than the initial estimate, because the futures price fell $1.00 and the basis strengthened 5 cents.

Prices Rise. As previously, assume that the price of November Soybean rises to $7.00 and that the Davenport cash price rises to $6.80. With November Soybean futures trading at $7.00 at the expiration of November options, the November 600 Call will be trading for approximately $1.00. Therefore, there will be a loss of 75 cents on the short call position. By selling soybeans in the Davenport cash market at $6.80 and covering the short call at $1.00, Lee can calculate the final sale price of soybeans at $6.05 as shown in Table 9–3C.

This example shows that selling calls makes it possible for short hedgers to benefit if commodity prices rise. In this example, the losses from the short call were 75 cents, but the call did not begin to lose until the underlying soybeans futures contract rose by 25 cents, the premium received. The premium received was a benefit to Lee, the soybean seller. As this example also shows, the basis also played a role in the determination of the final sale price. In this example, the price of soybeans rose $1.00, 20 cents of which accrued to Lee as a higher final sale price. The full $1.00 did not accrue to Lee, however, because (1) the loss on the short call was 75 cents and (2) the basis changed 5 cents against Lee's position.

Table 9–3B Short Calls as a Short Hedge: Prices Fall and Basis Strengthens

	Davenport Cash Market	November Futures	Basis	600 Call
June 15	$5.85	$6.00	($0.15)	$0.25
October 18	$4.90	$5.00	($0.10)	$0.00

Calculation of actual sale price:

Cash sale price	$ 4.90
Plus profit loss on call option	+ 0.25
Net sale price	$ 5.15

Table 9–3C Short Calls as a Short Hedge: Prices Rise and Basis Weakens

	Davenport Cash Market	November Futures	Basis	600 Call
June 15	$5.85	$6.00	($0.15)	$0.25
October 18	$6.80	$7.00	($0.10)	$1.00

Calculation of actual sale price:

Cash sale price	$ 6.80
Minus loss on call option	− 0.75
Final sale price	$ 6.05

Opportunity and Risks

The premium received from short calls creates an opportunity to raise the effective sale price of futures contracts. In stable or rising markets, the effective sale price is higher than the prevailing price at the time the call is sold. There are two risks, however. First, the premium received offers only limited downside protection if futures prices fall. Second, short calls establish a maximum sale price, and short hedgers do not benefit if prices rise above that level.

Forecast Justifying a Short Call Hedge

Short calls benefit short hedgers most if futures prices trade in a narrow range around the strike price of the call. Neutral price action must therefore be predicted.

Psychology for Hedging with Short Calls

The previous example shows that short calls have advantages and disadvantages different from those of either short futures or long puts. They also benefit short hedgers in different market scenarios. Whereas short futures lock in the current futures price and long puts lock in a futures price below the current level, the effective sale price for short calls is above the current futures price, assuming that the calls are assigned. If futures prices decline, however, the call premium offers only limited downside protection.

Since short calls offer a third set of trade-offs, it stands to reason that hedgers should use them when their forecasts are different. Short hedgers should sell calls when they are neutral on the market. Remember, short hedgers want to sell the underlying, and the call premium received raises the effective sale price only if futures prices do not fall or rise "too much."

An example of a period when a short hedger might be "neutral" is during the middle of a growing season when all seems to be going well, rainfall is adequate, weather is constructive, and crop reports are in line with expectations. Therefore, little price movement is expected. A short call position will bring in some option premium that increases profit if the forecast is correct. The call premium also offers some protection if prices fall. Since the risk is being unhedged if prices fall "too much," short hedgers who sell calls must be ready to sell futures if prices begin to fall dramatically.

THE BEARISH COLLAR AS A SHORT HEDGE

The Theory

A strategy known as the bearish collar was created with the goal of getting the advantages of the long put without its disadvantages. Purchasing a put with a strike price below the current futures price and simultaneously selling a call with a strike price above the current futures price creates a bearish collar. The put locks in a minimum sale price, and the call premium received reduces the cost of the put. The short call, however, establishes a maximum sale price. Table 9–4 and Figure 9–4 illustrate the theory of the bearish collar as a short hedge.

Table 9–4 is similar to Tables 9–1, 9–2, and 9–3 except that it has seven columns. Two columns are required to show the profit or loss from the two components of the hedging strategy. Column 3 shows the profit or loss from the long put, and column 4 shows the profit or loss from the short call. In this example, it is assumed that a 575 Put is purchased for 15 cents per bushel and that a 625 Call is sold for 15 cents per bushel. Column 5 contains the combined profit or loss of the long put, the short call, and the inherent long cash market position. The final sale price in column 7 is calculated by adding the combined profit in column 5 to the initial cash market price in column 6 or by subtracting the combined loss in column 5 from the initial cash market price in column 6.

The conclusion from Table 9–4 is that the bearish collar offers a fourth set of trade-offs. There are three positive aspects and two negative aspects. The bearish collar requires little or no initial cash payment. It leaves open the possibility for short hedgers to increase the sale price if prices rise, and it locks in a known, minimum sale price, assuming that the basis is unchanged. The negative aspects are that the possibility of increasing the sale price is limited and that the minimum price locked in is below the current price. This conclusion is presented graphically in Figure 9–4. The three lighter lines in Figure 9–4 represent the components of the strategy: the inherent long position, the long put, and the short call. The heavy solid line represents the final sale price and corresponds to column 7 in Table 9–4.

A Practical Example

Consider again the case of Farmer Lee, who wants to hedge a soybean crop for delivery in October. To estimate a sale price, Lee needs to know the current prices of the appropriate call and put and the basis.

Estimating a Sale Price

As in the examples above, assume a November Soybean futures price of $6.00 and a Davenport cash price of $5.85, so that the basis is "15 under." Assume also that Lee creates a bearish collar by buying a November 575 Put for 15 cents and simultaneously selling a November 625 Call for 15 cents. Given these assumptions, Lee can estimate the sale price as presented in Table 9–4A.

The effective selling price of the futures is equal to the current futures price minus the net premium paid or plus the net premium received. Since the futures price is 6.00 and the net cost of the bearish collar is zero in this example, the effective sale price of the futures is $6.00 (6.00+0.15 – 0.15). The following scenarios illustrate how the bearish collar can benefit short hedgers if the market behaves in a certain way.

Prices Fall. Fast-forward one last time to mid-October when Lee is ready to deliver soybeans. Assume that the price of November Soybean futures prices has fallen to $5.00 and that the Davenport cash price has fallen to $4.90.

Table 9–4 Calculating the Final Sale Price: Hedging an Inherent Long Position with a Bearish Collar

Initial cash market price: 6.00 per bushel
Hedge strategy: long a 575 Put at .15 and short a 625 Call at .15

	Col. 1 Futures Price at Expiration	Col. 2 Inherent Long Position P/(L)	Col. 3 Long 5.75 Put at .15 P/(L)	Col. 4 Short 6.25 Call at .15 P/(L)	Col. 5 Combined P/(L) (Col. 2 + Col. 3)	Col. 6 Initial Cash Market Price 6.00	Col. 7 Final Price (Sale Price) (Col. 5 + Col. 4)
Row 1	6.50	+.50	(.15)	(.10)	+.25	6.00	6.25
Row 2	6.40	+.40	(.15)	(.00)	+.25	6.00	6.25
Row 3	6.30	+.30	(.15)	+.10	+.25	6.00	6.20
Row 4	6.20	+.20	(.15)	+.15	+.20	6.00	6.20
Row 5	6.10	+.10	(.15)	+.15	+.10	6.00	6.10
Row 6	6.00	-0-	(.15)	+.15	-0-	6.00	6.00
Row 7	5.90	(.10)	(.15)	+.15	(.10)	6.00	5.90
Row 8	5.80	(.20)	(.15)	+.15	(.20)	6.00	5.80
Row 9	5.70	(.30)	(.10)	+.15	(.25)	6.00	5.75
Row 10	5.60	(.40)	-0-	+.15	(.25)	6.00	5.75
Row 11	5.50	(.50)	+.10	+.15	(.25)	6.00	5.75

Final sale price = initial cash market price plus combined profits or minus combined losses

190

Figure 9–4 Final Sale Price: Hedging an Inherent Long Position with a Bearish Collar

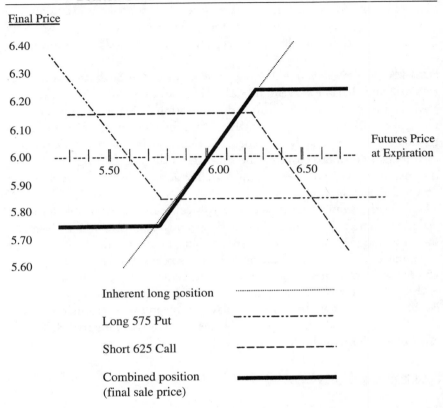

Final Price

Inherent long position	....
Long 575 Put	— · — · · — · · — · · —
Short 625 Call	— — — — — — — — ·
Combined position (final sale price)	▬▬▬▬▬▬▬

Table 9–4A The Bearish Collar as a Short Hedge: Estimating a Sale Price

Effective Futures Price	+	Expected Basis	=	Expected Sale Price
$6.00	+	($0.15)	=	$5.85

In this scenario, the November 575 Put will be trading for at least 75 cents, and the November 625 Call will expire worthless. Lee can sell soybeans in the Davenport cash market at $4.90, sell the 5.75 Put for 75 cents, and realize the 15-cent profit on the short 6.25 Call. As Table 9–4B shows, Lee will calculate the final sale price of soybeans as $5.65, 20 cents worse than initially estimated.

In this example, the total 75-cent profit from the two options partially offset the $1.00 decline in futures prices. As in previous examples, the
"strengthening basis" explained why the actual sale price of $5.65 was only
20 cents lower than initially estimated rather than being 25 cents lower.

Prices Rise. As above, assume that the price of November Soybean futures rises
to $7.00 and that the Davenport cash price rises to $6.80. With November
Soybean futures trading at $7.00 at the expiration of November options, the
November 575 Put will expire worthless, and the November 625 Call will be
trading for approximately 75 cents. By selling soybeans in the Davenport
cash market at $6.80, covering the short 625 Call, and writing off as a loss
the cost of the 575 Put, Lee can calculate the actual sale price of soybeans at
$6.05 as shown in Table 9–4C.

This example shows that a bearish collar makes it possible for short
hedgers to benefit if commodity prices rise. In this example, the losses from the
short call and long put positions were 75 cents. Losses did not begin to occur
at expiration, however, until the underlying soybeans futures contract rose by
25 cents, which is the distance from the initial futures price to the strike price
of the call. That rise in soybean prices was a benefit to Lee, the soybean seller.
As this example shows, the basis also played a role in the determination of the
actual final sale price. In this example, the price of soybeans rose $1.00, 20
cents of which accrued to Lee as a higher sale price for soybeans.

Opportunities and Risks

The positive aspects of a bearish collar are that the cost is lower than simply
buying a put, the opportunity to benefit from higher prices exists, and a
minimum price is locked in. The disadvantages are that the benefit from

**Table 9–4B The Bearish Collar as a Short Hedge: Prices Fall and
Basis Strengthens**

	Davenport Cash Market	November Futures	Basis	575 Put	625 Call
June 15	$5.85	$6.00	($0.15)	$0.15	$0.15
October 18	$4.90	$5.00	($0.10)	$0.75	$0.00

Calculation of actual sale price:		
	Cash sales price	$4.90
	Plus profit on put option	+0.60
	Plus profit on call option	+0.15
	Final sale price	$5.65

Table 9–4C The Bearish Collar as a Short Hedge: Prices Rise and Basis Weakens

	Davenport Cash Market	November Futures	Basis	575 Put	625 Call
June 15	$5.85	$6.00	($0.15)	$0.15	$0.15
October 18	$6.80	$7.00	($0.20)	$0.00	$0.75

Calculation of actual sale price:	Cash sale price	$6.80
	Minus loss on put option	−0.15
	Minus loss on call option	−0.60
	Final sale price	$6.05

higher prices is limited to the strike price of the call and that the minimum price that is locked in is below the current price.

Forecast Justifying a Bearish Collar Hedge

Short hedgers must predict neutral to bullish price action to choose a bearish collar, because the actual sale price is increased only if prices rise. As will be explained next, the motivations for choosing a bearish collar are complex.

Psychology for Hedging with a Bearish Collar

The motivation for buying puts as a short hedge was described as "bullish but worried." While the bearish collar strategy leaves intact the opportunity to benefit from rising prices, it also limits that opportunity. There must, therefore, be an additional twist to the motivation for selecting this strategy. Short hedgers should choose bearish collars for one of two reasons.

First, if a short hedger is "bullish but worried and puts are too expensive," a bearish collar is appropriate. The "bullish" part of the forecast explains why someone is willing to be at least partially unhedged in an attempt to benefit from rising prices. The "worried" part explains why someone feels the need to buy puts, and the "puts are too expensive" part explains why someone would sell calls.

The meaning of "too expensive" is subjective and will vary from hedger to hedger. The basis for making a judgment, however, is either a minimum necessary price or processing margins. If a price below a specified level would result in losses, the effective sale price of buying puts may be undesirable. Also, if the processing margin for a soybean crusher, for example, is 15 cents per bushel, it is hard for that crusher to justify buying a soybean oil put that costs 20 cents. However, if a call can be sold to reduce the cost of such a put, purchasing the put may be justified.

A second motivation for the bearish collar is the perceived need for "low-cost disaster insurance." Options, remember, are similar to insurance policies, and purchased puts for short hedgers act like insurance against falling prices. Remember also that an option's strike price and distance from current futures prices correspond to the deductible component of an insurance policy. The farther a strike price of a put is below the current futures price, the more like a disaster insurance policy that put is. Only if prices fall very dramatically will the put have a payoff value. Rather than "pay" for such a put, a short hedger can sell a call with a strike price equally far above the current futures price. The premium from the call can be applied toward the cost of the put, and the short hedger will have a low-cost insurance policy against an unforeseen very sharp decline in prices.

SUMMARY

There are four basic strategies that short hedgers can use to protect themselves against price risk. They can sell futures, buy puts, sell calls, and combine long puts and short calls to create a bearish collar.

Short futures should be used when short hedgers are forecasting declining prices. The opportunity is that today's prices can be locked in if prices fall as forecast. The risk is that prices rise, in which case the opportunity to benefit from rising prices has been eliminated.

Long puts should be purchased when short hedgers are "bullish but worried." Purchased puts lock in a minimum sale price and make it possible to benefit from rising prices, but the locked-in price is below the current price.

Selling calls is appropriate for short hedgers when neutral price action is forecast. The premium received from selling calls raises the effective sale price for futures contracts, but the downside protection of short calls is limited to the premium received.

Bearish collars can be used when short hedgers are bullish but worried and the price of puts is "too high." If the effective sale price locked in is too low or if processing margins are too low to justify the cost of puts, out-of-the-money calls can be sold to lower the net amount paid for puts. The advantages of bearish collars are that a minimum sale price is established, the opportunity to benefit from higher prices exists, and the net cost of the puts is reduced. The disadvantages, are that the locked-in price is below the current price and that the potential benefit from rising prices is limited to the strike price of the call.

Ten

Advanced Hedging Strategies

The term *advanced* undoubtedly means different things to different people. The goal of this chapter is to demonstrate a method of thinking and using options that can improve the hedging process. To use options in more than the basic ways described in the last two chapters, hedgers must learn to think in two steps. The first step is taken when a strategy is initiated, and the second step involves following through according to a plan on or before the option expiration date.

Five strategies are presented in this chapter: (1) the futures repair strategy, (2) increasing hedging exposure without increasing risk, (3) gaining on the spread, (4) trading the range, and (5) the El Niño hedge. The mechanics of each strategy are presented in the context of a hedging situation. The thinking process will be discussed, and each part of the two-step planning process is explained. Commissions and margin requirements are not included in the discussions, but they are important considerations that must be included in the analysis of real situations.

THE FUTURES REPAIR STRATEGY

Crushco, Inc. (CI), is a soybean processor in Nebraska that purchased one November Soybean futures contract at $6.50 in late May. The hedging manager forecast rising soybean prices over the summer, and the goal was to hedge part of CI's needs for the fall. Today is August 20, and the price of November Soybean futures is $6.00, 50 cents below CI's entry price. Ugh! This is a loser! What to do?

In any hedging decision, the most important element is the market forecast. If the hedging manager predicts a continued decrease in prices, the rational action is to sell the futures contract and take a loss. In this example,

195

however, the forecast is more bullish. November Soybean futures are expected to rise to $6.25 by late October, the expiration of November Soybean options.

"Doubling Up"

Given this situation—a 50-cent unrealized loss and a forecast for a 25-cent price rise—CI's hedging manager might consider the old standby strategy of "doubling up," as buying a second futures contract shares frequently is called. Purchasing a second futures contract at $6.00 creates a two-contract position with an average cost of $6.25 per contract. If a price rise to $6.25 occurs as predicted, the 50-cent unrealized loss on the first contract is recouped. The disadvantage of doubling up, however, is that losses mount at twice the rate of a one-contract exposure if prices continue to decline.

The Strategy

An alternative to doubling up is known as the futures repair strategy. In this strategy, a "ratio call spread" is established in conjunction with the existing long futures contract. A ratio call spread is created by purchasing one call and selling two calls with the same underlying and the same expiration date but with a higher strike price.

Table 10–1 and Figure 10–1 illustrate how the strategy of purchasing one November Soybean 600 Call for 20 cents and selling two November Soybean 625 Calls at 10 cents each offers CI a new alternative. First, the break-even futures price of $6.25 is achieved. This is the same break-even price achieved by purchasing a second futures contract. Second, there is no additional margin requirement. Third, the downside risk is not doubled. If the futures price declines below 6.00 in this example, CI's price exposure never exceeds one long contract.

Table 10–1 and Figure 10–1 also illustrate the negative trade-off of using the ratio call spread: Breaking even is the best result possible— it doesn't get any better. Above a futures price of 6.25, gains in the long futures and the long 600 Call are offset by losses in the short 625 Calls. Before the strategy mechanics are discussed in detail, some observations should be made about this strategy.

Some Observations

First, note that there are no "uncovered" short calls. One of the short 625 Calls is covered by the long futures contract, and the other is covered by the owned 600 Call. Second, this strategy is "futures-oriented," because losses from a price decline below 6.00 are equal to the initial one-futures-contract exposure to the market. Third, the profit potential of this strategy is limited. At expiration, if the futures price is above 6.25 in this example, the one long 600 Call will be exercised and the two short 625 Calls will be assigned. The result will be no position, but the initial loss will have been recovered.

Mechanics at Expiration

Exercise of the long 600 Call and/or assignment of the two short 625 Calls depend on the price of the underlying futures contract. There are three possible outcomes in the example presented above. The futures price might be (1) at or below 6.00, (2) above 6.00 and at or below 6.25, or (3) above 6.25. Each possibility is examined below.

If the futures price is at or below 6.00 at expiration, all options expire worthless. The amount of the loss depends entirely on the futures price since the option position, in this example, was established for zero cash outlay, not including transaction costs. At expiration, in this example, the strategy will lose 1 cent per futures contract for each 1-cent decline in futures price below 6.00. At a futures price of 5.70, for example, the result is an 80-cent loss. The futures contract was purchased for $6.50, resulting in an 80-cent loss, and all options expire worthless for a net loss of zero. The combined futures and options loss, therefore, is 80 cents.

If the futures price is above 6.00 and at or below 6.25 at expiration, the result is the same as long two futures contracts at an average price of 6.25. With the futures price at 6.10, for example, the loss on the entire position is 30 cents. This result is the combination of the three parts of the total position. First, there is a 40-cent loss from the futures contract that was purchased at 6.50; second, there is a 10-cent loss from the 600 Call that was purchased for 20 cents; third, there is a profit of 20 cents from the two short 625 Calls that were sold for 10 cents each and that expire worthless with the futures price at 6.10 at expiration. This combined loss of 30 cents is 10 cents better than the 40-cent loss on the initial long futures contract.

If the futures price is above 6.00 but not above 6.25 at expiration, the in-the-money 600 Call has both positive and negative consequences which must be anticipated. On the positive side, the value of this long call contributes to the improved results over owning just one futures contract. The potential negative consequence depends on exercise and related costs. Exercise of the 600 Call will create a second long futures contract. It must be decided whether to exercise this call and accept the risk of the additional

Table 10–1 The Futures Repair Strategy

Futures Price at Expiration	Long 1 Futures at 6.50	Long 1 600 Call at 0.20	Short 2 625 Calls at 0.10 each	Total P/(L) at Expiration
6.40	(0.10)	+0.20	(0.10)	0.00
6.35	(0.15)	+0.15	0.00	0.00
6.30	(0.20)	+0.10	+0.00	0.00
6.25	(0.25)	+0.05	+0.20	0.00
6.20	(0.30)	0.00	+0.20	(0.10)
6.15	(0.35)	(0.05)	+0.20	(0.20)
6.10	(0.40)	(0.10)	+0.20	(0.30)
6.05	(0.45)	(0.15)	+0.20	(0.40)
6.00	(0.50)	(0.20)	+0.20	(0.50)
5.95	(0.55)	(0.20)	+0.20	(0.55)
5.90	(0.60)	(0.20)	+0.20	(0.60)

futures contract or to sell the call immediately before expiration. Either decision adds transaction costs and potential risks.

If the call is exercised and the resulting long futures contract is sold, there may be a timing difference that creates price exposure. If the call is exercised on expiration Friday and if the futures contract is sold on the next Monday, there is "over-the-weekend risk." While the futures price might change favorably, it might also change adversely. These concerns must be thought through in advance of the expiration date when, at the latest, action is required.

Another risk to be considered is the price behavior of the options before the expiration date. Chapter 16 discusses the price behavior of ratio spreads in depth, and that chapter should be studied before attempting this strategy in a real situation. If the option position is closed prior to expiration, it is possible that a loss may result.

The third possible outcome is a futures price above 6.25 at expiration. Above this price at expiration, the maximum profit potential is realized, assuming that the long 600 Call is exercised and both 625 Calls are assigned. This means that a second futures contract is purchased by the call exercise and that both contracts are sold by the assignment. These transaction costs must be considered before this strategy is initiated.

Figure 10–1 The Futures Repair Strategy

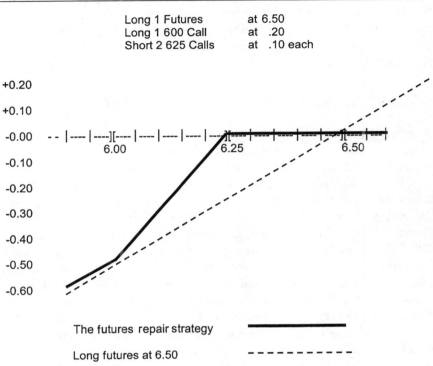

Long 1 Futures	at 6.50
Long 1 600 Call	at .20
Short 2 625 Calls	at .10 each

The futures repair strategy ————

Long futures at 6.50 — — — — — — —

With a futures price above the strike price of the short calls, 6.25 in this example, there is also the possibility of early assignment of one or both of the short calls. If one call is assigned early, the owned futures contract is sold. If both calls are assigned early, a short futures position is created. A decision must be made whether to exercise the long 600 Call or to close the position by selling the 600 Call and covering the short futures contract. Although these many possible outcomes and follow-up decisions may sound complicated or even scary to inexperienced option users, these intricacies are part of hedging and trading with options. These intricacies can be learned by anyone who examines each step in the exercise and assignment process and thinks through the timing at which each step might occur.

Analyzing the Trade-offs

Which is better, doubling up or using the futures repair strategy? Unfortunately, there is no "better." Each strategy offers different trade-offs. Doubling up lowers the break-even price and allows unlimited profit potential in return for the doubling of risk. The futures repair strategy, in contrast, lowers the break-even price without increasing risk, but it sacrifices participation in a price rise above the upper strike price, 6.25 in this example. Neither strategy is better. The choice depends on a hedger's forecast and tolerance for risk.

INCREASING HEDGING EXPOSURE WITHOUT INCREASING RISK

Another way for long hedgers to use the ratio call spread is to initiate it at the same time that a futures position is established. As the following example shows, the result is that market exposure is doubled over a limited price range.

Consider the case of Snaxco, a snack food manufacturer which uses wheat futures to hedge its purchasing needs. Assume that today is October 20, 90 days from the expiration of March Wheat options. Also assume that March Wheat futures are trading at 2.50 and that the March Wheat 250 and 270 Calls are trading at 12 cents and 6 cents, respectively. If Snaxco's hedging manager wants to create a two-contract hedge exposure over a limited price range while taking only a one-contract risk, this can be accomplished by initiating a 250–270 ratio call spread along with buying one March Wheat futures contract. Let's see how this strategy might be implemented.

The Snaxco hedging manager can initiate a three-part position by simultaneously purchasing one March Wheat futures contract at 2.50, purchasing one March 250 Call and selling two March 270 Calls. If the 250 Call is purchased for 12 cents and the two 270 Calls are sold for 6 cents each, the ratio call spread portion of this strategy will be established for a zero net cost, not including commissions.

Many brokers will accept an order to execute a ratio call spread at a net debit or net credit. Rather than entering spread orders "at the market," such "limit-price" orders guarantee that the trade will be executed at the customer's price or better or not at all. The risk of limit-price orders is that the market moves away from the stated price and the order is never executed.

Table 10–2 and Figure 10–2 show the results of Snaxco's long wheat futures with ratio call spread at expiration. If the futures price is between 2.50 and 2.70 at expiration, profits are equal to two long futures contracts at 2.50 each. Below 2.50 at expiration, however, losses are equal to only one long futures contract at 2.50. The maximum profit that can be earned from this position is 40 cents, and that profit is earned if the futures price is 2.70 or higher at expiration. Above a futures price of 270 at expiration, the one long 250 Call is exercised and the two short 270 Calls are assigned. The result is that a second futures contract is purchased at 2.50 and then both contracts are sold at 2.70.

Snaxco would then be left with a 40-cent profit and no position. If wheat futures were trading at or slightly above 2.70, this result would undoubtedly be satisfactory. If, however, prices were dramatically higher, at 3.20, for example, this strategy would underperform one long futures contract from 2.50. With futures at 3.20, one contract purchased at 2.50 would earn 70 cents.

Motivations for this Strategy

Option strategies, remember, are not better in an absolute sense; they just offer different trade-offs. Strategies therefore should be chosen on the basis of a market forecast and tolerance for risk. Table 10–3 and Figure 10–3 compare three long-hedge strategies: (1) buying futures outright, (2) a ratio call spread with a long futures, and (3) selling a put. The prices for the first two strategies are the same as they are in the example above. The futures price is 250, the price of the 2.50 Call is 12 cents, and the price of the 270 Calls is 6 cents each. The price of the 250 Put in the third strategy is 12 cents.

The positive and negative aspects of each strategy are apparent from Figure 10–3 and can be summed up as follows. Buying one futures contract at 2.50 has unlimited profit potential and the risk of one long futures contract at a break-even price of 2.50. The ratio call spread with one long futures has two positive aspects. First, there is the potential of making twice as much as one long futures if the price is between 2.50 and 2.70 at expiration; second, the risk is equal to only one long futures at 2.50. The negative aspect is that profits are limited, to 40 cents in this example. The short put has the advantage of a lower break-even point, 2.38 in this example, and the disadvantage of limited profit potential, 12 cents in this example.

Choosing between strategies depends on the forecast. A sideways price forecast favors selling the put. Forecasting a price rise above 2.90 favors buying one futures contract outright, and forecasting a modest price rise, between 2.50 and 2.90 in this example, favors the ratio call spread with one long futures. When a hedger thoroughly understands what each strategy offers, an informed selection can be made.

Realistic Prices

The prices in the last two examples work perfectly. The futures price exactly equals the strike price of the long call, and the price of the short calls is exactly half the price of the long call. As a result, the ratio call spread is established for no cash outlay, not including commissions. It is therefore

Table 10-2 Ratio Call Spread with Long Futures

Futures Price at Expiration	Long 1 Futures at 2.50 each	Long 1 250 Call at 0.12 each	Short 2 270 Calls at 0.06 each	Total P/(L) at Expiration
2.80	+0.30	+0.18	−0.08	+0.40
2.75	+0.25	+0.13	+0.02	+0.40
2.70	+0.20	+0.08	+0.12	+0.40
2.65	+0.15	+0.03	+0.12	+0.30
2.60	+0.10	−0.02	+0.12	+0.20
2.55	+0.05	−0.07	+0.12	+0.10
2.50	0.00	−0.12	+0.12	0.00
2.45	−0.05	−0.12	+0.12	−0.05
2.40	−0.10	−0.12	+0.12	−0.10

reasonable to ask, Are these examples made up for the purpose of this book, or do such opportunities actually exist in the real world?

In fact, prices of at-the-money calls are frequently approximately twice the price of calls with the next higher or second higher strike price if the time to expiration is 60 days or longer. Although actual ratio spreads with more than 60 days to expiration may be established for a slight net debit or net credit, the examples presented above are realistic. It is suggested that readers look at real prices in the current market to verify this.

Not a Trading Strategy

The tables and figures in this chapter have illustrated the ratio call spread with long futures strategy at expiration. The short-term price behavior of this strategy makes it an undesirable trading vehicle. The combined position of long one futures contract, long one call, and two short calls does not change sufficiently with 10-cent or even 20-cent changes in futures prices over short time periods to justify entering and exiting the position with any frequency. When this strategy is established, a hedger must be committed to holding the position until expiration. Market conditions and forecasts do change and such changes may dictate closing a ratio call spread and futures position, but this strategy should not be initiated with the intention of "trading in and out."

Figure 10–2 Ratio Call Spread with Long Futures

Buy Futures   at 2.50
Buy 1 250 Call   at 0.12
Sell 2 270 Calls   at 0.06 each

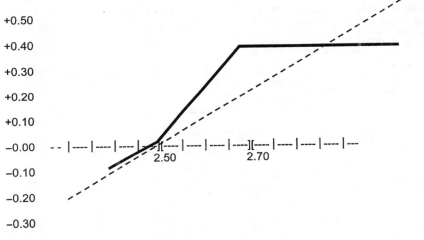

Ratio call spread with long futures   ▬▬▬▬▬

Long futures at 2.50   – – – – – – – –

GAINING ON THE SPREAD

1: Selling Calls to Improve the Price of a Long Roll

There are occasions when hedgers find it necessary to "roll their hedges." *Rolling a hedge* means closing out one position and reestablishing a position with a similar market exposure but a later expiration date. A hedger who is long December Corn futures, for example, may find it desirable to extend the hedge to March of the next year. Typically, this is accomplished by selling the existing long December Corn futures contract to close the position and simultaneously purchasing a new March Corn futures contract to open that position.

       Assume that today is November 15, one week before the expiration of December options. Also assume that December Corn futures are trading

Table 10–3 Comparison of Three Strategies:
- **Long Futures**
- **Ratio Call Spread with Long Futures**
- **Short Put**

Stock Price at Expiration	Long Futures at 2.50	Long Futures @ 2.50 and Long 1 2.50 Call at 0.12 and Short 2 2.70 Calls at 0.06 each	Short 1 2.50 Put at 0.12
3.00	+0.50	+0.40	+0.12
2.90	+0.40	+0.40	+0.12
2.80	+0.30	+0.40	+0.12
2.70	+0.20	+0.40	+0.12
2.60	+0.10	+0.20	+0.12
2.50	0.00	0.00	+0.12
2.40	−0.10	−0.10	+0.02
2.30	−0.20	−0.20	−0.08
2.20	−0.30	−0.30	−0.18
2.10	−0.40	−0.40	−0.28
2.00	−0.50	−0.50	−0.38

at 2.35 and that March Corn futures are trading at 2.50. Finally, assume that Cerealco, a cereal manufacturer in Minnesota, is long a December Corn futures contract and that the company's hedging manager wants to roll this position out to March of next year.

Cerealco could execute a traditional long roll by selling its long December contract at 2.35 and simultaneously purchasing a March contract for 2.50. At these prices, the spread would be executed for a 15-cent debit; i.e., the difference of 15 cents is an amount paid.

The question is, How might Cerealco use options to do better? If the December Corn 220 Call is trading at 17 cents, the following example shows how this call might be used to improve the price at which the spread is executed.

Instead of simply selling the December contract and buying the March contract, the hedging manager at Cerealco might consider selling the December Corn 220 Call at 17 cents and buying March Corn futures at 2.50. After this transaction, the new position will be long December Corn futures, short the December 220 Call, and long March Corn futures.

Figure 10–3 Comparison of Three Strategies
• **Buy futures**
• **Ratio call spread with long futures**
• **Short put**

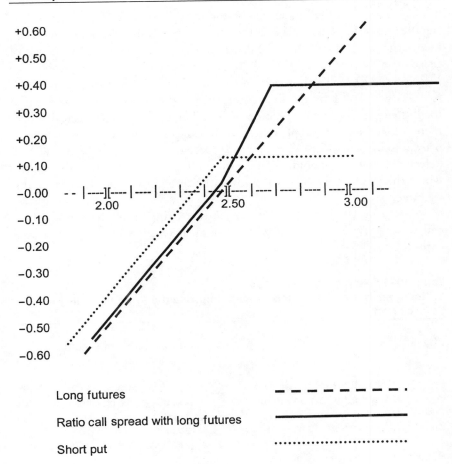

Long futures	– – – – – – – –
Ratio call spread with long futures	——————
Short put	··················

Fast-forward 1 week to the expiration of December options. If December Corn futures are above 2.20, the December 220 Call will be assigned, and Cerealco will sell its December Corn futures contract at an effective price of 2.37, 2 cents better than the price of 2.35. Remember, from Chapter 1, that the *effective price* is the price of a futures transaction that takes into account the option premium. In this example, if the short

December 220 Call is assigned, a futures contract is sold at 2.20. The premium received from selling the 220 Call, however, was 17 cents. Consequently, the effective price of this futures transaction would be 2.37 (2.20 + 0.17).

The risk of selling an in-the-money call to roll a hedge is that during the remaining life of the call, the price of the futures contract could drop below the strike price of the call. In the example above, if the price of December Corn drops below 2.20 before December options expire, the December 220 Call will expire worthless. If the 220 Call is not assigned, Cerealco will still have the long December futures contract and be exposed to all the risks that such a position entails. The price at which Cerealco ultimately sells the contract, plus the 17-cent call premium, will be the effective price of selling that futures contract. If December futures drops below 2.20 before the contract is sold, the effective selling price could be substantially worse than 2.35, which was the initial price of December futures in this example.

Table 10–4 shows the three steps in using an in-the-money short call to improve the price at which a long hedge is rolled out to a later expiration.

Table 10–4 Gaining on the Spread
1: Using an In-the-Money Short Call to Improve the Price of Rolling a Long Futures Hedge

Step 1:	The existing position	Long 1 December Futures (current price 2.35)
Step 2:	Sell in-the-money call *and* buy further expiration futures	Sell 1 December 220 Call at 0.17 *and* buy 1 March futures at 2.50
Step 3:	At expiration, if call is assigned	December futures sold (effective price of 2.37)
Result:	If futures price is above strike price of call at expiration	December futures sold at 2.37 March futures purchased for 2.50 Net debit paid for spread: 0.13 (2 cents better than initial spread price)
Risk:	If the front-month futures price is below the strike price of the call at option expiration and if the contract is ultimately sold at a price below the strike price, the effective price of the spread can be worse than the original price of the futures spread.	

2: Selling Puts to Improve the Price of a Short Roll

Now consider the case of Mashco, a soybean crushing company which is short May Soybean Meal futures as a hedge against falling prices. If Mashco's hedging manager wants to roll the May hedge to July, in-the-money short puts can be used in an attempt to improve the price at which the roll is executed.

Assume that today is April 9, eight days before the expiration of May options. Also assume that May Soybean Meal futures are trading at 180.00, that July Soybean Meal futures are trading at 190.00, and that the May 200 Put is trading at 21.00. The traditional roll would involve purchasing the May contract at 180.00 to close the position and selling a July contract at 190.00 to establish a new short position. If Mashco executed this transaction at these prices, the roll would be executed for a $10 net credit. Now consider how the May 200 Put might be used to improve the situation.

Instead of simply buying the May contract and selling the July contract, the hedging manager might consider selling the May 200 Put at 21.00 and selling July futures at 190.00. After this transaction, the new position will be short May Soybean Meal, short the May 200 Put, and short July Soybean Meal.

In 8 days, when May options expire, if the price of May futures is below 200.00, the May 200 Put will be assigned. As a result, Mashco will purchase a May contract that closes its existing short position. The effective price at which this purchase occurs is 179.00 (200.00 − 21.00). The final result, then, would be that the May–July roll is executed for an $11 net credit, 1 dollar better than the traditional futures roll.

The risk of selling an in-the-money put for the purpose of rolling a hedge is that the futures price could rise above the strike price of the put before expiration. In the example above, if the price of May Soybean Meal futures is above 200 at May expiration, the May 200 Put will expire worthless. If the 200 Put is not assigned, Mashco will still have the short May futures contract and be exposed to the risks that such a position entails. The price at which Mashco ultimately buys the contract, minus the $21 put premium, will be the effective price. If the price of May Soybean Meal futures is above 200 when the contract is covered, the effective purchase price could be substantially higher than 180.00, the initial price of May futures in this example.

Table 10–5 shows the three steps in using an in-the-money short put to improve the price at which a short hedge is rolled out to a later expiration.

Table 10–5 Gaining on the Spread
2:Using an In-the-Money Short Put to Improve the Price of Rolling a Short
Futures Hedge

Step 1:	The existing position	Short 1 May futures (current price 180.00)
Step 2:	Sell in-the-money put *and* sell further expiration futures	Sell 1 May 200 Put at 21.00 *and* sell 1 July futures at 190.00
Step 3:	At expiration, if put is assigned	May futures purchased (effective price of 179.00)
Result:	If futures price is below strike price at expiration	May futures purchased at 179.00 July futures sold at 190.00 Net credit received for spread: 11.00 ($1 better than initial spread price)
Risk:	If the futures price is above the strike price of the put at option expiration, and if the contract is ultimately purchased at a price above the strike price, the effective price of the spread can be worse than the price of the original futures spread.	

Forecast Justifying Selling Options to Roll Hedges

What do the cases of Cerealco and Mashco have in common? In both cases, the hedging managers were forecasting that the price of the near-term futures contract *would not move beyond the strike price of the short option.* In the case of the long hedger, Cerealco, the hedging manager did not want the price of December Corn futures to drop below 2.20, the strike price of the call that was sold. Mashco, the short hedger, did not want the price of May Soybean Meal futures to rise above 200.00, the strike price of the put that was sold.

Hedgers who sell in-the-money options to improve the prices of rolling hedges must have a neutral forecast. At the very least, they should believe that the price of the futures contract will not move beyond the strike price of the sold option.

3: Buying Puts to Improve the Price of a Long Roll

Hedgers also can use options to improve the price of a roll when they have a strong directional opinion about the market. Consider the case of Bakery,

Inc. (BAKI), which is long September Wheat and wants to roll to December. BAKI's hedging manager is also very bullish on wheat and believes that prices could rally 15 cents in the next 2 weeks.

Assume that today is August 6, 2 weeks before the expiration of September Wheat options. Also assume that September Wheat futures are trading at 3.15, that December Wheat futures are trading at 3.25, and that the September Wheat 320 Put is trading at 9 cents. If the September contract were sold at 3.15 and the December contract were purchased for 3.25, the traditional futures spread would be executed for a 10-cent debit.

Instead of selling the September contract and buying the December contract, however, the hedging manager at BAKI might consider buying the September 320 Put for 9 cents and buying December futures at 3.25. After this transaction, the new position will be long September futures, long the September 320 Put, and long December futures.

If in 2 weeks the price of September futures is 15 cents higher at 3.30, as the BAKI hedging manager predicts, the September 3.20 Put will expire worthless. BAKI, however, could sell its long September Wheat futures contract at the prevailing price of 3.30. The effective selling price of this transaction would be 3.21, 6 cents better than the original price of 3.15. Consequently, the effective price of the spread would also be 6 cents better.

The effective selling price of the futures contract is calculated by subtracting the cost of the put from the actual selling price of the futures. In this case, the September futures contract was sold for 3.30 and the cost of the 320 Put was 9 cents. Therefore, the effective selling price was 3.21 (3.30 − 0.09).

The risk of buying an in-the-money put to roll a long futures hedge is that the price of the futures contract does not rise high enough to offset the cost of the put. In this example, if the price of September Wheat does not rise above 3.24, the effective selling price of the September futures will not be above 3.15. The worst case is that the price of September futures stays below 3.20, and the 3.20 Put is exercised. If this happens, the effective selling price of the September futures will be 3.11 (3.20 − 0.09), which is 4 cents worse than the initial price of 3.15.

Table 10–6 shows the three steps in using an in-the-money long put to improve the price at which a long hedge is rolled out to a later expiration.

4: Buying Calls to Improve the Price of a Short Roll

If a short hedger has a bearish opinion, calls can be purchased to improve the price of rolling a short hedge. Consider the case of The Elevator Company (TECOM), which is short January Soybean futures and wants to roll to

Table 10–6 Gaining on the Spread
3: Using an In-the-Money Long Put to Improve the Price of Rolling a Long
Futures Hedge

Step 1:   The existing position   Long 1 September Futures
                                          (current price 3.15)

Step 2:   Buy in-the-money put *and*   Buy 1 September 3.20 Put at 0.09
          buy further expiration futures buy 1 December futures at 3.25

Step 3:   At expiration,   Put expires, sell September
          with September futures   futures
             at 3.30   (effective price of 3.21)

Result: If futures price is above   September futures sold at 3.21
          strike price plus cost of put   December futures purchased at 3.25
                                          Net Debit paid for spread: 0.04
                                          (6 cents better than initial spread
                                            price)

Risk: If the futures price at option expiration is less than the strike price of
          the put plus the time premium of the put, the effective price of the
          spread can be worse than the original futures spread. The worst that
          can happen is that the put is exercised. Exercise of the put causes
          the futures to be sold at an effective price equal to the strike price of
          the put minus its cost, 3.11 in this example.

March. TECOM's hedging manager is also very bearish on soybean futures
and believes that prices will fall 30 cents in the next month.

Assume that today is November 15, one month before the expiration of January Soybean options. Also assume that January Soybean futures
are trading at 5.35, that March Soybean futures are trading at 5.45, and that
the January Soybean 525 Call is trading at 20 cents. If the January contract
were purchased at 5.35 and the March contract were sold at 5.45, the spread
would be executed for a 10-cent credit.

Instead of buying the January contract and selling the March contract, however, the hedging manager at TECOM might consider buying the
January 525 Call for 20 cents and selling March futures at 5.45. After this
transaction, the new position will be short January futures, long the January
525 Call, and short March futures.

If the price of January Soybean futures is 30 cents lower at 5.05 at
the expiration of January options as the TECOM hedging manager predicts,

the January 525 Call will expire worthless. TECOM, however, could buy a January Soybean futures contract at the prevailing price of 5.05 to cover its short position. The effective purchase price of this transaction would be 5.25, or 10 cents better than the original price of 5.35. Consequently, the effective price of the spread would also be 10 cents better.

The effective purchase price of the futures contract in this example is calculated by adding the cost of the call to the actual buying price of the futures. In this case, the January futures contract was purchased at 5.05, and the cost of the 525 Call was 20 cents. Therefore, the effective purchase price was 5.25 (5.05 + 0.20).

The risk of buying an in-the-money call to roll a short futures hedge is that the price of the futures contract does not drop low enough to offset the cost of the call. In this example, if the price of January Soybeans does not fall below 5.15, the effective purchase price of the January futures will not be below 5.35. The worst case is that the price of January futures stays above 5.25, and the 525 Call has to be exercised at expiration. If this happens, then the effective purchase price of the January futures will be 5.45 (5.25 + 0.20), or 10 cents worse than the initial price of 5.35.

Table 10–7 shows the three steps in using an in-the-money long call to improve the price at which a short hedge is rolled out to a later expiration.

Forecast Justifying Buying Options to Roll Hedges

What do the cases of BAKI and TECOM have in common? In both cases, the hedging managers were forecasting that the futures price *would move beyond the strike price of the long option.* In the case of the long hedger, BAKI, the hedging manager predicted that September Wheat futures prices would rise above 2.24, the strike price of the put plus the time premium paid. TECOM, the short hedger, wanted the price of January Soybeans to fall below 5.15, a price equal to the strike price of the purchased call less the time premium paid.

Hedgers who buy options to improve the prices of rolling hedges must have a strong directional forecast. They should predict that the futures price will move beyond the strike price of the purchased option by at least the time premium portion of the option's cost.

TRADING THE RANGE

For those who believe that hedging is partly trading, options can be used to facilitate the task of targeting buy and sell prices. Consider the case of Oleoco, an oleo manufacturer that uses soybean oil futures to hedge its

Table 10–7 Gaining on the Spread
4: Using an In-the-Money Long Call to Improve the Price of Rolling a Short Futures Hedge

Step 1:	The existing position	Short 1 January Soybean futures (current price 5.35)
Step 2:	Buy in-the-money call *and* sell further expiration futures	Buy 1 January 5.25 Call at 0.20 *and* sell 1 March futures at 5.45
Step 3:	At expiration, with January futures at 5.05	Call expires, purchase January futures (effective price of 5.25)
Result:	If futures price is 5.05 at	January futures purchased for 5.25 March futures sold at 5.45 Net credit received for spread: 0.20 expiration (10 cents better than ini tial spread price)
Risk:	If the futures price at option expiration is higher than the strike price of the call minus the time premium of the call, the effective price of the spread can be worse than the original futures spread. The worst that can happen is that the call is exercised. If the call is exercised, the futures is purchased at an effective price equal to the strike price of the call plus the cost of the call, 5.45 in this example.	

purchasing needs. The hedging manager at Oleoco has established a partial hedge by purchasing 20 October Soybean Oil futures contracts at 18 cents per pound, or 18.00. The hedger believes that October Soybean Oil will trade in a 1-cent range around its current price for the next 60 days. The hedging-trading plan is to add to longs as the price dips near 17.00 and to sell some contracts on rallies toward 19.00. An option strategy known as "long futures plus short straddle" might be just what this hedger needs.

This strategy, as its name implies, involves three parts: the purchase of a futures contract, the sale of a call, and the sale of a put. The put and the call have the same strike price and expiration. Writing both a call and a put means the hedger is taking on two obligations: the obligation to sell the long futures (if the calls are assigned) and the obligation to buy additional contracts (if the puts are assigned).

For the example of Oleoco, assume that 20 October Soybean Oil futures are owned at a price of 18.00, that 10 October Soybean Oil 18.00

Calls are sold for 0.60 each, and that 10 October Soybean Oil 18.00 Puts are sold for 0.60 each

Since the number of calls sold is less than the number of long futures contracts, the short calls in this strategy are covered. The willingness and the financial ability to purchase futures contracts cover the short puts.

When the mechanics of this strategy are fully understood, it is possible to determine whether it meets a hedger's objectives. To review the mechanics, a futures price at expiration is selected and then what happens to each component is explained.

Futures Price Above 18.00 at Expiration

Consider first an October Soybean Oil futures price of 18.40 (or any other price above 18.00) at expiration. The question is, What happens, and what is the final position?

With a futures price of 18.40 at expiration, the 10 short 18.00 Puts expire worthless and the 10 short 18.00 Calls are assigned. Assignment of the short calls means that 10 of the long futures contracts are sold at 18.00 each. The effective selling price, however, is 19.20 (18.00 + 0.60 + 0.60). The result is long 10 futures, but 1.20 of option premium on 10 contracts is kept as income even though futures prices have risen only 0.40.

At any futures price above 18.00, at expiration, the same profit will result. The short puts expire, the short calls are assigned, and some of the futures contracts are sold. Given this outcome, the hedger is faced with the decision of what to do next. The hedger may hold or sell the remaining contracts, or the sold contracts may be repurchased. Any action should be based on the market forecast. Whatever is decided, a profit will have been earned.

Futures Price Below 18.00 at Expiration

If the price is below 18.00 at expiration, say, 17.60, then the 10 short 18.00 Calls expire, and the 10 short 18.00 Puts are assigned. Assignment on the puts means that an additional 10 October Soybean Oil futures contracts are purchased at 18.00 each. The effective purchase price, however, is 16.80 (18.00 − 0.60 − 0.60). The average price on 30 contracts, therefore, is 17.60 [(18.00 × 20) + (16.80 × 10)].

At this point the hedging manager will also have a decision to make: All 30 contracts can be held, more could be purchased, or some or all could be sold. Again, the action should be based on the hedging need and the market forecast.

Futures Price at the Strike Price at Expiration

A third possibility is that the futures price is exactly equal to the strike price at expiration, 18.00 in this example. If this happens, both the calls and the puts expire worthless, and the total option premiums are kept as income. The resulting position is long 20 October Soybean Oil futures contracts, and again, the hedging manager will have a decision to make.

Objectives Versus Results

Oleoco's hedging manager initially forecast a trading range between 17.00 and 19.00. In the outcomes presented, even though the futures price never reached one of those levels, assignment of a short option made the effective price of buying or selling some contracts better than the manager's target. This is how the strategy is supposed to work. The premiums received from selling two options make it possible to target a wider range than might otherwise be achievable.

Common Objections

As good as all the examples above appear, hedgers learning about this strategy for the first time have some reasonable questions. First, one might ask: What if the futures price trades outside of the predicted range, to 16.50 or lower or to 20.00 or higher? Second, The 1.20 profit on 10 contracts is attractive, but how do I know I can earn it again? These are reasonable questions and are addressed in order below.

A "Large" Price Rise.   It is true that this strategy limits participation in a rising market, but remember that the hedging manager's forecast and objectives were very specific. If the futures price rallies outside of the predicted range, it is the forecast, not the option strategy, that is too blame. If the hedging manager had predicted sharply rising prices, another strategy would have been chosen.

A "Large" Price Decline.   A similar answer applies to the objection about a sharp price decline. If the forecast called for a large price decline, a neutral to bullish strategy was not appropriate. Again, any loss must be attributed to an inaccurate forecast rather than to the option strategy.

Repeating the Results.   Although there is no guarantee that new options will have the same price as the ones initially sold, the concern over the possibility of repeating the profit involves a misunderstanding of an important point. Profit calculations are only one element of the subjective process of forecasting markets and choosing strategies. The profit potential, remember, is accompanied by the risk of a futures position. On the downside, in this example, the hedging manager is assuming the risk of an additional 10 long futures contracts. On the upside, the risk of selling 10 contracts and possibly being underhedged is being assumed.

Balancing the Positives and Negatives

The most important element of the hedging manager's decision is the market forecast. In this example, selling 10 straddles in conjunction with 20 long futures contracts matched the forecast, but only the hedging manager can decide how much confidence should be placed in the forecast. The objections about potential missed opportunities or negative futures price action should be addressed to the market forecast.

Hedgers with experience using futures contracts must adapt their style to the two-step thinking required for successful hedging with options. The initiation of an option strategy has implications for what happens at option expiration, and that depends on the futures price. Hedgers who use options must consider all possible outcomes and plan accordingly.

THE EL NIÑO HEDGE

Wouldn't it be nice if good, cheap disaster insurance could be purchased for the next drought, the next Chernobyl, or the next Southeast Asian monsoon?

In order to purchase insurance, you need to select a time period and a deductible. With regard to the analogy between options and insurance, the time period corresponds to the expiration date and the deductible corresponds to the strike price. In the agricultural markets, option expirations correspond to the delivery months of the futures contracts that are open for trading. Typically, option expirations extend out approximately 8 months, and strike prices typically are created at least five strike prices above the current futures price. This means that with soybeans at 6.00, for example, options with expirations out 8 months and strike prices up to 7.50 are available. Also, if wheat futures are trading at 3.00, then 3.60-strike options exist out eight months.

A strategy known as a ratio volatility spread with calls sometimes can be used by long hedgers to fill the need for affordable disaster insurance.

Although the trading aspects of this strategy will be discussed in depth in Chapter 16, this explanation of the strategy will focus on hedging uses.

A 1 × 2 ratio volatility spread with calls is created by selling one call and purchasing two calls with the same underlying and the same expiration but with a higher strike price. Figure 10–4 illustrates a 575–625 1 × 2 ratio volatility spread with calls. In this strategy, one 575 Call is sold for 58 cents and two 625 Calls are purchased for 36 cents each. This means that the spread is established for a net debit of 14 cents. This means that 14 cents is paid, not including commissions.

Profit or Loss at Expiration

At expiration, there are three possible outcomes. The futures price can be at or below the lower strike, above the lower strike but not above the upper strike, or above the upper strike. The straight line in Figure 10–4 illustrates these possibilities. If the futures price is at or below the lower strike of a ratio volatility spread with calls at expiration, all calls expire worthless and the full amount paid for the position, 14 cents in this example, is lost. This does not imply, however, that this is the maximum risk. The maximum risk will be calculated shortly.

If the futures price is above the lower strike but not above the upper strike, the short call (lower strike) is assigned and the two long calls (higher

Figure 10–4 Ratio Volatility Spread with Calls:

Short 1 575 Call at 0.58 and Long 2 625 Calls at 0.36 Each (Net Debit of 0.14)

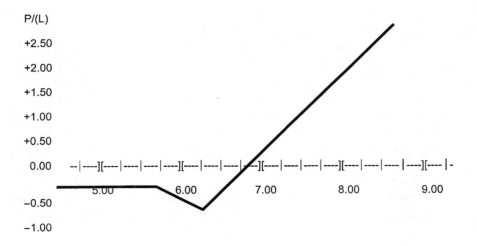

strike) expire worthless. If the futures price is 6.05 at expiration, assignment of the 575 Call results in selling a futures contract at 5.75 The 625 Calls expire worthless, and so the final profit or loss result is calculated by adding the cost paid or the credit received when establishing the position to the profit or loss from the futures position. If the short futures contract is covered at 6.05, then a futures loss of 30 cents is realized. Adding this 30-cent loss to the net debit of 14 cents paid to establish the position results in a total loss of 44 cents, or $2,200, not including commissions.

The maximum loss occurs if the futures price is exactly at the higher strike at expiration. With the futures price at 6.25 at expiration in this example, assignment of the 575 Call results in selling one futures contract at 5.75. If this contract is covered at 6.25, a 50-cent loss is realized. Since the 625 Calls expire worthless with the futures at 6.25 at expiration, the futures loss of 50 cents is added to the initial net debit of 14 cents for a total loss of 64 cents. Figure 10–4 confirms that 6.25 is the futures price at expiration where the maximum loss occurs.

If the futures price is above the higher strike at expiration, the short call (lower strike) is assigned and the two long calls (higher strike) are assigned. As Figure 10–4 illustrates, either a net profit or a net loss can result if the futures price is above the higher strike. If the futures is at 6.50 at expiration, for example, assignment of the 575 Call results in selling one futures contract at 5.75 and exercising the two 625 Calls results in purchasing two contracts at 6.25 each. These two events result in one long futures contract at 6.25 and a realized loss of 50 cents. If the one long futures contract is sold at 6.50, the final result is calculated by combining futures profits and losses with the initial net debit. In this case, with the futures at 6.50, the initial net debit of 14 cents is added to the net 25-cent loss on the two futures transactions. One contract is sold at 5.75 and repurchased at 6.25 for a loss of 50 cents, and the second contract is purchased at 6.25 and sold at 6.50 for a profit of 25 cents. The final result, with the futures price at 6.50, in this example is a net loss of 39 cents, not including commissions.

A net profit is the result, however, if the futures price is at 7.00 at expiration. In this case, the short 575 Call is assigned and the two long 625 Calls are exercised. These two events cause a realized loss of 50 cents on one short futures contract and create a long futures position at 6.25. If that long futures contract is sold at 7.00, a profit of 75 cents is realized on that contract. Subtracting the initial net debit of 14 cents from the net 25-cent profit from the futures transactions results in the final profit of 11 cents, or $550, not including commissions.

While analysis of the strategy at expiration is a starting point, the price behavior of the strategy before expiration is important to hedgers.

Price Behavior: Ratio Volatility Spreads with Calls

Table 10–8 contains theoretical values of a 575–625 1 × 2 ratio volatility spread with calls at various futures prices and days to expiration. This table was created using the OP-EVALF™ computer program that accompanies this text, the use of which is explained in Chapter 11. The value in each box assumes that one 575 Call is sold and that two 625 Calls are purchased. Column 1, row 7, in Table 10–8, for example, assumes a futures price of 6.00, 8 months to expiration, and the assumptions about volatility and interest rates listed at the top of the table. Although the individual call values are not shown, selling one 575 Call at 58 cents and purchasing two 625 Calls at 36 cents each results in a net debit of 14 cents, not including commissions, and 14 is the number which appears in this box. Consequently, given the assumptions stated above, the strategy could be established for a net debit of 14 cents.

Parentheses in Table 10–8 indicate that the strategy can be established for a net credit. The number in parentheses appearing in column 7, row 7, for example, indicates that selling one 575 Call and purchasing two 625 Calls results in a credit of 10 cents. Table 10–8 can be difficult to interpret. Calculating profit or loss requires knowing the debit or credit when a position is opened and when it is closed and then combining them correctly.

Long hedgers can use a table such as Table 10–8 to estimate how much will be made or lost if the market behaves in certain ways. Suppose, for example, soybean prices rally to 8.00 at 3 months from today which is 5 months to expiration in this example. The cell in column 4 and row 3 shows that, with Soybean futures at 8.00 and 5 months to expiration, the 575–625 ratio volatility spread will be trading for a net debit of 1.27. Paying a net 14-cent debit to open a position and receiving 1.27 when closing it results in a profit of 1.13. Even though the futures prices had moved $2.50 per bushel, a profit of 1.13 has value to a hedger.

The next question is, What is the cost if the market does not rally as feared? Table 10–8 also shows the results if soybean futures have not moved dramatically before expiration. If soybean futures are unchanged at 6.00 with 2 months to expiration, for example, the cell in column 7, row 7, indicates that the price of the spread will be a credit of 10 cents. If the position is closed at this price, a 24-cent loss will be realized. Opening a position for a payment of 14 cents and closing it at a payment of 10 cents results in

Table 10–8 575–625 1 x 2 Ratio Volatility Spread with Calls—Theoretical Values Volatility 25%, Interest Rates 5%

	Col. 1	Col. 2	Col. 3	Col. 4	Col. 5	Col. 6	Col. 7	Col. 8	Col. 9
Futures Price	8 Months	7 Months	6 Months	5 Months	4 Months	3 Months	2 Months	1 Month	Exp.
Row 1	9.00	2.20	2.20	2.20	2.20	2.21	2.22	2.23	2.24	2.25
Row 2	8.50	1.75	1.75	1.75	1.73	1.73	1.73	1.73	1.74	1.75
Row 3	8.00	1.33	1.31	1.29	1.27	1.26	1.25	1.25	1.25	1.25
Row 4	7.50	0.94	0.91	0.88	0.85	0.82	0.79	0.76	0.75	0.75
Row 5	7.00	0.60	0.56	0.52	0.48	0.44	0.38	0.33	0.27	0.25
Row 6	6.50	0.33	0.29	0.25	0.21	0.16	0.10	0.02	(0.09)	(0.25)
Row 7	6.00	0.14	0.11	0.08	0.04	0.00	(0.04)	(0.10)	(0.17)	(0.25)
Row 8	5.50	0.04	0.02	0.00	(0.02)	(0.04)	(0.06)	(0.06)	(0.05)	0.00

8 months at 6.00:   Short 1 575 Call at 58 cents
Long 2 625 Calls at 36 cents each
Net debit: 14 cents

Numbers *not in* parentheses mean that the spread can be established for a debit and closed for a credit.
Numbers *in* parentheses mean that the spread can be established for a credit and closed for a debit.

219

a loss of 24 cents. This means that if the market does not move, this position can be closed out after 6 months for a loss of approximately 24 cents. Consequently, this strategy is similar conceptually to purchasing a 6-month call for 24 cents.

Now consider the "strike price." Given that the upside break-even point of this strategy is 6.89 and that its estimated cost is 24 cents, this strategy is similar conceptually to buying a 6.65 strike call for 24 cents.

SUMMARY

Options can be used in a number of creative ways to add to the list of available hedging strategies.

A ratio call spread with a long futures contract can be used as an initial strategy to add leverage without increasing risk, or it can be used as a "futures repair" strategy to lower the break-even point of a long futures position. This strategy offers a different set of trade-offs than does doubling up or selling puts. If the ratio call spread can be established at the right prices, risk is not increased beyond owning one futures contract. The negative aspect is that upside participation is limited. Regardless of how this strategy is used, this is not a "trading strategy."

In-the-money options can be used in an attempt to improve the price at which futures hedges are rolled out to a further expiration. In-the-money options can be sold in an attempt to improve spread prices when hedgers have a neutral forecast. At the very least, they should believe that the price of the futures contract will not move beyond the strike price of the sold option. Hedgers who buy options to improve the prices of rolling hedges, by contrast, must have a strong directional forecast. They should predict that the futures price will move beyond the strike price of the purchased option by at least the time premium portion of the option's cost.

Selling straddles in conjunction with long futures involves the purchase of futures contracts and the simultaneous sale of calls and puts. This strategy can be used by hedgers who are forecasting a trading range and want to increase a long futures position at the low end of the predicted range and decrease exposure at the high end. The effective buy and sell prices established by the sold options provide reference points which can be used as part of the subjective decision-making process.

Ratio volatility spreads with calls can be used as an alternative to purchasing out-of-the-money calls when low-cost disaster insurance is desired. If the market moves dramatically as feared, the extra long call provides long market exposure above the break-even point. If no large price change has occurred by some predetermined time before expiration, the goal is to close out the position at little or no loss.

Hedgers with experience using futures contracts must adapt their style to the two-step thinking required for successful hedging with options. The initiation of an option strategy has implications for what happens at option expiration, and that depends on the futures price. Hedgers who use options must consider all the possible outcomes and plan accordingly.

Part 3

Trading Strategies

Eleven

Pricing and Graphing Strategies with OP-EVALF™

omputer programs are tools designed to perform calculations quickly and improve analysis. They are not designed to take over the decision-making process. Although the profit and loss diagrams in Chapters 2 and 3 can be drawn by hand, the calculations needed to calculate theoretical values require a computer. The computer program OP-EVALF™ which accompanies this text can perform both of these tasks. This chapter explains how to install and operate the program. Later chapters will show how the program can be used to analyze alternative strategies in hedging and trading situations.

OP-EVALF™

Included with this book is a CD labeled "OP-EVALF™ Setup Disk." This CD is designed to work on computers with Windows operating systems. Although the installation procedures are straightforward, if you have little experience with computers, you may want assistance with installing the program. Once the program is installed, you will find that it is easy to use.

The installation instructions are as follows:

1. Insert Setup Disk in drive D (or drive E).

2. Click on Start, then click on Run.

3. Type d:\setup (or e:\setup), press Enter, and follow the instructions.

To Run: Click on Start. Move the arrow to Programs in the first menu column and then to OP-EVAL Programs in the second menu column; then click on OP-EVALF™ in the third menu column.

When you start the program, the first few pages you will see are Disclaimers and Disclosures that contain important information about the assumptions made by the program. You should read these pages carefully.

225

Only with a thorough understanding of the limitations of this program (or any program) can you make informed decisions. If you rely on your own intuition and uninformed perceptions, you are not likely to do well in any area of trading, let alone option trading. After you have read all the Disclosures and Disclaimers carefully, you will be instructed to press Y if you accept the conditions or press any other key to exit the program.

If you have read and understand the Disclosures and Disclaimers and are willing to accept the risks you are undertaking by using the information provided by this program with all its limitations, press Y to indicate your willingness to accept. If you have not read the Disclosures and Disclaimer pages, if you would like to study them again, or if you do not want to proceed for any other reason, press any other key and you will exit the program. At that point, if you wish, you can restart the program in accordance with the instructions above.

When in Doubt, Seek Help

This chapter will review the major pricing and graphing capabilities of OP-EVALF™, but from time to time, you will undoubtedly have questions. It is therefore, useful to familiarize yourself with the Help pages that contain information on all aspects of the program, including operational techniques and definitions of terms.

MOST COMMONLY ASKED QUESTIONS

Operation of the program will be reviewed from the beginning below, but for the benefit of experienced computer users, the two most frequently asked questions will be answered first. Question number 1 is typically about the operation of the graphing capability. The graphing capability is available only from the Four Option Analysis page. Click on the Four Option Analysis item on the Menu bar and simply enter the desired position according to the procedures presented in this chapter. Then click on the Graph item on the Menu bar, and a graph of the position will appear. The Graph item on the Menu bar cannot be accessed from other pages in the program.

Question number 2 is typically about the ability to graph a position in a futures contract. To graph a futures position, again using the Four Option Analysis page, set the strike of Option 1 to zero (0.000) and set the Option Type to Call. You will then observe that the title Option 1 has changed to Underlying. A futures position will be graphed when you click on the Graph item on the Menu bar, assuming a non-zero number appears in the Quantity row in the Underlying column.

A complete discussion of operating OP-EVALF™ will now be presented. Even experienced computer users should read this section to learn the full range of capabilities of the program.

STARTING OP-EVALF™

When you have pressed Y in response to the question on the last page of the Disclosures and Disclaimers, which means you have read the Disclaimers and Disclosures and are willing to accept the limitations of the program, you will see a screen that looks like Figure 11–1.

Figure 11–1 shows the Call/Put Pricer page, the first of three calculation pages. This page provides theoretical values, delta, gamma, theta, and vega for a call and a put with the same strike, same expiration, and same underlying. Chapter 7 explained how this information can be used to analyze option prices and estimate how those prices may change given your forecast. This chapter only describes how the Call/Put Pricer and other aspects of the program work.

Figure 11–1 OP-EVALF™ Call/Put Pricer Page

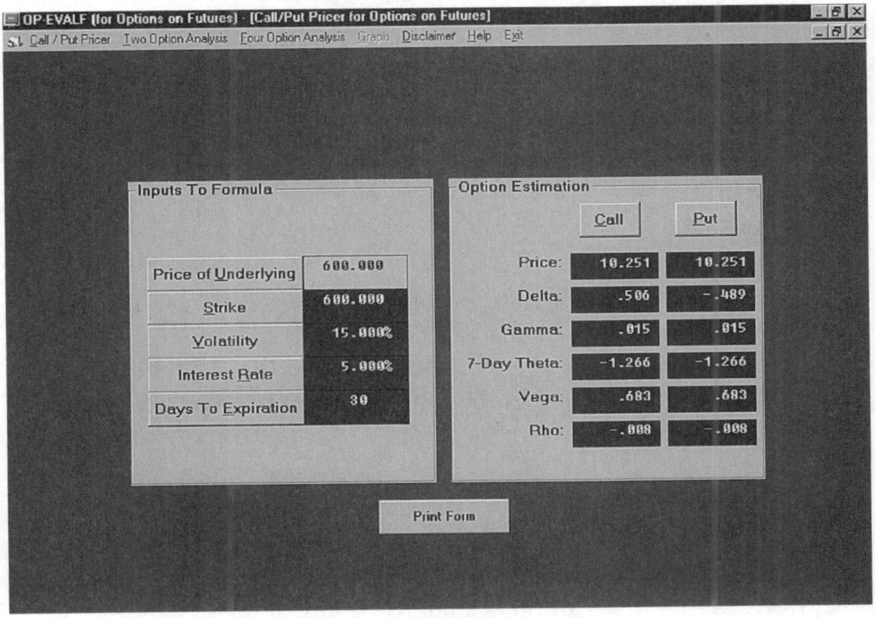

Moving Around the Call/Put Pricer Page

The highlighted rectangle can be changed either by clicking on a desired rectangle or by pressing the arrow keys. The down arrow (↓) and the right arrow (→) move the highlighted rectangle down the Inputs to Formula column first, then over to the Call rectangle, then to the Put rectangle, and, finally, back to the Price of Underlying rectangle. The rectangles below Call and Put cannot be highlighted, as they are "output only." The up arrow (↑) and the left arrow (←) move the highlighted rectangle in the opposite direction.

After familiarizing yourself with movement around the calculation page, highlight the Price of Underlying rectangle and make sure the default settings appear as in Figure 11–1. These are 600.000 for Price of Underling, 600.000 for Strike, etc. Given these inputs, OP-EVALF™ has calculated the theoretical value of the 600 Call as 10.251, which appears on the top line of the right side of the Call/Put Pricer page in the Price rectangle under Call.

Changing Price of Underlying

With the Price of Underlying rectangle highlighted, you can input any price from 0.001 to 99,999.999. If a whole number such as 805 is entered, OP-EVALF™ assumes that all three numbers to the right of the decimal point are zeros. After 805 (or some other number) is entered, then, when the Enter key or an arrow key is pressed or when another rectangle is highlighted by clicking, the number 805.000 appears in the Price of Underlying rectangle, and all output values are recalculated.

You can now practice with the different input rectangles and observe how OP-EVALF™ calculates option theoretical values, given your inputs.

Changing Strike Price

Strike price intervals vary by futures contract. Although strike prices are set at whole numbers such as 2.50 and 2.60, etc., OP-EVALF™ has the flexibility to set the strike price at any number between 0 and 99,999.999. This feature allows OP-EVALF™ to be used for options on a wide variety of underlying instruments.

Changing Volatility

Volatility, as discussed in Chapters 4 and 6, is a statistical measure of potential price changes in an option's underlying instrument. If other factors remain constant, a wider range of possible futures prices (i.e., higher volatility) means options have higher theoretical values. It is common practice to express volatility as a percentage, and this practice is followed in OP-EVALF™. The default setting for volatility is 15.000, or 15 percent. When the Volatility rectangle is highlighted, it is possible to enter any number from 0.000 to 999.999. If all inputs are at their default settings (as in Figure 11–1), changing the volatility to 16 and pressing Enter results in 16.000 appearing in the Volatility rectangle and 10.934 appearing under both Call and Put, as illustrated in Figure 11–2. Experiment with the volatility input and develop a feel for how changes in volatility affect option prices.

Changing the Interest Rate

Interest rates are a factor in the values of options, because time and the cost of money directly affect purchasing decisions. The default setting for interest rates is 5.000, or 5 percent. After experimenting with this input, observe that changes in interest rates have the smallest impact on option prices of any of the inputs. This is consistent with the discussion in Chapter 7, specifically, Table 7–6.

Figure 11–2 Call/Put Pricer with Volatility of 16%

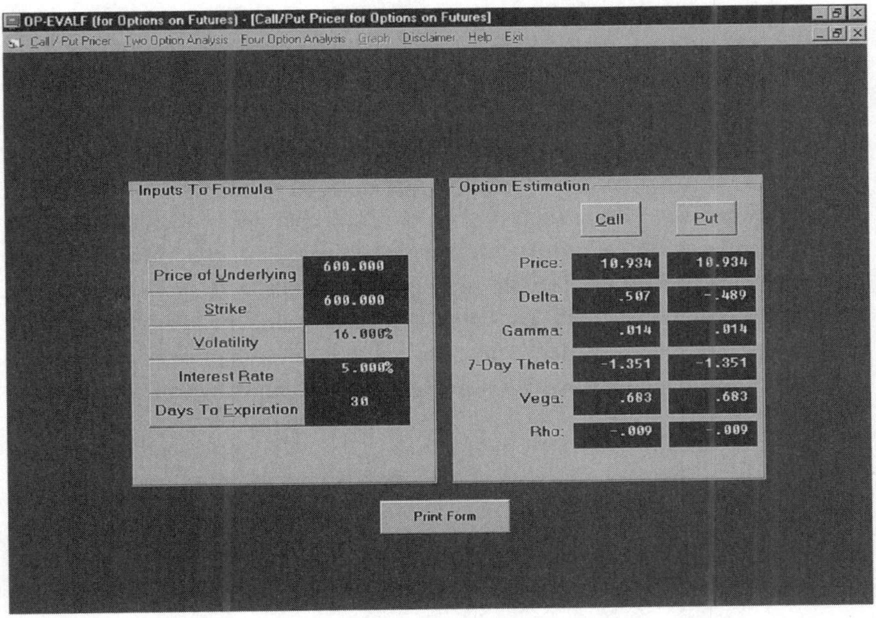

Changing Days to Expiration

The effect of time on option values was introduced in Chapter 5, and there will be more discussion of this issue in later chapters. The default setting for Days to Expiration is 30. When counting the days to expiration, include the current day if it is before or during market hours but do not include the current day if it is after the market close. Also, be sure to use the correct last day of trading as the expiration day. Even though expiration is technically on the Saturday following the last trading day, it is the last trading day that is the last opportunity to exercise.

Although all in-the-money futures options are typically subject to automatic exercise by the exchange's clearing corporation at expiration, option traders should be sure to know the brokerage firm's exact exercise procedures. While you may think that you will never need to know these procedures, it takes little effort to learn these details. Not needing something and knowing it is not costly. Needing something and not knowing it, however, can be very costly!

Changing Call and Put Prices: Estimating Implied Volatility

Given the default setting of inputs (as in Figure 11–1) the Call rectangle reads 10.251. Highlight this rectangle, type in 12 and press Enter. The first change you will notice is that the number in the Call rectangle is now 12.000. But another change is far more important. Can you tell what it is?

Look at the Volatility rectangle. You will observe that the volatility number has been recalculated from 15.000 to 17.560. Figure 11–3 shows the computer screen with a call price of 12.000 and volatility of 17.560. As was explained in Chapter 6, 17.560 is the implied volatility of this call.

When the value in the Call rectangle is changed, OP-EVALF™ not only recalculates the volatility, but also recalculates the Put value using the new volatility percentage and all other outputs as well.

OP-EVALF™ will also calculate an implied volatility percentage given a new Put value. When a new Put value is entered, a new Call value is calculated using the new volatility percentage, and all other outputs are also recalculated.

THE TWO OPTION ANALYSIS PAGE

Clicking on the Two Option Analysis item on the Menu bar at the top of the screen brings up a new screen that looks like Figure 11–4.

Figure 11–3 Input Call Price 12 and New Implied Volatility

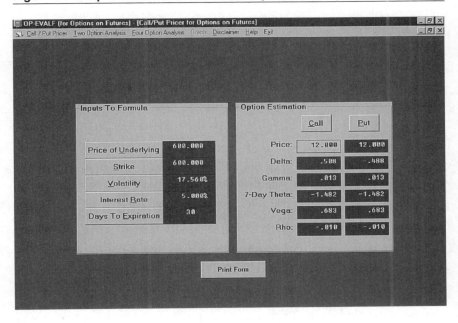

Figure 11–4 Two Option Analysis Page: Default Settings

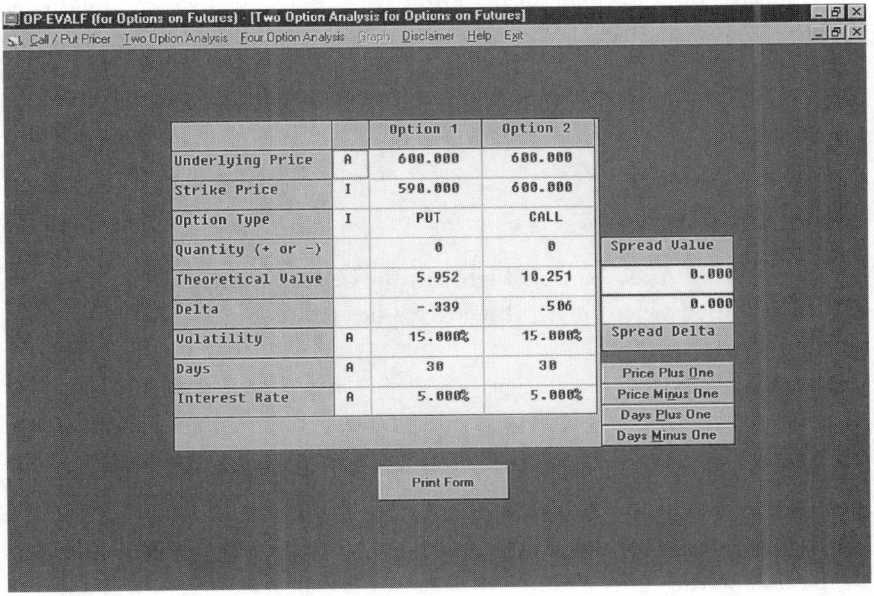

		Option 1	Option 2	
Underlying Price	A	600.000	600.000	
Strike Price	I	590.000	600.000	
Option Type	I	PUT	CALL	
Quantity (+ or -)		0	0	Spread Value
Theoretical Value		5.952	10.251	0.000
Delta		-.339	.506	0.000
Volatility	A	15.000%	15.000%	Spread Delta
Days	A	30	30	Price Plus One
Interest Rate	A	5.000%	5.000%	Price Minus One
				Days Plus One
				Days Minus One

Print Form

The purpose of the Two Option Analysis page is to analyze two-option positions. The Two Option Analysis page operates in a similar way to the Call/Put Pricer page. Left clicking highlights rectangles, and highlighted rectangles can have their values changed. Arrow keys can also be used to change the highlighted rectangle and recalculate outputs. Pressing the Enter key recalculates the outputs while leaving the highlighted rectangle unchanged. The following features on this page do not appear on the Call/Put Pricer Page.

A and I

The Two Option Analysis page can be used to analyze two options with the same volatility or different volatilities or two options with the same days to expiration or different days to expiration. It is also possible to analyze spreads involving calls only, puts only, or both calls and puts. The A and I buttons make this possible.

An A indicates that all numbers in that row are set to the input in the Option 1 column and that a change in the contents of one rectangle will change the contents of the other rectangles in that row. For example, if the Two Option Analysis page is set to the default settings as in Figure 11–4, a change in the Underlying Price of Option 1 will also change the Underlying Price of Option 2. Similarly, a change in the Volatility of Option 2 will change the Volatility of Option 1.

An I indicates that all the numbers in that row are set individually. A change in the contents of one rectangle will not change the contents of the other rectangles in that row. Referring to Figure 11–4, if the Strike Price of Option 1, for example, is changed, this will not change the Strike Price of Option 2.

Changing from A to I

To change from A to I, simply highlight the desired rectangle containing an A or I, and then type I or A, whichever is desired.

Changing Call to Put

To change from Call to Put or vice versa, simply highlight the desired rectangle containing Call or Put and press any letter or number key. If the row setting is A, pressing on any letter or number key, when a Call or Put rectangle is highlighted, will change the contents of every rectangle in that row to the new setting. If the row setting is I, only that rectangle will change.

ANALYZING A HYPOTHETICAL SPREAD

The Two Option Analysis page can be used to analyze ratio spreads and positions involving calls and puts, but the most common spread is a one-to-one vertical spread with only calls or only puts. An example of a one-to-one vertical call spread is the simultaneous purchase of one 600 Call and sale of one 625 Call. Both calls are assumed to have the same expiration and the same underlying instrument. A one-to-one vertical call spread is illustrated in Figure 11–5. The following example illustrates how a one-to-one 600–625 vertical call spread might be analyzed.

Setting Up the Two Option Analysis Page

The first step in estimating the value of a hypothetical 600–625 Call spread is entering all the inputs: futures price, days to expiration, volatility, etc. An example of how this can be accomplished is presented in Figure 11–5.

     After entering the standard information such as the Underlying Price, which is assumed to be 600 in this example; days to expiration, assumed to be 45 days; the volatility, assumed to be 17 percent; and other inputs, as indicated in Figure 11–5, the position must also be entered.

Figure 11–5 Hypothetical 600-625 Call Spread

		Option 1	Option 2	
Underlying Price	A	600.000	600.000	
Strike Price	I	600.000	625.000	
Option Type	I	CALL	CALL	
Quantity (+ or –)		+1	–1	Spread Value
Theoretical Value		14.198	5.332	+8.866
Delta		.509	.255	+0.254
Volatility	A	17.000%	17.000%	Spread Delta
Days	A	45	45	Price Plus One
Interest Rate	A	5.000%	5.000%	Price Minus One
				Days Plus One
				Days Minus One

Print Form

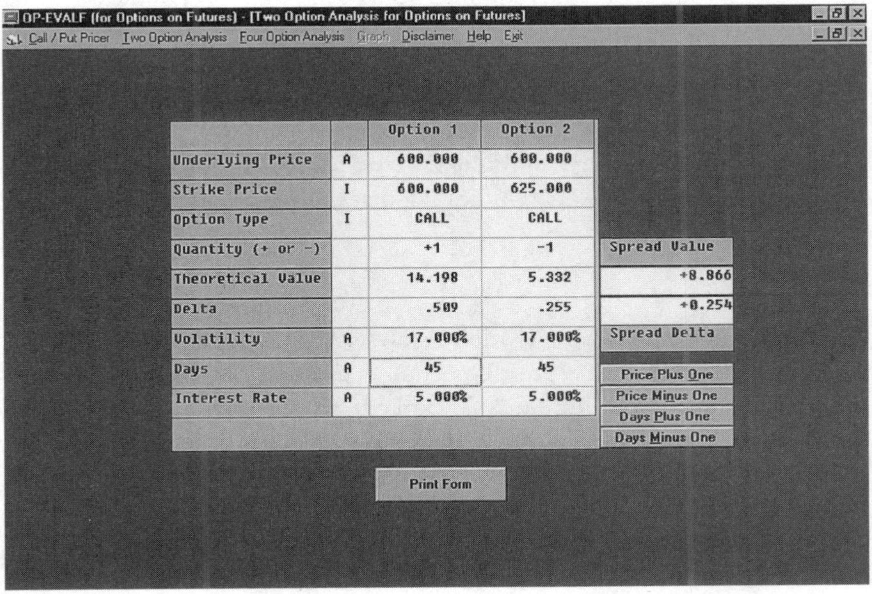

The Quantity Row

To enter a position, the Quantity row is used. The +1 in the Option 1 column of Figure 11–5 indicates that one of these options, the 600 Call, was purchased. The –1 in the Option 2 column indicates that one 625 Call was sold. The result is a position consisting of one long (or purchased) 600 Call at 14.198 and one short (or sold) 625 Call at 5.332.

Spread Value

For the simple 600–625 Call Spread position in Figure 11–5, one might be able to calculate the net spread value of 8.866 mentally by subtracting the 625 Call value from the 600 Call value. But for more complicated positions, it is nice to have the help of the computer. The Spread Value rectangle which appears at the right of the Two Option Analysis page contains the result of this calculation. OP-EVALF™ did the work for us!

    A positive number in the Spread Value rectangle indicates a debit, i.e., the position is established for a net payment, or cost, not including transaction costs. In the case in Figure 11–5, the 600 Call is purchased for 14.198 and the 625 Call is sold for 5.332. The net cost therefore is 8.866, and this is what the plus sign and the number in the Spread Value rectangle indicate.

    A negative number in the Spread Value rectangle indicates a Credit, i.e., the position is established for a net receipt of money as opposed to a net payment. Some traders speak of this as "selling a spread." Suppose, for example, that the 600 Call had been sold for 14.198 and the 625 Call had been purchased for 5.332. In this case, a –1 would appear in the Quantity row under Option 1 indicating that this option was sold, and a +1 would appear under Option 2 indicating that this option was purchased. The Spread Value in this case would then be –8.866 indicating that this net amount was received.

Spread Delta

Another feature of the Two Option Analysis page is the Spread Delta rectangle, which presents the "position delta." A position delta is the sum of the deltas of Option 1 and Option 2. As explained in Chapter 5, the delta of an option is an estimate of how much that option will change in price for a one-point price change in the underlying futures. A *spread delta* is an estimate of how much a multiple-part option position will change in price when the futures changes by one point, assuming that all other inputs remain constant. The Spread Delta of +0.254 in Figure 11–5 indicates that the value of the 600–625 Call spread will increase by 0.254 if the price of the underlying futures is raised by 1.00 and that the value will decrease by a like amount after a one-point decrease in the futures price.

Plus One and Minus One Buttons

In the lower right corner of the Two Option Analysis Page are four command buttons. Click on one and see what happens. As expected, a click on the Price Plus One button raises all the numbers in the Underlying Price row by one full point and recalculates the option values, their deltas, the spread value, and the spread delta. Click on one of the other three buttons, and a one-unit change in either the price of the underlying or the days to expiration, as indicated, will occur and all outputs will be recalculated.

These Plus One and Minus One buttons make it easy to estimate how a position will change in value given a change in the underlying (in whole points) and/or a change in the specific number of days to expiration. For example, a trader might want to know how much the 600–625 Call spread value illustrated in Figure 11–5 will change if the index rises five points in 2 days. To answer this question, just click on the Price Plus One button five times (raising the futures price from 6.00 to 6.05) and then click on the Days Minus One button two times (decreasing the days from 45 to 43). The result is that the spread value has increased to 10.124.

Changing Theoretical Value: Estimating Implied Volatility

On the Two Option Analysis page, the rectangles in the Theoretical Value row are equivalent to the Call or Put rectangles on the Call/Put Pricer page. Theoretical values are normally a calculated output. However, it is possible to enter a price as an input. To do this, first highlight a rectangle in the Theoretical Value row. Then, type in the market price of the option, and, finally, press the Enter key. Volatility now becomes a calculated output, and this is the implied volatility of the option whose price was entered. Also, note that the Setting in the Volatility row defaults to I. This means that calculating an implied volatility for one option in one column does not affect the value of the option in the other column even if the Setting for Volatility is A.

THE FOUR OPTION ANALYSIS PAGE

Get ready for a shock! The Four Option Analysis page illustrated in Figure 11–6 may initially seem overwhelming, but it is just an expansion of the Two

Option Analysis page. The Four Option Analysis page makes it possible to analyze and graph an option position involving from one to four options or a position with one underlying and from zero to three options.

The A, I, Call, and Put rectangles operate in the same way they do on the Two Option Analysis page. The Plus One and Minus One buttons operate the same way, and the Spread Value and Spread Delta are calculated as they are on the Two Option Analysis page.

Graphing Profit and Loss Diagram

As was explained in earlier chapters, profit and loss diagrams are valuable for educational purposes and trading analysis. The graphing capability of OP-EVALF™ makes it possible to quickly prepare and print diagrams such as the ones that appear throughout this book. The graphing capability is available only from the Four Option Analysis page.

If you use the following three steps, any position involving up to four options or one underlying instrument and three options can be graphed

Figure 11–6 The Four Option Analysis Page

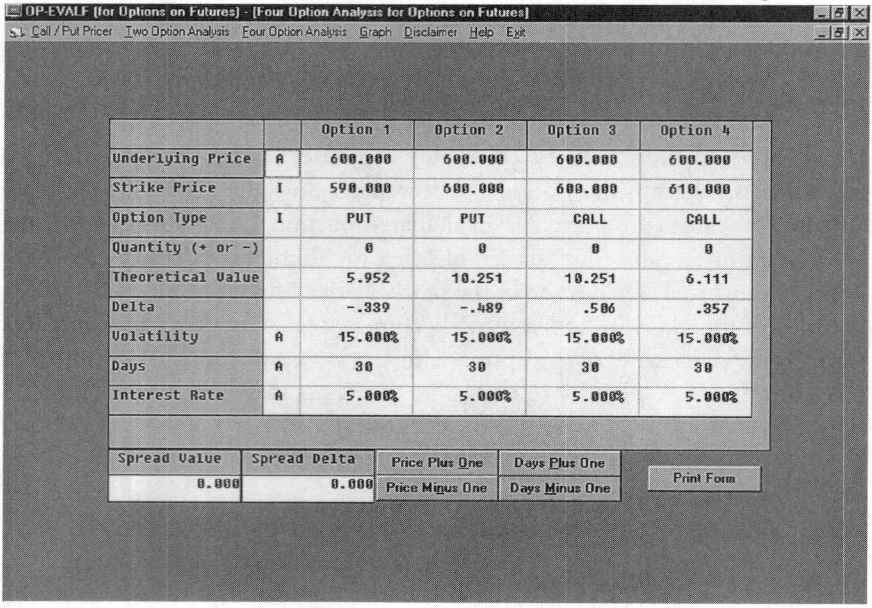

		Option 1	Option 2	Option 3	Option 4
Underlying Price	A	600.000	600.000	600.000	600.000
Strike Price	I	590.000	600.000	600.000	610.000
Option Type	I	PUT	PUT	CALL	CALL
Quantity (+ or −)		0	0	0	0
Theoretical Value		5.952	10.251	10.251	6.111
Delta		−.339	−.489	.506	.357
Volatility	A	15.000%	15.000%	15.000%	15.000%
Days	A	30	30	30	30
Interest Rate	A	5.000%	5.000%	5.000%	5.000%

Spread Value	Spread Delta	Price Plus One	Days Plus One	Print Form
0.000	0.000	Price Minus One	Days Minus One	

quickly and easily. As an example, the process of graphing a 600–625–650 Long Call butterfly spread is illustrated below. Commissions, other transaction costs, and margin requirements will not be included in this example. A futures price of 6.05, a volatility of 20 percent, 10 days to expiration, and interest rates of 5 percent are assumed.

Step 1 : Value the Options.   The first step is to enter the necessary information on the Four Option Analysis page so that the values of all options involved can be estimated.

On the Four Option Analysis page, the assumed futures price of 6.05 must be entered in the Underlying Price row under Option 1. Note that when the Enter key is pressed, all the rectangles in this row change to 605.000. This happens because of the A setting to the left of the 6.05 that was typed in. Next, type 600, 625 and 650 in the Strike Price row under Option 1, Option 2, and Option 3, respectively. In the Option Type row, change the I to A, then highlight the rectangle under Option 1 in which Put appears, and press any letter or number key. All the rectangles in the Option Type row now contain Call. Finally, under Option 1, enter the assumptions of 20 for Volatility, 10 for Days, and 5 for Interest Rate. Pressing the Enter key after each of these entries changes the contents of all the rectangles in these rows because of the A settings in all these rows. At this point, the Four Option Analysis page will look like Figure 11–7. All three options that are involved in the 600–625–650 Call butterfly spread have values in the Theoretical Value row. You can ignore the information in the Option 4 column, because it is not needed to create the desired butterfly spread. We are ready for the next step.

Step 2 : Create the Position Using the Quantity Row   There must be a non-zero number in the Quantity row for a position to be graphed. A plus (+) sign before a number indicates a long, or purchased, option. A minus (–) sign indicates a short, or written, option. Therefore, step 2 entails entering the appropriate numbers in the Quantity row on the Four Option Analysis page.

A 600–625–650 Long Call butterfly spread is created by simultaneously purchasing one 600 Call, selling two 625 Calls, and purchasing one 650 Call. Type +1 in the Quantity row under Option 1 and under Option 3 to indicate that one 600 Call and one 650 Call are purchased. Then type –2 under Option 2 to indicate that two 625 Calls are sold. Our Four Option Analysis page will now look like Figure 11–8, and we are ready for the final step.

Figure 11–7 Inputs Prepared for 600–625–650 Long Call Butterfly Spread

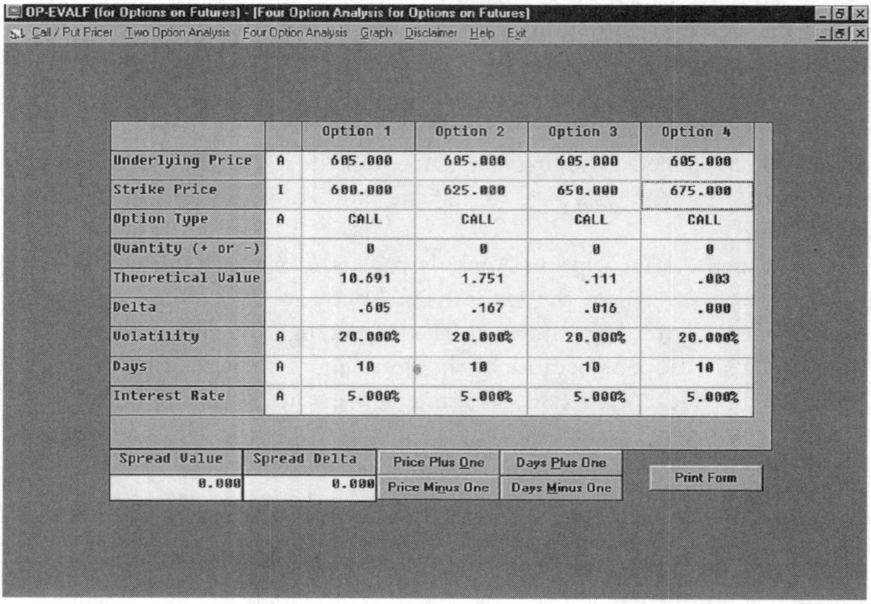

OP-EVALF (for Options on Futures) - [Four Option Analysis for Options on Futures]

Call / Put Pricer   Two Option Analysis   Four Option Analysis   Graph   Disclaimer   Help   Exit

		Option 1	Option 2	Option 3	Option 4
Underlying Price	A	605.000	605.000	605.000	605.000
Strike Price	I	600.000	625.000	650.000	675.000
Option Type	A	CALL	CALL	CALL	CALL
Quantity (+ or −)		0	0	0	0
Theoretical Value		10.691	1.751	.111	.003
Delta		.605	.167	.016	.000
Volatility	A	20.000%	20.000%	20.000%	20.000%
Days	A	10	10	10	10
Interest Rate	A	5.000%	5.000%	5.000%	5.000%

Spread Value	Spread Delta	Price Plus One	Days Plus One	
0.000	0.000	Price Minus One	Days Minus One	Print Form

Step 3: Graphing. Check Figure 11–8 to make sure all the information is correct. Are the Volatility and other inputs correct? Is the "Quantity" under each option correct? Be careful, because it is easy to make mistakes until you become familiar with the layout of the Four Option Analysis page. When all the inputs are correct, you are ready to graph the butterfly spread.

Just click on the Graph item on the Menu bar at the top of the screen, and the screen will look like Figure 11–9.

THE GRAPH PAGE

The Graph page shows three lines. The line with straight segments is a graph of the strategy at expiration. The middle line (in red) is a graph of the strategy at half the days to expiration indicated on the Four Option Analysis page in the Days row. The middle line may be recalculated by clicking on the up arrow or down arrow on the middle box in the lower right corner of the Graph page. The third line (in blue) is a graph of the strategy at the number of days before expiration indicated on the Four Option Analysis page.

Figure 11–8 Four Option Analysis Page with Quantity Row Completed

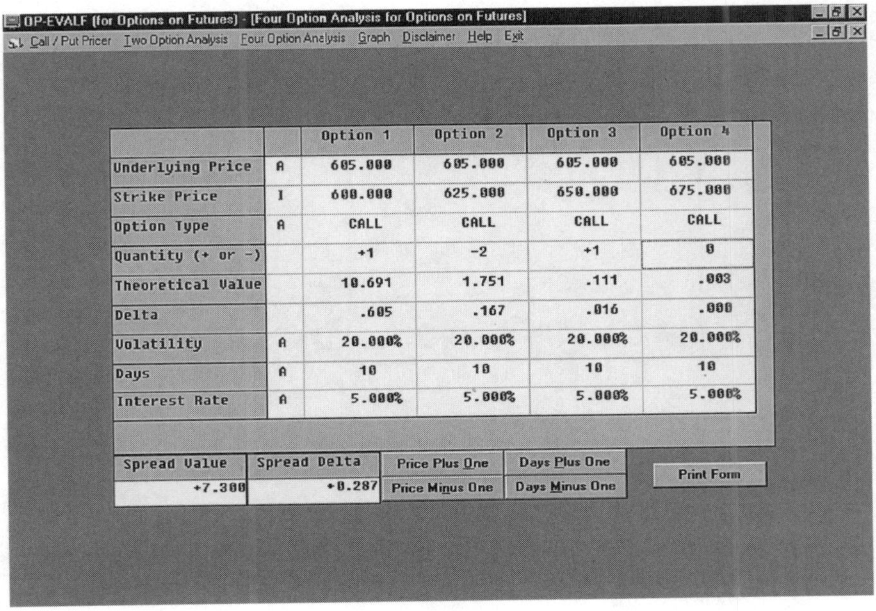

OP-EVALF (for Options on Futures) - [Four Option Analysis for Options on Futures]

Call / Put Pricer   Two Option Analysis   Four Option Analysis   Graph   Disclaimer   Help   Exit

		Option 1	Option 2	Option 3	Option 4
Underlying Price	A	605.000	605.000	605.000	605.000
Strike Price	I	600.000	625.000	650.000	675.000
Option Type	A	CALL	CALL	CALL	CALL
Quantity (+ or -)		+1	-2	+1	0
Theoretical Value		10.691	1.751	.111	.003
Delta		.605	.167	.016	.000
Volatility	A	20.000%	20.000%	20.000%	20.000%
Days	A	10	10	10	10
Interest Rate	A	5.000%	5.000%	5.000%	5.000%

Spread Value	Spread Delta	Price Plus One	Days Plus One	Print Form
+7.300	+0.287	Price Minus One	Days Minus One	

Quick-Change to Graph

In the lower left corner of the Graph page are four lines that describe the strike price and quantity of Options 1, 2, 3, and 4 from the Four Option Analysis page. These lines also have up and down arrow buttons. A click on an up arrow will increase by one the quantity of that particular option. Changing the quantity of a particular option in a position will, of course, change the total position, and OP-EVALF™ will immediately graph the new position. Clicking on a down arrow will decrease by one the quantity of a particular option, and the new position will be graphed.

Figure 11–10 shows how the graph of the 600–625–650 Long Call butterfly spread is changed by clicking on the up arrow next to the 625 Call position. Originally, the butterfly spread had two short 625 Calls, indicated by the –2 in Figure 11–9. After clicking on the up arrow next to the 625 Call, there is only one short 625 Call. The new position is long one 600 Call, short one 625 Call, and long one 650 Call, and this position is graphed in Figure 11–10.

Figure 11–9 Graph of 600–625–650 Long Call Butterfly Spread

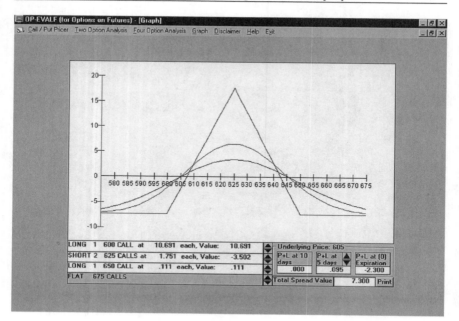

Graphing a Futures Position

OP-EVALF™ has the ability to graph a futures position. When the Option Type of Option 1 is set to Call and the Strike Price is set to 0.000, the heading in that column becomes Underlying, and the Theoretical Value is equal to the underlying price. If +1 is in the Quantity row of the Underlying column and the other rectangles in the Quantity row are set to zero, clicking on the Graph item on the Menu bar brings up a screen like Figure 11–11. This is a graph of a long position in an underlying instrument.

BE AWARE THAT MULTIPLIERS ARE CONSISTENT

OP-EVALF™ assumes a multiplier of 1 for all option types. This allows positions to be valued and graphs to be drawn on a per-unit basis. As a result of this feature, however, care must be taken in setting a Quantity to be sure that the number of units (i.e., the multiplier) is consistent between the options and the underlying futures contract.

Figure 11–10 Changed Graph after Clicking on Up Arrow Next to 625 Calls

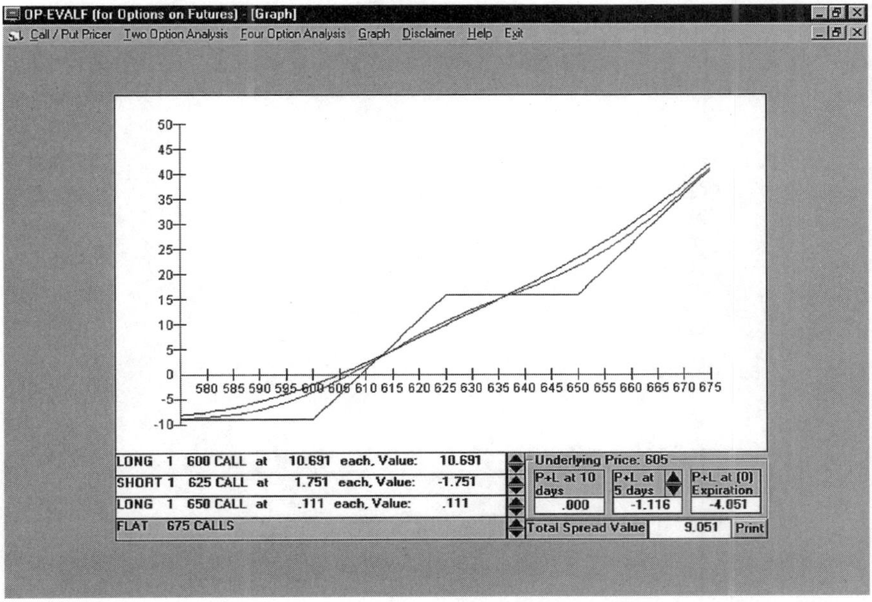

LONG	1	600 CALL at	10.691 each, Value:	10.691
SHORT	1	625 CALL at	1.751 each, Value:	-1.751
LONG	1	650 CALL at	.111 each, Value:	.111
FLAT		675 CALLS		

Underlying Price: 605

P+L at 10 days	P+L at 5 days	P+L at [0] Expiration
.000	-1.116	-4.051

Total Spread Value   9.051   Print

SUMMARY

Computer programs such as OP-EVALF™ are designed to perform calculations and draw diagrams quickly and to improve the analytic process. They are not designed to take over the decision-making process.

After installing the program, you must carefully read and thoroughly understand the Disclosures and Disclaimers before attempting to use the program to analyze individual options or multiple-option strategies.

The Call/Put Pricer page presents theoretical values of a call and a put with the same strike price, same underlying, and same expiration date along with their respective deltas, gammas, thetas, and vegas (see Chapter 7). Starting with the default settings, any one or more of the six inputs may be changed by highlighting the desired rectangle and typing in the new information. When the Enter key is pressed, OP-EVALF™ recalculates all outputs and leaves the highlighted rectangle the same. Pressing an up arrow or down arrow or clicking on a different rectangle recalculates all outputs and changes the highlighted rectangle.

Figure 11–11 Graph of a Long Futures Position

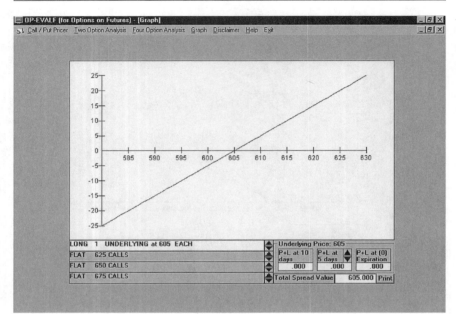

If the Call or Put or Theoretical Value is changed on any page, OP-EVALF™ recalculates the volatility percentage which is known as the implied volatility. On the Call/Put Pricer page, the Put or Call is recalculated using the new volatility percentage. On the Two Option Analysis and Four Option Analysis pages, an A setting in the Volatility row is set to I and the calculation of no other option value is affected.

The graphing feature is available only from the Four Option Analysis page. The line with straight segments on the Graph page is a graph of the strategy at expiration. The middle line is a graph of the strategy at half the days to expiration and may be recalculated by clicking on the up arrow or down arrow on the middle box in the lower right corner of the Graph page. The third line is a graph of the strategy at the number of days before expiration indicated on the Four Option Analysis page.

A futures position can be graphed by setting the Option Type of Option 1 to Call and setting the Strike Price to zero. OP-EVALF™ assumes that the multiplier is 1 in all cases.

It is important to practice with the many pages and features of OP-EVALF™ because it is easy to make mistakes inputting information if you are not familiar with the layout of the various pages. Once you become familiar with the many features of OP-EVALF™, you will find it a valuable tool for trading futures options.

Twelve

Buying Options

uying options seems simple enough. It is generally low in cost, the risk is limited, and as an added benefit, profits are leveraged if the forecast is right.

Is it really this simple?

Like most activities, trading options involves a number of nuances. The purpose of this section on trading strategies is to discuss those nuances.

The first question option buyers typically ask is: How does a trader find "the right option"? There are, after all, many options to choose from, and one option is undoubtedly better suited to a particular forecast than are others. In the process of looking for "the right option," other questions are raised: How are results measured? How should trading capital be managed? What must a trader know about volatility?

This chapter goes through the steps of making a market forecast, analyzing several potential options, and using the results of the analysis to select a particular option. OP-EVALF™ is used first to illustrate how implied volatility is calculated, and second to track how implied volatility changes so that a volatility forecast can be made with greater confidence. The program then is used to estimate the results of various specific forecasts. Capital management is discussed, and the chapter concludes with a description of a three-part market forecasting technique that helps traders focus on the important elements of option trading decisions.

Commissions and other transaction costs are not included in the examples in this chapter, but they are important factors to consider when analyzing real trading decisions.

STARTING THE ANALYSIS

The trader in this example is an office manager named Sue in Ames, Iowa. She grew up on a farm and learned to trade agricultural futures from her father. Sue subscribes to a weekly futures charting service, and spends from 1 to 3 hours a week analyzing her charts and planning trades. She typically makes one to four trades per month. She prefers buying calls and puts because of the limited risk feature.

Right now it is 42 days before the expiration of September options, September Soybean Meal futures are trading at 199.0, and Sue believes that the market is ready for a rally to 204.0. She is considering whether to buy some September 200 Calls for 3.60 each or some September 205 Calls for 1.80 each. We will follow Sue as she examines the issues in making this decision.

Step 1 is making a market forecast, and Sue has made one: She is forecasting a rise in September Soybean Meal futures from the current level of 199.0 to 204.0. The topic of market forecasting is beyond the scope of this book, and so Sue's forecast will be taken as presented and the justification for the forecast will not be addressed. However, the biggest risk in any trading decision is that the forecast is wrong and a loss will be incurred. Sue is well aware of this risk. She is financially capable of bearing it, and she is ready to move forward.

Step 2 is creating profit and loss diagrams of alternative strategies. Experienced traders may be able to do this quickly in their heads. For the sake of this example, however, Sue uses OP-EVALF™ to create Figure 12–1 which illustrates the purchase of one 200 Call at 3.60, and Figure 12–2 which illustrates the purchase of one 205 Call at 1.80. These graphs show that the strategies have different maximum risks and different break-even points. Although these diagrams may be unnecessary for experienced traders when basic strategies are being considered, this step should not be overlooked when complex strategies are being studied.

Step 3 is estimating the implied volatility of the options under consideration. As explained in Chapter 7, implied volatility is the volatility percentage which, if used in an option pricing formula with the known inputs of time to expiration, interest rates, etc., will produce the current market price of an option as the theoretical value. The current level of implied volatility will be the basis for creating theoretical value tables that are used to estimate strategy results. The current level of implied volatility also will be compared to historic levels so that a volatility forecast can be included in estimating strategy results.

To estimate the implied volatility of the 200 Call, Sue uses the Call/Put Pricer page in OP-EVALF™. She creates Figure 12–3 by entering the inputs, based on her knowledge of current market conditions. In Sue's case, September Soybean Meal futures are 199.0 and the Strike is 200.000.

Figure 12–1 Long 1 200 Call at 3.60

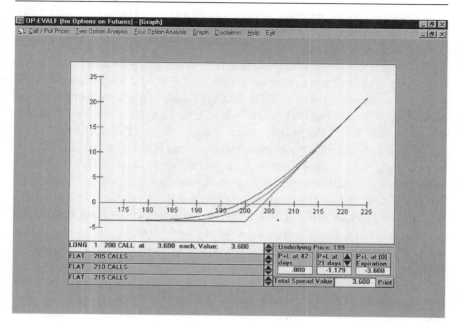

Figure 12–2 Long 1 205 Call at 1.80

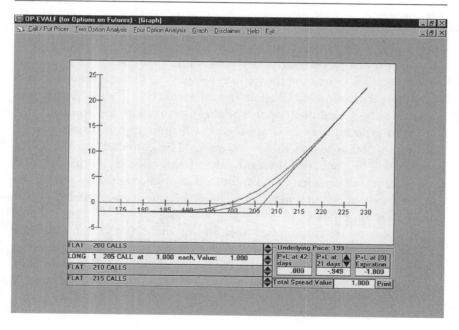

Figure 12–3 Calculating Implied Volatility of the 200 Call

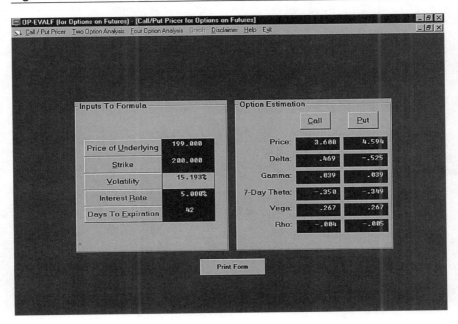

According to a well-known business newspaper, the 90-day Treasury bill interest rate is 5 percent. As was mentioned earlier, the Days to Expiration of the September options is 42. When these inputs are entered along with the market price of the 200 Call of 3.60, OP-EVALF™ calculates an implied volatility of 15.193%. Sue will round this number to 15 percent when creating a theoretical value table for the 200 Call.

　　　Repeating this process to estimate the implied volatility of the 205 Call, Sue creates Figure 12–4 by changing the Strike to 205.000, entering 1.800 by Price under Call and then pressing Enter. By doing this, Sue ascertains that the implied volatility of the 205 Call is 15.135 percent. Sue will also round this number to 15 percent when creating a theoretical value table for the 205 Call.

　　　Step 4 is creating theoretical value tables that will be used to estimate the results of different strategies over a range of futures prices and different times to expiration. Tables 12–1 and 12–2 are tables Sue might create for the 200 and 205 Calls, respectively. The rows in these tables represent 1-dollar increments in the soybean meal futures price, and the columns represent 7-day time intervals. Although OP-EVALF™ generates theoretical

Figure 12–4 Calculating Implied Volatility of the 205 Call

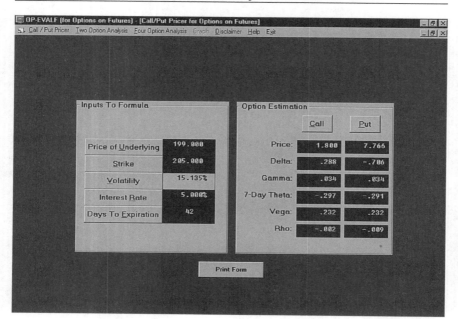

values in numbers with three decimal places, the numbers in Tables 12–1 and 12–2 have been rounded to the first decimal for the sake of simplicity.

Sue's current situation in both tables is row 8, column 1. September Soybean Meal futures are 199.0, it is 42 days to expiration, the 200 Call is 3.60 in Table 12–1, and the 205 Call is 1.80 in Table 12–2. These tables assume interest rates of 5 percent and volatility of 15 percent. The issue of changing volatility will be discussed later. Sue now has two tools to help her make a trading decision.

So how does Sue use those tools? She starts with her forecast and uses the tables to estimate how the calls will perform. Sue believes that the futures price, now 199.0, will rise to 204.0, but she is not exactly sure when. Although she typically buys 10 or more options, to keep the analysis simple, Sue will start by comparing the purchase of one 200 Call to the purchase of one 205 Call. Later, she will examine purchasing more than one of each option.

First, consider a 1-week time frame. If the futures price rises from 199.0 at 42 days to 204.0 at 35 days, Table 12–1 estimates that the 200 Call

Table 12–1 Theoretical Values of 200 Call at Various Futures Prices and Days to Expiration (Interest Rates, 5%; Volatility, 15%)

Row	Futures Price	Col. 1 42 Days	Col. 2 35 Days	Col. 3 28 Days	Col. 4 21 Days	Col. 5 14 Days	Col. 6 7 Days	Col. 7 Exp.
1	206.0	7.80	7.50	7.20	6.80	6.50	6.10	6.00
2	205.0	7.00	6.70	6.40	6.10	5.70	5.20	5.00
3	204.0	6.40	6.10	5.70	5.30	4.90	4.40	4.00
4	203.0	5.70	5.40	5.00	4.60	4.20	3.60	3.00
5	202.0	5.10	4.80	4.40	4.00	3.50	2.90	2.00
6	201.0	4.60	4.20	3.80	3.40	2.90	2.20	1.00
7	200.0	4.00	3.70	3.30	2.90	2.30	1.70	0.00
8	199.0	3.60	3.20	2.80	2.40	1.90	1.20	0.00
9	198.0	3.10	2.80	2.40	2.00	1.50	0.80	0.00

Table 12–2 Theoretical Values of 205 Call at Various Futures Prices and Days to Expiration (Interest Rates, 5%; Volatility, 15%)

Row	Futures Price	Col. 1 42 Days	Col. 2 35 Days	Col. 3 28 Days	Col. 4 21 Days	Col. 5 14 Days	Col. 6 7 Days	Col. 7 Exp.
1	206.0	4.70	4.30	3.90	3.50	2.90	2.30	1.00
2	205.0	4.10	3.80	3.40	2.90	2.40	1.70	0.00
3	204.0	3.60	3.30	2.90	2.50	1.90	1.20	0.00
4	203.0	3.20	2.90	2.50	2.00	1.50	0.90	0.00
5	202.0	2.80	2.50	2.10	1.70	1.20	0.60	0.00
6	201.0	2.40	2.10	1.70	1.30	0.90	0.40	0.00
7	200.0	2.10	1.80	1.40	1.10	0.70	0.30	0.00
8	199.0	1.80	1.50	1.20	0.80	0.50	0.20	0.00
9	198.0	1.50	1.20	0.90	0.60	0.30	0.10	0.00

will rise from 3.60 to 6.10 (row 3, column 2) for a profit of 2.50, or $250, before transaction costs. Table 12–2 estimates that the 205 Call will rise from 1.80 to 3.30 for a profit of 1.50 ($150) before transaction costs.

Now consider 2-week and 3-week time frames. Table 12–1 estimates that with futures at 204.0, the 200 Call will be trading at 5.70 at 28 days to expiration (row 3, column 3) and at 5.30 at 21 days (row 3, column 4), for profits of 2.10 ($210) and 1.70 ($170), respectively. Table 12–2 estimates that with the futures price at 204.0 in 2 weeks and 3 weeks, the 205 Call will be trading at 2.90 and 2.50, respectively, for profits of 1.10 ($110) and 0.70 ($70), respectively.

Of course, Sue's bullish forecast might not be realized, and a loss could result. Table 12–1 estimates that if the futures declines to 198.0, the 200 Call will fall to 2.40 in 2 weeks (row 9, column 3) and to 2.00 in three weeks (row 9, column 4), for losses of 1.20 ($120) and 1.60 ($160), respectively. Table 12–2 estimates that the 205 Call will fall to 0.90 and to 0.60 in 2 and 3 weeks, respectively, for losses of 0.90 ($90) and 1.20 ($120), respectively.

What conclusion can be drawn from Sue's initial analysis? Simply stated, if the results are measured in dollars, *the two strategies are not equal.*

The purchase of one 210 Call has a higher profit potential, in dollars, in all the positive outcomes than does the purchase of one 205 Call. However, the 200 Call also has higher risk potential, in dollars, in all the negative outcomes. *Conclusion: The choice between buying a number of calls at one strike and buying an equal number of calls at a different strike is not a choice between equal alternatives; it is a choice between trade-offs.* Lower-strike options have higher profit potential and a higher risk potential when results are measured in dollars.

If the results are measured in percentage terms, however, there is a different conclusion.

MEASURING RESULTS IN PERCENTAGE TERMS

Table 12–3 summarizes, in dollar terms and in percentage terms, the information in rows 3 and 9 in Tables 12–1 and 12–2. The positive outcomes assume that the futures price rises from 199.0 to 204.0 in 1-week intervals up to 5 weeks (row 3 in both tables). The negative outcomes assume a decline to 198.0 in similar time periods (row 9 in both tables).

Looking at the percentage results in Table 12–3, the choice between the 200 Call and the 205 Call depends on something other than futures price change or the amount at risk. Can you see what it is?

Table 12–3 200 Call versus 205 Call

	Soybean Meal Futures 199.0 → 204.0					
	200 Call Purchased for 3.60			205 Call Purchased for 1.80		
Time Frame	200 Call Price Futures at 198.0	Dollar Change	Percent Change	205 Call Price Futures at 204.0	Dollar Change	Percent Change
1 week	6.10	+$250	+69%	3.30	+$150	+83%
2 weeks	5.70	+$210	+58%	2.90	+$110	+61%
3 weeks	5.30	+$170	+47%	2.50	+$ 70	+39%
4 weeks	4.90	+$130	+36%	1.90	+$ 10	+ 0%
5 weeks	4.40	+$ 80	+22%	1.20	($ 60)	(33%)

	Soybean Meal Futures 199.0 → 198.0					
	200 Call Purchased for 3.60			205 Call Purchased for 1.80		
Time Frame	200 Call Price Futures at 198.0	Dollar Change	Percent Change	205 Call Price Futures at 198.0	Dollar Change	Percent Change
1 week	2.80	($ 80)	(23%)	1.20	($ 60)	(33%)
2 weeks	2.40	($120)	(33%)	0.90	($ 90)	(50%)
3 weeks	2.00	($160)	(44%)	0.60	($120)	(66%)
4 weeks	1.50	($210)	(58%)	0.30	($150)	(83%)
5 weeks	0.80	($280)	(78%)	0.10	($170)	(96%)

Time is the critical variable in comparing the percentage results of same-type options with different strikes. If, for example, futures rise from 199.0 to 204.0 in 1 week, Table 12–3 indicates that the profit from the 200 Call is 69 percent versus 83 percent from the 205 Call. If the price rise takes 2 weeks, in percentage terms, the strategies have approximately equal results. Both make approximately a 60 percent profit in the 2-week time frame.

If the forecasted rise takes 4 or 5 weeks, however, the percentage profits of the 200 Call surpass the results of the 205 Call. Table 12–3 indicates the 200 Call earns profits of 36 percent and 22 percent in 4 and 5 weeks, respectively. But the 205 Call earns a 6 percent profit in 4 weeks and has a 33 percent loss in 5 weeks.

It is interesting to observe that if Sue's forecast is incorrect and the futures price drops to 198.0, the percentage losses of the 205 Call are always greater than the losses of the 200 Call. Both strategies, of course, risk the total loss of the price of the call in the worst possible outcome. Table 12–3 indicates that if soybean meal futures decline to 198.0 in 1 week, the 200 Call loses 23 percent and the 205 Call loses 33 percent.

So what has Sue learned? First, comparing equal quantities of 200 Calls and 205 Calls is not a comparison of equals. Second, when examining percentage results, time is the critical variable. Consequently, the question becomes, How does Sue find trading alternatives that are more equal in terms of risk?

This is an important question but first we will discuss a method of getting information more quickly and efficiently. Tables 12–1 and 12–2 have given Sue much information about the performance of these two options, but they are time-consuming to create. Is there an easier, more efficient way to get the same information? The answer is a resounding yes!

USING THE GREEKS

Position Greeks offer a quick and easy way to estimate how strategies will perform, and understanding position Greeks reduces the need for theoretical value tables. That is why experienced traders learn to interpret the delta, gamma, vega, and theta of a position: It saves time!

Sue can use the Call/Put Pricer page in OP-EVAL3™ to create Table 12–4 to evaluate the purchase of one 200 Call and the purchase of one 205 Call. Table 12–4 compares the position Greeks of the two strategies. First, the long 200 Call has a position delta of +0.469 versus +0.288 for the long 205 Call. This difference in delta explains both the short-term higher profit potential and the higher risk potential of the 200 Call.

Table 12–4 Position Greeks: Long 1 200 Call versus Long 1 205 Call
Futures Price, 199.0; Days to Expiration, 42;
Interest Rates, 5%; Volatility, 15%

	Long 1 200 Call	Long 1 205 Call
Price	3.600	1.800
Delta	+0.469	+0.288
Gamma	+0.039	+0.034
Vega	+1.267	+0.232
Theta	−0.350	−0.297

Both positions have positive vegas, and so both will benefit from a rise in volatility and be hurt by a decline, but analysis of vega is not as simple as it may seem. The question is, If Sue forecasts that implied volatility will increase, should she be more inclined to buy the 200 Call or the 205 Call?

The vega of the 200 Call is 1.267. This means that if implied volatility rises 1 percent, the 200 Call will rise in price from 3.60 to 3.867. This is approximately a 7.4 percent increase. At 0.232, the vega of the 205 Call is smaller on an absolute basis, but it is larger on a percentage basis. If implied volatility rises 1 percent, the 205 Call will rise from 1.80 to 2.032, or approximately 12.9 percent. Thus, if Sue were looking at percentage results, a forecast for increasing implied volatility would make her favor the 205 Call.

The position thetas indicate that the 200 Call will lose more per unit of time than will the 205 Call, but the percentage erosion of the two calls is nearly equal: 19 percent for the 200 Call versus 16.5 percent for the 205 Call. On a 1-week-only basis, therefore, Sue would be almost indifferent between the two calls. Remember, however, that thetas change as time passes toward expiration, and so Sue should do much more analysis if she expects to hold a position for more than 1 week.

The gammas of the two calls are nearly equal in absolute terms but are higher in percentage terms for the 205 Call. If Sue is expecting a "sharp price rise," this would favor purchasing the 205 Call, because its price would rise faster, as a percentage, than would the price of the 200 Call.

The position Greeks confirm the message from Tables 12–1 and 12–2 that choosing between buying one 200 Call and buying one 205 Call is not a choice between equal alternatives. Now we can return to the issue of looking for strategy alternatives that are "more equal."

CAPITAL MANAGEMENT

What makes two limited-risk strategies equal? The amount of the risk is certainly one factor. If the maximum theoretical risk is equal, then at least in some basic sense, the two strategies are comparable. There may still be some trade-offs, i.e., relative advantages and disadvantages, but at least the strategies have the same maximum theoretical risk.

Sue can make alternative strategies equal from a risk standpoint by deciding on the amount of capital she is willing to invest and risk. From that amount, she can then determine the number of calls of each strike that can be purchased. She will then be comparing alternatives that do not exceed her risk limit.

If Sue is willing to invest and risk $3,600, for example, she can purchase 10 of the 200 Calls at 3.60 each (10 × $360 = $3,600) or purchase 20 of the 205 Calls at 1.80 each (20 × $180 = $3,600). For a picture of these strategies, Sue creates Figures 12–5 and 12–6. Both strategies risk a maximum of $3,600, but they have different break-even points at expiration.

The strategies also have different market exposure above the respective strike prices at expiration. In Figure 12–5, the upward-sloping line of the 200 Call position, at expiration, has a slope of positive 10, because 10 of the calls are owned, and each one becomes a long futures contract if they are in-the-money at expiration. The upward-sloping line in Figure 12–6, however, has a slope of positive 20, because twice as many of the 205 Calls are owned.

CHOOSING BETWEEN ALTERNATIVES

Since the capital at risk is the same for these two strategies, the analysis of profits in percentage terms in Table 12–3 is appropriate. The conclusion from that analysis was that time is the critical factor. Sue must add time to her forecast. It is not enough for her to believe that soybean meal futures will rally from 199.0 to 204.0. This is the first major difference between trading options and trading futures.

Figure 12–5 Long 10 200 Calls at 3.60 Each

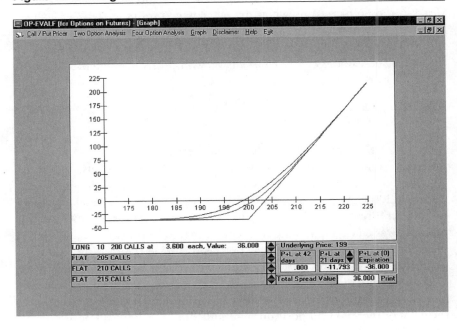

Figure 12–6 Long 20 205 Calls at 1.80 Each

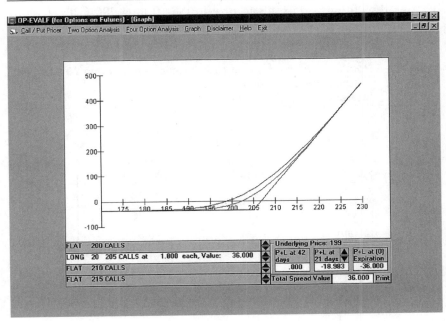

Regarding time and the observations made from Table 12–3, 2 weeks is the point in time when the percentage profits of the 205 Call no longer exceed those of the 200 Call. The question Sue must address is, Will futures rise to 204.0 before two weeks or later? This is a subjective question that only Sue can answer, but her answer will determine whether she purchases 10 of the 200 Calls or 20 of the 205 Calls.

USING THE GREEKS II

Position Greeks can help Sue evaluate the alternatives. Table 12–5 compares the position Greeks of 10 long 200 Calls and 20 long 205 Calls.

Table 12–5 shows that the two positions have very different Greeks. Ten long 200 Calls have a position delta of +4.69, which is equal, in theory to long 4.69 futures. Twenty long 205 Calls, however, are like owning one more futures contract, because the delta of that position is +5.76. While the difference in position gammas may not seem large at 0.39 for the 200 Calls versus 0.68 for the 205 Calls, the gamma of the 205 Calls is nearly twice that of the 200 Calls. This means that as the futures price rises and other factors remain constant, the delta of the 205 Call position increases faster than does the delta of the 200 Call position. Not only does the 205 Call position start out with a higher delta, its higher gamma means that its delta will also increase more rapidly. "Longer and getting longer faster" is how one would describe the 20 long 205 Calls relative to the 10 long 200 Calls. Judging from the position delta and the position gamma, buying 20 of the 205 Calls

Table 12–5 Position Greeks II: Long 10 200 Calls versus Long 20 205 Call
Futures Price, 199.0; Days to Expiration, 42;
Interest Rates, 5%; Volatility, 15%

	Long 10 200 Call	Long 20 205 Call
Price	36.00	36.00
Delta	+4.69	+5.76
Gamma	+0.39	+0.68
Vega	+2.67	+4.64
Theta	−3.50	−5.94

appears to be preferable to buying 10 of the 200 Calls. Sue must, however, look at the position vegas and position thetas to see what information they provide.

Table 12–5 shows that 20 long 205 Calls have a bigger vega than do 10 long 200 Calls: +4.64 versus +2.67. Is this an advantage or a disadvantage for the 205 Call position? Unfortunately, there is no definitive answer to this question, because the answer depends on whether implied volatility increases or decreases. If implied volatility increases, a larger position vega is an advantage, but if implied volatility decreases, it is a disadvantage. What are the implications of this observation?

Sue must add a third component to her forecast: volatility. We will see how Sue might gather information for forecasting volatility later in this chapter.

The position thetas point out a clear advantage for the 10 200 Calls. With a position theta of –3.50, the 200 Call position will lose $350 over the first 7 days if the futures price and other factors do not change. The 205 Call position, however, will lose $594.

SUMMARIZING THE TWO POSITIONS

The Greeks tell Sue that the 205 Call position is "longer and getting longer faster" than the 200 Call position. But the 205 Call position has greater exposure to changes in volatility and to time decay than does the 200 Call position. Can it be said that one position is "better" than the other? Unfortunately, no.

Conceptually, in an efficient market, there is no such thing as "better." If there were a "better" strategy, the market would find that strategy and bid up its price. The higher price, in theory, would eliminate the advantage.

There is a trade-off between Sue's alternatives. The advantage of the 205 Call position is the greater market exposure from its higher delta. The disadvantage is the greater risk from time decay. In short, the greater profit potential from a bullish move in the underlying futures comes at the cost of a greater risk from time decay if the forecast move does not occur soon.

If there is no "better," what is the conclusion? The main point is that trading options is different from trading futures. "Being bullish" is not enough when one is trading options! Futures do not have the exposure to time erosion that options have, but futures involve substantially more risk than options do. So how do traders conceptualize the differences?

A THREE-PART FORECAST

Sue needs to forecast market direction just as futures traders do, but the message from Table 12–3 is that Sue needs to have a different emphasis on time. The effect of volatility on option values also has implications for the way Sue thinks. Having decided how much to invest and risk, in this case $3,600, Sue must concentrate on all three aspects: futures price, time, and implied volatility.

      The missing element in the analysis up to now is implied volatility. In Tables 12–1, 12–2 and 12–3, implied volatility was assumed to remain constant. However, implied volatility is likely to change, and Sue must factor this into her forecast. The following discussion will show how Sue might gather information about implied volatility that can be included in her forecast and ultimately in her trading decision.

FORECASTING IMPLIED VOLATILITY

How does a trader forecast implied volatility? There is no proven method, but one can gain insights by looking at history. When forecasting anything, a starting point is to gather historical information. There is, of course, absolutely no guarantee that this information, or any information, will lead to an accurate forecast, but it is the nature of trading to make forecasts and act on those forecasts.

      For Sue to gather information on implied volatility, she starts with readily observable information such as closing futures and option prices. Columns 1 through 4 in Table 12–6 contain information that Sue has gathered. The information in the table is not actual data taken from any actual trading period; it is simulated for the purpose of creating a realistic example.

      To create a table such as Table 12–6, Sue would start with observable information from a period of time. Table 12–6 uses 15 consecutive days, but the time period could be different, and the observations need not be consecutive, because the information will be used in a subjective decision-making process. Generally, the longer the period, the better, because more information may offer more clues.

      Column 1 in Table 12–6 contains closing futures prices. Column 2 identifies the at-the-money strike price on each day. Since the futures price changes daily, the at-the-money strike price also will change. Column 3 contains the number of days to expiration of the option being studied. Over time, as monthly expirations come and go, the number of days in this column gradually declines and then increases by approximately 28 or 35 as options with a

Table 12–6 Sue's Implied Volatility Tracker
Interest Rates: 5%

	Col. 1	Col. 2	Col. 3	Col. 4	Col. 5
Day	Futures Price	Expiration/ ATM Strike	Days to Expiration	Call Price	Implied Volatility
1	196.1	Aug 195	34	3.30	13.68
2	196.7	Aug 195	33	3.50	13.39
3	202.3	Sep 200	58	5.75	14.24
4	201.9	Sep 200	57	5.50	14.30
5	204.1	Sep 205	56	4.40	15.24
6	203.5	Sep 205	55	4.05	15.16
7	200.7	Sep 200	54	4.85	14.73
8	198.0	Sep 200	51	3.45	14.49
9	194.8	Sep 195	50	4.35	15.57
10	195.9	Sep 195	49	4.80	15.29
11	198.6	Sep 200	48	3.80	15.58
12	198.2	Sep 200	47	3.50	15.31
13	196.8	Sep 195	44	2.75	15.19
14	200.1	Sep 200	43	4.25	15.42
15	199.0	Sep 200	42	3.60	15.19

new expiration in 4 or 5 weeks are added to the table. From day 2 to day 3 in the table, for example, the number of days increases from 33 to 58. This occurs because the 195-strike Call being analyzed in the day 2 row has a different expiration date than does the 200-strike Call in the day 3 row.

Column 4 contains the closing prices of the options being analyzed, and column 5 contains the level of implied volatility. The implied volatility numbers in column 5 were calculated with the OP-EVALF™ program, and they were calculated in exactly the same way as the implied volatility of the 200 and 205 Calls were calculated in Figures 12–1 and 12–2, respectively. The known information, such as strike, interest rate, and days to expiration, are entered along with the market price of the option. When the Enter key is pressed, OP-EVALF™ calculates the implied volatility of that option.

How is the information in Table 12–6 helpful? Column 6 provides historical information about implied volatility. While there is no assured method of using this information, one might be able to identify a trend that might be forecast to continue. Alternatively, if implied volatility has been in a range, a trader might forecast that it will stay in that range or break out of that range. Let's see how Sue might use this information.

The first observation is that the implied volatility of the 200 Call, 15.19 percent, is noticeably higher than the 13.68 percent on day 1. This information might be the basis for a forecast that implied volatility is "in an up trend." Alternatively, it might be the basis for a forecast that implied volatility is "high" and likely to decline. Because forecasting techniques are not within the scope of this book, Sue's forecast that implied volatility is "in an up trend" will be accepted. Sue, of course, must be willing to assume the risk that her forecast is wrong and a loss will result.

The next step in Sue's analysis is to make a range of forecasts and evaluate the results. In this example, Sue will make an "optimistic" forecast, a "most likely" forecast, and a "pessimistic" forecast. In each case, Sue will forecast the amount the futures price will change, the time it will take for that change to occur, and the implied volatility level after the change has occurred.

An Optimistic Forecast

In her optimistic forecast Sue predicts that futures will rise beyond her target level to 206.0 in 10 days and that implied volatility will rise to 16.5 percent. Table 12–7 estimates that, given these assumptions, the 200 Call will rise to 7.60, and the purchase of 10 of these calls will earn a profit of $4,000. Table 12–7 also estimates that the 205 Call will rise to 4.50 and that the buying 20 of these calls will earn a profit of $5,400. In this optimistic forecast, buying 20 of the 205 Calls is the preferred choice.

A Most Likely Forecast

The most likely outcome, in Sue's opinion, is that futures will rise to 204.0 in 2 weeks and implied volatility will rise slightly to 15.5 percent. Table 12–8 estimates that given these assumptions, the 200 Call will rise to 5.80 and the 205 Call will rise to 3.00. In this scenario, the results are nearly equal, but

Table 12–7 Sue's Optimistic Forecast

	Initial Inputs		Inputs Changed to Optimistic Forecast
Inputs:			
Futures price	199.0	→	206.0
Strike price	200/205		
Volatility	15%	→	16.5%
Interest rates	5%		
Days to expiration	42	→	32
Outputs:			
200 Call price	3.60	→	7.60
205 Call price	1.80	→	3.50

Strategy Results

Long 10 200 Calls at 3.60		Long 20 205 Calls at 1.80	
Sale price	7.60	Sale price	4.50
Purchase price	3.60	Purchase price	1.80
Profit/loss per option	4.00	Profit/loss per option	2.70
Times quantity	× 10	Times quantity	× 20
Strategy profit/loss	40.00	Strategy profit/loss	54.00
Profit/loss in dollars	$4,000	Profit/loss in dollars	$5,400

purchasing 20 205 Calls has a slight edge with an estimated profit of $2,400 versus $2,200 for 10 200 Calls.

A Pessimistic Forecast

To be realistic, Sue must also estimate a loss outcome. Table 12–9 estimates the results if futures fall to 198.0 in 2 weeks and implied volatility falls to 14.7 percent. Under these assumptions, OP-EVALF™ calculates that the 200 Call will fall to 2.30 and that the 205 Call will fall to 0.90. The purchase of 10 of the 200 Calls results in a loss of $1,300, and the purchase of 20 of the 205 Calls loses $1,800. In this pessimistic forecast, the 200 Calls are the preferred choice, because they lose less than the 205 Calls do. It should be noted that Sue's pessimistic forecast is not the worst case. It is possible for Sue to lose her entire investment in either the 200 Call or the 205 Calls if those options expire worthless.

Table 12–8 Sue's Most Likely Forecast

	Initial Inputs		Inputs Changed to Most Likely Forecast
Inputs:			
Futures price	199.0	→	204.0
Strike price	200/205		
Volatility	15%	→	15.5%
Interest rates	5%		
Days to expiration	42	→	28
Outputs:			
200 Call price	3.60	→	5.80
205 Call price	1.80	→	3.00

Strategy Results

Long 10 200 Calls at 3.60		Long 20 205 Calls at 1.80	
Sale price	5.80	Sale price	3.00
Purchase price	3.60	Purchase price	1.80
Profit/loss per option	2.20	Profit/loss per option	1.20
Times quantity	× 10	Times quantity	× 20
Strategy profit/loss	22.00	Strategy profit/loss	24.00
Profit/loss in dollars	$2,200	Profit/loss in dollars	$2,400

SUE'S DECISION

Sue has done a lot of work to arrive at the point of making a decision. To summarize the results of her forecasts, Sue creates Table 12–10 which summarizes the results of the two strategies under the three forecasts.

Table 12–10 is not intended to provide an "answer" to Sue's strategy-selection decision. It simply shows that if either Sue's optimistic or most likely scenario is correct, buying 20 205 Calls will yield a higher profit than will buying 10 200 Calls. Regarding risk, however, the 205 Call position is also forecast to lose more than will the 200 Call position. But compare the results. If her optimistic or most likely forecast is correct, then Sue makes $1,400 or $200 more, respectively, by buying 20 205 Calls. If her pessimistic forecast occurs, the 205 Call position loses $500 more than does the 200 Call position. To Sue, the possibility of earning $1,400 more if she is right is worth the risk of losing $500 more if she is wrong, and so she decides to buy the 20 205 Calls.

Table 12–9 Sue's Pessimistic Forecast

	Initial Inputs		Inputs Changed to Pessimistic Forecast
Inputs:			
Futures price	199.0	→	198.0
Strike price	200/205		
Volatility	15%	→	14.7%
Interest rates	5%		
Days to expiration	42	→	28
Outputs:			
200 Call price	3.60	→	2.30
205 Call price	1.80	→	.90

Strategy Results

Long 10 200 Calls at 3.60		Long 20 205 Calls at 1.80	
Sale price	2.30	Sale price	0.90
Purchase price	3.60	Purchase price	1.80
Profit/loss per option	(1.30)	Profit/loss per option	(.90)
Times quantity	× 10	Times quantity	× 20
Strategy profit/loss	(13.00)	Strategy profit/loss	(18.00)
Profit/loss in dollars	($1,300)	Profit/loss in dollars	($1,800)

Table 12–10 Comparison of Strategy Results

Index Level / Time / Volatility	Results of Purchasing 10 200 Calls	Results of Purchasing 20 205 Calls
Sue's optimistic forecast 206.0 / 10 days / 16.5%	$4,000	$5,400
Sue's most likely forecast 204.0 / 14 days / 15.5%	$2,200	$2,400
Sue's pessimistic forecast 198.0 / 14 days / 14.7%	($1,300)	($1,800)

Not all traders, of course, would interpret this information this way or make the same decision as Sue, but that is not the point. The point is to demonstrate the analysis and the decision-making process.

SUMMARY

Buying options is different from buying futures. Option prices behave differently, and the forecasting process is different. For options, a three-part forecast is essential. Option traders should start with a specific price forecast for the underlying futures contract. Second, a specific forecast for time is required. The third element is a forecast for implied volatility.

It is not a comparison of equal alternatives to compare equal numbers of different strike options of the same type and the same expiration. Such a comparison involves trade-offs.

The process for analyzing alternatives and choosing a strategy involves five steps. First, draw a profit and loss diagram of each strategy being considered. Profit and loss diagrams illustrate the maximum profit and risk potential and break-even point(s) at expiration. Second, estimate the implied volatility of all the options under consideration. Knowing the implied volatility is necessary to create theoretical value tables which estimate how option prices will behave under forecast market conditions.

The third step is making a capital management decision by deciding on an amount to invest and risk. Choosing an amount to commit to a particular trade is one method of making several alternatives "more equal." After an amount is chosen, determine the number of options of a particular strike that can be purchased. Fourth, create theoretical value tables or use the position Greeks to evaluate the trade-offs of the various alternatives. Fifth, make a range of forecasts that include three parts: the amount of the futures price change, the time for the price change to occur, and the implied volatility level after the price change. Regarding the implied volatility forecast, it may be helpful to track the history of implied volatility over a recent period of time so that more information can be brought to bear on the forecast. However, no method of forecasting volatility, time, or price is guaranteed to succeed, and traders must be prepared to withstand the risk of their forecasts being wrong. When these five steps have been completed, reaching a decision that makes sense is easy.

Thirteen

Selling Options

Selling options is *not* simply the opposite of buying options! Traders who use strategies that involve short option positions must think differently about capital management, risk, and profit potential than they do when using strategies that involve only long options.

Selling uncovered futures options involves substantial or unlimited risk and is only suitable only for experienced traders. Traders with no experience or only limited experience should learn the techniques for the analysis of trading decisions and the tracking of positions explained in this chapter before attempting to use these strategies.

This chapter presents a disciplined thinking process for planning trades and tracking the performance of positions that involve uncovered short options. After a review of the basics of risk, profit potential, and sensitivities to changes in market conditions, capital management is discussed. A consistent method for measuring profit potential is explained next, and the chapter concludes with a trading example in which a short option position is initiated and then followed through three possible outcomes. Criteria will be suggested for when to close a short option position at either a profit or a loss.

THE BASICS OF SHORT OPTIONS

Short option positions have limited profit potential and substantial or unlimited risk potential. Figure 13–1 illustrates a short 250 Corn Call sold at 8 cents. The Figure 13–1 shows that if corn futures are below 2.50 at option expiration, the call expires worthless and the maximum potential profit of 8 cents, or $400, is realized. If the futures price is above 2.50 at expiration, the 250 Call has value, and a 250 Call that is sold for 8 cents realizes a profit at expiration if the futures price is below 2.58. A loss is incurred, however, if the futures price is above this level at expiration. The potential risk of a short call position is unlimited, because losses increase as the price of the underlying futures contract rises.

A short call position has a negative delta, a negative gamma, a negative vega, and a positive theta. Table 13–1 contains the numbers calculated by OP-EVALF™ for the short 250 Call in this example. The negative sign in front of the delta indicates that the position will make money if the futures price falls and lose money if it rises. Specifically, the delta estimates that if futures rise by 1 cent, the price of this call will rise by 0.466. Since this is a short call, that is how much will be lost. Similarly, if futures fall by 1 cent, the call price will decline by 0.466 and that amount will be made, assuming that other factors remain constant.

The minus sign in front of the gamma means that as the futures price changes, the delta will change in the opposite direction to the change in futures price. Specifically, if corn futures rise by 1 cent, the gamma estimates that the delta will decrease by 0.017 from –0.466 to –0.483. Similarly, if futures rise by 1 cent, the gamma estimates that the delta will increase from –0.466 to –0.449.

Figure 13–1 Short 1 250 Call at 8

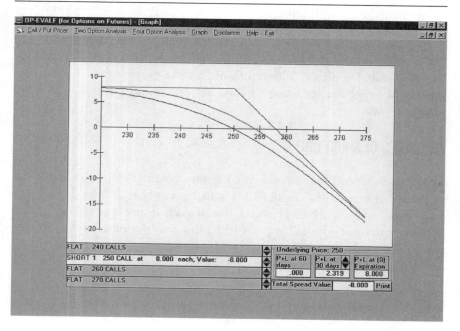

Table 13-1 Position Greeks: Short 1 250 Call

(Futures Price, 2.47; Days to Expiration, 50; Interest Rates, 5%; Volatility, 26%)

	Short 1 250 Call
Price	8.000
Delta	−0.466
Gamma	−0.017
Vega	−0.361
Theta	+0.675

Taken together, the delta and the gamma indicate that a 1-cent rise in the futures price will result in a loss greater than 0.466. A greater loss occurs because the delta of the short call position is decreasing as the futures price rises. What started out as a position with a delta of −0.466 gradually becomes a position with a delta of −0.483. Consequently, more than 0.466, the initial delta, will be lost. Similar reasoning leads to the conclusion that a 1-cent fall in the futures price will result in a profit of less than 0.466. In the case of a futures price decline, what started out as a position with a delta of −0.466 gradually becomes a position with a delta of −0.449. This means that less than 0.466 will be made.

The minus sign in front of the vega means that losses occur if implied volatility increases and profits occur if implied volatility decreases and other factors remain constant. The implication for options sellers is that the forecast must predict an unchanged or decreasing level of implied volatility. Specifically, the vega of −0.361 means that the call price will increase by this amount, and this amount will be lost, if implied volatility increases by 1 percent. Alternatively, the call price will decrease by 0.361, and the profit will equal this amount, if implied volatility decreases by 1 percent.

The plus sign in front the theta means that time erosion benefits the position. Specifically, the call price will decrease by 0.675, and this amount will be made, if 7 days passes and the futures price and other factors remain constant.

To summarize Table 13-1, a short call benefits from a decrease in the price of the underlying, a decrease in implied volatility, and a decrease in time to expiration.

MARGIN REQUIREMENTS

Sellers of uncovered futures options must deposit a preset amount of equity capital in their trading accounts when initiating such positions. This deposit is known as an *initial margin deposit.* There is no guarantee that an initial margin deposit will cover the risk of a position requiring the deposit, and a trader may be called upon by the brokerage firm to deposit additional margin, close the position, or both. If a trader fails to respond to the brokerage firm's request, the firm has the right to close the position without the trader's knowledge or consent.

Minimum margin requirements are established by exchanges on which products requiring margin deposits are traded, but brokerage firms may require higher deposits. It is therefore essential that traders who employ strategies requiring margin deposits be familiar with the firm's policies.

MARGIN CALL

If the price of the underlying futures contract rises (falls), the margin requirement for a short call (put) will increase. A brokerage firm, however, will not immediately require a customer to increase the account equity. If, however, the account equity drops to a predetermined level known as the *minimum margin level,* then the brokerage firm will require a customer to deposit additional funds into the account so that the account will be increased to a level known as the *maintenance margin level.* Such a request is known as a *margin call.* If a customer fails to increase the account equity within a defined time period as requested, the brokerage firm will close the position.

PROFIT MEASUREMENT INTRODUCED

Profit and loss results frequently are stated in annualized percentage terms, because annualized percentages take into account differences in capital at risk and time. To calculate the annualized percentage results of a strategy, its profit or loss is divided by the initial investment, and the resulting quotient is multiplied by an annualization factor which is the quotient of the days per year divided by the number of days the trade was open. The results of such calculations are sometimes an impressive annualized return, and traders should note that it is unlikely that such a performance can be repeated for an entire year. In fact, the purpose of such calculations is to compare two or more alternative strategies. The purpose is not to estimate what annualized percentage profits will be.

Consider the profitable trading results of two traders who purchased options. The first trader, Ken, purchased an option for 10 cents, or $500, and sold it 90 days later for 20 cents, or $1,000. The second trader, Sharon, purchased an option for 30 cents, or $1,500, and sold it 75 days later for 50 cents, or $2,500. Since Ken and Sharon invested different amounts and held their options for different periods of time, the typical method of comparing these trades is to look at the annualized percentage profits.

For Ken, his profit of $500 is divided by his investment of $500, and the quotient, 1.00, is multiplied by 365 divided by 90 (the number of days Ken's position was held). The result is a 400 percent annualized profit. For Sharon, her profit of $1,000 is divided by her investment of $1,500, and the quotient, 1.67, is multiplied by 365 divided by 75 (the number of days her position was held). Sharon's result is a 324 percent annualized profit. Note that these impressive annualized returns are for only one trade and that it is unlikely that such results can be repeated over the course of a year of making several trades. The only purpose of these calculations is to compare Ken's and Sharon's results, and the comparison indicates that Ken's profit was higher on an annualized percentage basis. It also should be noted that this comparison does not include other potential criteria that may lead to a different conclusion, such as absolute dollar profit and the ratio of profitable trades to losing trades.

MEASURING THE PROFIT POTENTIAL OF SHORT OPTIONS

The same formula can be used to evaluate the profit potential of a strategy involving short options. Assuming that the option expires without being assigned, the "profit" is the option premium received. The "investment" is the initial margin requirement, and assuming that the position will be held to expiration, the annualization factor is the number of days in a year divided by the number of days to expiration.

As an example, assume that a 50-day 250 Call is sold for 8 cents, or $400, and that the initial margin requirement is $1,500. Given these assumptions, the annualized percentage profit potential is calculated as follows: The option premium, $400, is divided by the margin requirement of $1,500, and the quotient is multiplied by 365 days per year divided by 50 days to expiration. The resulting annualized percentage potential profit is approximately 194 percent, and the calculations are shown in Table 13–2.

RETURN CALCULATIONS MUST BE INTERPRETED CAREFULLY

Selling uncovered options involves substantial risk and is suitable only for experienced, well-capitalized traders who meet the financial requirements of

Table 13–2 Annualized Percentage Calculation of Profit Potential (Assumes Sold Option Expires without Being Assigned): Formula and Example

Formula: $\dfrac{\text{profit}}{\text{investment}} \times \dfrac{\text{days per year}}{\text{days to expiration}}$

where   Profit = option premium received
        Investment =   margin requirement

Example: 50-Day 250 Call sold for 8 cents

Option premium received	=	$ 400
Margin requirement	=	1,500
Days per year	=	365
Days until expiration	=	50

Formula: $\dfrac{\$400}{\$1,500} - \dfrac{365}{50} \times \dfrac{\text{days per year}}{\text{days to expiration}}$

Note: Annualized percentage calculations assume that the results can be repeated during the course of a year, which is unlikely. Calculations of this nature are for comparison purposes only.

a brokerage firm and maintain the required account balances. Potential percentage returns such as those in Table 13–2 should not be seen as enticements to employ short option strategies. Furthermore, a decision between two short option trades should not be based on annualized percentage calculations. It is possible to compare alternatives only if "all other factors are equal," and this is almost never true. Rarely, if ever, are forecasts for different futures contracts exactly the same.

The advantage of annualized percentage return calculations is that they are specific. The disadvantage is that they do not include subjective elements such as a market forecast and a tolerance for risk. These subjective considerations are the most important elements of trading decisions. With experience, traders can use annualized percentage return calculations as part of a subjective decision-making process.

Now that the basics of short option positions and profit measurement have been reviewed, we will follow a trader through the process of establishing a short option position and tracking it as market conditions change. Since is it impossible to know in advance what will happen after a position has been established, three possible outcomes will be examined.

A SHORT OPTION TRADING EXAMPLE

Felecia is a senior administrator at a large food-processing company in the Midwest, and she is an experienced option trader who frequently takes aggressive positions. In this example we will accept Felecia's market forecast as given. She is, of course, taking the risk that her forecast is wrong and that a loss will result. But Felecia is not hesitant about taking a loss if her forecast does not materialize. Felecia will first analyze three options that she might sell to profit from her forecast and then she will choose one. Next, three possible outcomes an optimistic scenario, a pessimistic scenario, and an expected scenario—will be presented. We will watch Felecia's analysis and action in each situation.

Felecia follows wheat futures, and December Wheat is currently trading at 3.15. Felecia is forecasting that December Wheat will trade between 3.10 and 3.25 for the next 24 days until the expiration of December Wheat options. Felecia also believes that the implied volatility will stay at its current level or decline slightly. Consequently, she is planning to sell puts to profit from her forecast.

Table 13–3 shows the information Felecia has gathered on implied volatility. Column 1 contains recent closing levels of December Wheat, and columns 2 through 5 contain information about an at-the-money call option and implied volatility. Column 2 identifies the at-the-money strike price that is nearest to the closing futures price in column 1. Column 3 contains the days to expiration of the call in column 2, and column 4 shows the closing price of that call.

From the information in columns 1 through 4 and the interest rate listed at the top of the table, the implied volatility in column 5 is calculated by using OP-EVALF™ as described in Chapter 11. Although some traders may disagree, Felecia believes that concrete information about the recent history of implied volatility is helpful in making trading decisions.

The daily information-gathering process takes Felecia about 5 minutes. She gets the closing futures prices and closing option prices either by looking in a national business newspaper or by calling her broker.

In Felecia's opinion, Table 13–3 and her knowledge of market conditions indicate that the implied volatility of December Wheat options is likely to remain constant or decline. She believes that since her forecast is for neutral market action, she can profit from both a decline in implied volatility and time erosion. The risk is that Felecia's forecast is wrong and she will have a losing trade. Furthermore, an unexpected adverse move in the futures

Table 13–3 Felecia's Implied Volatility Tracker
Interest Rate: 5%

	Col. 1	Col. 2	Col. 3	Col. 4	Col. 5
	Dec. Wheat	ATM Strike	Days to Expiration	Call Price	Implied Volatility
Day 1	3.21¼	320	22	8½	25.1%
Day 2	3.20¾	320	21	7⅞	24.5%
Day 3	3.22½	320	18	8½	25.3%
Day 4	3.20¾	320	17	7¼	24.9%
Day 5	3.20	320	16	6⅝	24.5%
Day 6	3.21¼	320	15	7	24.5%
Day 7	3.19¼	320	14	5⅝	24.0%
Day 8	3.17	320	40	8¾	24.3%
Day 9	3.18¼	320	39	9⅛	24.0%
Day 10	3.18	320	38	8¾	23.8%
Day 11	3.19½	320	37	9½	24.1%
Day 12	3.18½	320	36	8¾	24.1%
Day 13	3.17¾	320	33	8⅛	24.1%
Day 14	3.18	320	32	8⅛	24.2%
Day 15	3.17½	320	31	7¾	24.2%
Day 16	3.17	320	30	7⅜	24.2%
Day 17	3.16½	320	29	7⅛	24.6%
Day 18	3.14¾	320	26	6	24.8%
Day 19	3.15½	320	25	6⅛	24.7%
Day 20	3.15	320	25	5¾	24.7%

could mean that Felecia's loss will be substantially bigger than she expects. Prepared to take these risks, Felecia begins her analysis of three options.

Options Under Consideration

It is 24 days before the expiration of December Wheat options, and Felecia is considering the sale of the December 300 Put for 2½, the December 310 Put for 5⅜, or the December 320 Put for 10¾. Table 13–4 shows the delta, gamma, vega, and theta for each put.

Table 13–4 Position Greeks: Short 1 300 Put, Short 1 310 Put, Short 1 320 Put (Futures Price, 3.15; Days to Expiration, 24; Interest Rates, 5%; Volatility, 24.7%)

	Short 1 300 Put	Short 1 310 Put	Short 1 320 Put
Price	2½	5⅝	10¾
Delta	+0.211	+0.387	+0.584
Gamma	−0.014	−0.019	−0.020
Vega	−0.236	−0.309	−0.314
Theta	+0.861	+1.195	+1.211
Margin requirement	$900	$1,500	$2,000
Annualized percentage profit potential*	158%	285%	408%

* Annualized percentage profit potential assumes that the futures price is above the strike price at expiration and that the option expires without assignment.

Table 13–4 shows that these three put positions are not directly comparable! Each has a different delta and a different profit potential. The short 320 Put has the highest maximum profit potential, but that potential is not realized unless December Wheat futures are above 320 at expiration, 5 cents above the current futures price. Also, that highest potential profit is accompanied by the highest short-term market exposure. A short 320 Put has a delta of +0.584 compared to +0.387 and +0.211 for the short 310 Put and 300 Put, respectively. A short 300 Put, while having the lowest delta, and therefore the lowest short-term market exposure, also has the lowest profit potential.

How does Felecia choose between alternatives that are not directly comparable? She must make a subjective decision that is based on her forecast and her tolerance for risk. Since her forecast is for "neutral price action in a range between 3.10 and 3.25," Felecia decides to sell five 310 Puts at 5⅝ each. This is a subjective decision that only Felecia can make, and we will accept her decision as given and watch the three scenarios develop. It is important to note that Felecia did not automatically choose the strategy with the highest profit potential. She chose the strategy best suited to her market forecast.

Preparing the Trade

Having chosen to sell five 310 Puts at 5⅝ each, Felecia prepares Table 13–5 which shows her initial risk exposures, i.e., the Greeks. The delta of +1.935 indicates that with factors other than the futures price unchanged, Felecia's short put position will profit by 1.93 cents, or approximately $95, if futures rise by 1 cent and lose this amount if futures fall by 1 cent. The negative gamma means that the position delta will change in the opposite direction to the change in the futures price. Specifically, if December Wheat futures rise by 1 cent, the position delta will decline by 0.095 from +1.935 to +1.840. The vega of −1.545 means that the position will lose approximately 1½ cents, or $75, if implied volatility rises by 1 percent. This amount will be made if implied volatility decreases by 1 percent. The theta of +5.975 means that approximately 6 cents, or $300, will be earned from time erosion if 7 days pass and other factors remain constant. These sensitivities, the "Greeks," indicate whether a position meets a trader's risk parameters. It takes some practice to understand what they are saying, but given time, anyone can learn to interpret these numbers.

Felecia's next step is to create Table 13–6 which shows estimated prices of the 310 Put at different futures prices and days to expiration. Although Felecia's forecast is for December Wheat futures to stay above 3.10, Table 13–6 contains option price estimates with futures prices as low as 2.90, because she wants to estimate what her potential losses will be if her forecast is wrong. The futures price, of course, could drop significantly, and Felecia's loss could be substantially larger than the largest estimated loss from Table 13–6. As was stated earlier, this is the risk Felecia is taking.

Using Table 13–6 and the Call/Put Pricer page of OP-EVALF™, Felecia can estimate how her short option position will behave and how her risk exposures will change under various scenarios. We will watch as Felecia considers three scenarios.

Scenario 1: Better Than Expected

In this scenario, Felecia's neutral to bullish forecast is too conservative. December Wheat futures rally to 3.30 in 4 days, and her puts decline in price to 1⅜ (row 1, column 2 in Table 13–6) for an unrealized profit of 4¼ per option, or $1,062.50 on five options, not including commissions. What should Felecia do? Although Felecia has many alternatives, in this scenario she is choosing between holding her position and closing it by repurchasing the short puts at 1⅜ cents each.

Table 13–5 Position Greeks   Short 5 310 Puts
(Futures Price, 3.15; Days to Expiration,
24; Interest Rates, 5%; Volatility, 24.7%)

	Short 5 310 Puts
Total premium received	28⅛
Position delta	+1.935
Position gamma	−0.096
Position vega	−1.545
Position theta	+5.975

There are a number of factors to consider when making this decision. First, has the forecast changed? Second, has the target profit and/or futures price been achieved? Third, if the trade is profitable, what percentage of the total maximum profit could be realized if the position is closed? Is closing the position justified? Fourth, regardless of whether the trade is profitable, how do the current risk measures, i.e., the Greeks, compare to the position's original risk measures? If the trade is unprofitable, have the risks changed sufficiently to warrant closing the position and realizing a loss? We will address these questions in order.

1. *Has the forecast changed?* As was mentioned above, forecasting the market is a subjective process that is not within the scope of this book. If Felecia changes her forecast, the possibilities are endless. We will therefore assume that Felecia has not changed her forecast.

2. *Has the target profit or target futures price been achieved?* In Felecia's case, she picked a futures price of 325 as the top of her predicted range. Her forecast, remember, was that the futures would trade in a range from 3.10 to 3.25 With the futures now at 3.30, Felecia's forecast implies that the futures price is more likely to decline from its current level than it is to rise. The answer to the question about the target being achieved is a definite yes! Although it is possible for the futures to decline at a sufficiently slow rate so that time erosion of the options is greater than the tendency of the puts to rise with a decline in the futures price, such a prediction is far too precise to be reliable. Since the upper end of the futures price range has been exceeded, many traders would close the position and move on to the next trade.

3. *What percentage of the total maximum profit has been realized?* Felecia's maximum profit potential is 5⅜ cents per put. With the price now at 1⅛, the decline of 4¼ cents represents approximately 79 percent of the maximum profit potential (4¼/5⅜). Also, since only four out of 24 days has

Table 13–6 Theoretical Values of 310 Put at Various Futures Prices and Days to Expiration (Interest Rates, 5%; Volatility, 24.7%)

		Col. 1	Col. 2	Col. 3	Col. 4	Col. 5	Col. 6	Col. 7
Row	Futures Price	24 Days	20 Days	16 Days	12 Days	8 Days	4 Days	Exp.
1	3.30	1¾	1⅜	⅞	½	¼	0	0
2	3.25	2⅝	2⅛	1⅝	1	½	⅛	0
3	3.20	3⅞	3⅜	2⅝	2	1¼	⅜	0
4	3.15	5⅝	5	4¼	3⅜	2½	1⅜	0
5	3.10	7¾	7⅛	6⅜	5½	4½	3⅛	5
6	3.05	10½	9⅞	9⅛	8⅜	7⅜	6¼	10
7	3.00	13⅝	13⅛	12½	11⅞	11⅛	10⅜	15
8	2.95	17⅜	16⅞	16⅜	15⅞	15⅜	15⅛	20
9	2.90	21⅜	21	20⅝	20⅜	20⅛	20	25

passed, Felecia has earned 79 percent of her maximum potential profit in just 16 percent of the expected time (4 days/24 days). While an opinion about these percentages is subjective, many traders would think, Getting this much, this soon is too good to pass up. This is a second argument in favor of closing the position.

4. *How has the market exposure changed?* Table 13–7 compares Felecia's short put position under the new market conditions to the position when initiated. The comparison clearly indicates that the market exposure has changed. With the rise in the futures price and the decrease in the put price, the total premium has declined to 6⅞ cents from 28⅛ cents. The delta is now +0.665, approximately 30 percent of the original delta of +1.935. The new gamma and vega indicate less exposure, and the new theta indicates that 3.460 cents will be made from time erosion in the next 7 days compared to 5.975 for the original position.

Weighing the Evidence. Although weighing the available evidence is subjective, the answers to these four questions seem to indicate a strong preponderance of evidence in favor of closing the position, realizing the profit, and moving on to the next trade. In real trading situations, of course, analysis of the new

Table 13–7 Outcome 1: Better Than Expected
       Position Greeks
       Current Exposure versus Original Exposure

(Current Futures Price, 3.30; Current Days to Expiration 20; Interest Rates, 5%; Volatility, 24.7%)

	Current Position	Original Position
Option price	1⅜	5⅜
Total premium	6⅞	28⅛
Position delta	+0.665	+1.935
Position gamma	−0.055	−0.095
Position vega	−0.850	−1.545
Position theta	+3.460	+5.975

Greeks may not as clearly indicate a course of action. But when this happens, traders should act.

Scenario 2: Worse Than Expected

In this scenario, December Wheat futures fall to 3.05 in 8 days and Felecia's puts rise in price to 9⅛ cents each (row 6, column 3 in Table 13–6) for an unrealized loss of 3½ cents per option, or $870 on five options, not including commissions.

Table 13–8 shows Felecia's risk exposures under the new market conditions. First, the position delta has increased from +1.935 to +3.060. This delta estimates that, assuming that other factors remain constant, another 1-cent decline in the futures price will cause Felecia's position to lose approximately 3 cents or $150. This loss is approximately 50 percent larger than the loss caused by the first 1-cent futures price drop from 3.15 to 3.14. Felecia's short put position has more risk! The slight change in vega, from −1.545 to −1.220, means that there is less exposure to an adverse change in implied volatility, but this benefit is outweighed by the increase in delta risk.

What should Felecia do in this case?

First, Felecia must maintain a rational view of the situation. Given the decline in the futures price, which she did not predict (her estimate of the low end of the futures price range was 3.10), the simple fact is that Felecia's forecast is wrong. The biggest mistake Felecia could make is to become emotionally involved in this losing trade, to look for more reasons why "*this really is a good trade*," or decide that "*I wasn't wrong, I was just early*," or come up with some other rationalization.

Second, Felecia must know her stop-loss limit, the point at which, no matter what else she may think, she recognizes that she is wrong and that it is time to close the position, realize a loss, and move on to the next trade.

Generally, stop-loss limits are established in "price terms" or in "dollar terms." An example of setting a stop-loss limit in price terms is having a price limit at which a position is closed. A purchaser of calls at 12 cents each, for example, might set a stop-loss limit of 4 cents per option. Therefore, if the price drops to 8 cents each, then the calls will be sold and a loss will be realized.

In Felecia's situation, which involves a short option position, a loss limit per option translates into a price above which the option was sold. Since Felecia established her short put position by selling the 310 Puts for 5⅝ cents each, a loss of 3½ cents on each would be realized if she repurchased these options at 9⅛ cents each.

Table 13–8 Outcome 2: Worse Than Expected
Position Greeks
Current Exposure versus Original Exposure

(Current Futures Price, 3.05; Current Days to Expiration 16; Interest Rates, 5%; Volatility, 24.7%)

	Current Position	Original Position
Option price	9⅛	5⅝
Total premium	45⅝	28⅛
Position delta	+3.060	+1.935
Position gamma	−0.120	−0.095
Position vega	−1.220	−1.545
Position theta	+7.370	+5.975

When a loss limit is established in dollar terms, the stated maximum dollar amount must be translated into a price at which a position is closed. A purchaser of 10 options who has a loss limit of $2,000, for example, would have a loss limit of 4 cents, or $200, per option. If the 10 options were purchased at 12 cents each, the price at which a $2,000 loss would be realized would be 8 cents each.

For short option positions, the dollar loss limit is converted into a maximum loss per option in the same manner as above, but that loss-per-option figure is added to the price at which the short option position was established. If Felecia had an $875 loss limit, for example, a loss of 3½ cents, or $175, on each of five options would equal this figure. Consequently, if "3½ cents per option" is Felecia's stop-loss limit, the price of 9⅛ cents is her stop-loss point.

Setting Stop-Loss Limits. There are no firmly established rules about stop-loss limits, but some traders establish such limits in relation to the potential profits of a trade. It makes little sense, for example, to risk $10,000 on a trade that has a maximum profit potential of $1,000. Consequently, given that Felecia's five short puts have a maximum profit potential of 5⅝ cents each, or $281.25, a stop-loss limit of 3½ cents each, or $175, seems reasonable.

Actual or Mental Stop-Loss Orders. Although Felecia should have a maximum-loss point in mind, this does not necessarily mean that she should place a stop-loss order with her broker. First, some brokerage firms do not accept stop-

Table 13–9 Outcome 3: About as Expected
            Position Greeks
            Current Exposure versus Original Exposure

(Current Futures Price, 3.15; Current Days to Expiration 12;
            Interest Rates, 5%; Volatility, 24.7%)

	Current Position	Original Position
Option price	3⅜	5⅝
Total premium	16⅞	28⅛
Position delta	+1.760	+1.935
Position gamma	–0.130	–0.095
Position vega	–1.060	–1.545
Position theta	+8.945	+5.975

loss orders. Second, stop-loss orders are inflexible, and flexibility is sometimes an advantage for traders. If a broker has a stop-loss order, its specific
instructions must be followed if certain market conditions are met. If, however, a trader is watching the market and can give the broker a market order,
the trader has flexibility as to timing.

There is, however, a difference between being flexible and lacking
discipline. Closing a trade "at or near a maximum-loss point" is being flexible. Lacking discipline, in contrast, is failing to close a position until a margin call that cannot be met is received.

In Felecia's case, her forecast for December Wheat to trade in a range
between 3.10 and 3.25 was made when the futures price was 3.15. Consequently, with the price at 3.05, it has declined more than she feared. With the
310 Puts now trading a 9⅛, her unrealized loss of 3½ cents per option is almost
two-thirds of her potential profit of 5⅝ cents. Consequently, a strong case can
be made that Felecia should close the position, realize the loss, and move on
to the next trade. Of course, only Felecia can make this decision, but experienced traders know that losing trades are inevitable. There is an old saying:
"Your first loss is your best loss." Arguably, in this "worse than expected" scenario, Felecia should take her 3½ cent loss, close her short put position by
repurchasing them in the market, and move on to the next trade.

Scenario 3: About as Expected

In the third scenario, the market is living up to the "neutral" in Felecia's
forecast. December Wheat futures have changed little from where they

started. With 12 days to expiration, the futures price is 3.15, and Felecia's 310 Puts are trading at 3⅜ (row 4, column 4, in Table 13–6). In this case, Felecia has an unrealized profit of 2¼ cents per option, or $562.50 on five options, not including commissions. Since "success is no excuse for complacency," Felecia should review the initial premises on which she based her strategy selection and ask herself if anything has changed. The four factors introduced above will be reviewed in order. These questions will guide Felecia in deciding between keeping the position open and closing it.

First, has the forecast changed? As was mentioned above, forecasting the market is a subjective process that is not within the scope of this book. In real trading situations, forecasts change frequently. Traders must constantly study the market, looking for clues about changes in direction. Felecia's forecast has been accurate so far in this example, but she must still look for clues that things are about to change. To complete the decision-making process regarding this position, we assume that Felecia has not changed her forecast.

The second question—Has the target price been achieved?—is moot, because there has been no change in the futures price. Felecia originally picked a futures price of 3.25 as the top of her predicted range. Consequently, the answer to this question is a certain no! Given that her forecast has not changed, this is a point in favor of keeping the position open.

What percentage of the total maximum profit has been realized? Felecia's maximum profit potential is 5⅝ per put. With the put price now at 3⅜ and 12 of 24 days having passed, this means that 40 percent of the maximum profit potential has been earned in 50 percent of the time. Realistically, if the position is closed today, the actual percentage may be lower if bid-ask spreads and transaction costs are taken into account. Right now, assuming that the futures price stays above 3.10 until expiration, Felecia will realize the balance of 60 percent of the original maximum profit potential in 50 percent of the time. Her future profit potential over the next 12 days is greater than her results over the past 12 days, assuming that the futures price cooperates. This is another argument in favor of keeping the position open.

How has the market exposure changed? Table 13–9 shows Felecia's risk exposures under the new market conditions. The position delta has decreased slightly from +1.935 to +1.760. This should be expected, because the absolute values of deltas of out-of-the-money options decline toward zero as expiration approaches. The gamma has increased slightly, which means that the delta will now change slightly faster than previously, and the smaller absolute value of the vega indicates a reduced sensitivity to volatility. The higher theta means that more profit will be earned if factors other than time are unchanged for the next 7 days relative to the first 7 days after the position was established. This is another argument in favor of keeping the position open.

The weight of evidence in this scenario is clearly in favor of keeping the position open. The key assumption, though, is that Felecia's forecast has not changed.

SUMMARY

Uncovered short option positions have limited profit potential and substantial or unlimited risk potential. When considering strategies that involve short options, traders must think differently about capital management, risk, and profit potential than they do when buying options.

Traders should select strategies on the basis of their market forecast and their tolerance for risk rather than on annualized percentage return calculations of a strategy's profit potential.

After a short option position is established, it should be monitored closely, and the decision to keep it open or to close it and realize a profit or a loss should be based on four considerations. First, has the forecast changed? Second, has the target been achieved? Third, if the trade is profitable, what percentage of the maximum profit potential will be realized if the position is closed? Is this profit sufficient to justify closing the trade? Fourth, regardless of whether the trade is profitable, how do the position's current risk measures compare to the original measures? If the trade is unprofitable, has the risk changed sufficiently to warrant closing the position and taking a loss?

Although risk sensitivity numbers, i.e., the Greeks, are difficult to understand at first, with practice, any trader can learn to interpret and use these numbers.

Fourteen

Vertical Spreads

Bob made what is perhaps the most common mistake in trading options: He purchased 10 bull call spreads, because they were "cheaper" than simply buying 10 at-the-money calls. When the market moved up as Bob predicted, the at-the-money calls rose nicely, but his call spread hardly moved! We will spend a lot of time with Bob in this chapter, discussing his motivations, his market forecast, and his alternatives. In the process, many aspects of vertical spreads will be explained.

The goal of this chapter is to explain the unique aspects of vertical spreads, how to analyze them and how to determine when they are appropriate for a particular market forecast and when they are not. First, the term *vertical spread* is defined, and four basic examples are presented. Second, commonly used terminology regarding vertical spreads is defined. Third, the price behavior of vertical spreads is examined. Finally, the impact of changes in volatility on vertical spreads is discussed.

The examples in this chapter do not include commissions, other transaction costs or margin requirements. Since vertical spreads involve two option positions, commissions and margin requirements can be higher than they are for single-option positions. Consequently, these factors can significantly affect the desirability of the strategies discussed in this chapter, and they must be included in the analysis of any real strategy involving real options.

VERTICAL SPREAD DEFINED

A *vertical spread* involves the purchase of one option and the sale of a second option of the same type with the same underlying and the same expiration but with a different strike price. The term *vertical* describes the relationship of the strike prices, with one being higher, or over, or "vertical to" the other. Also, unless stated otherwise, the term *vertical spread* refers to one-to-one

283

vertical spreads in which one option is purchased and one is sold. *Ratio vertical spreads,* as the name implies, involve the purchase (or sale) of one option and the sale (or purchase) of more than one of a second option. Ratio vertical spreads will be discussed in Chapter 16.

Bull Call Spread

The purchase of one call and the simultaneous sale of a second call with the same underlying and the same expiration but with a higher strike price is known as a bull call spread. Figure 14–1 illustrates a 600–625 Bull Call spread in which one 600 Call is purchased and one 625 Call is sold.

The name *bull call spread* describes three aspects of the position. First, this is a *bull* call spread, because the position has a tendency to profit as the underlying futures rises in price. In Figure 14–1, for example, the bull call spread achieves its maximum profit potential at expiration only if the futures price is at or above 6.25. Second, this is a bull *call* spread, because only call options are involved: the 600 and 625 Calls in this example. Third, this is a *spread,* because two different options are involved. The term spread is used loosely to describe a wide range of multiple-option positions, but in

Figure 14–1 600–625 Bull Call Spread

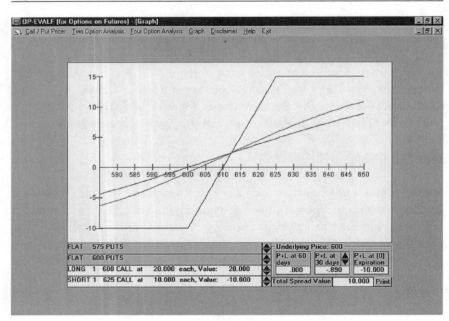

this example it refers to the 25-cent difference, or spread, between the strike prices of the 600 Call and the 625 Call.

Bull call spreads sometimes are referred to as "debit call spreads" because they are established for a net cost, or net debit. The spread in Figure 14–1, for example, is established by purchasing the 600 Call for 20 cents, or $1,000, and simultaneously selling the 625 Call at 10 cents, or $500, for a net cost, or net debit, of 10 cents, or $500.

Also, it is common practice to describe a spread by using the lower strike first regardless of whether calls or puts are involved; hence, the name for the position in Figure 14–1 is a "600–625 Bull Call spread."

Profit or Loss at Expiration.   At expiration, there are three possible outcomes. The futures price can be at or below the lower strike, above the lower strike but not above the higher strike, or above the higher strike. The straight line in Figure 14–1 illustrates these possibilities. If the futures price is at or below the lower strike of a bull call spread at expiration, both calls expire worthless and the full amount paid for the position, $500 plus commissions in this example, is lost.

If the futures price is above the lower strike but not above the higher strike, then the long call (lower strike) is exercised, and the short call (higher strike) expires worthless. The futures price at expiration at which a bull call spread breaks even is equal to the lower strike price plus the net premium paid for the position. In Figure 14–1, for example, the break-even futures price at expiration is 6.10, the lower strike of 6.00 plus the net cost of 10 cents.

If the futures price is above the higher strike at expiration, the long call is exercised and the short call is assigned. If the futures price is 6.30 at expiration, for example, exercising the 600 Call results in purchase of a futures contract at 6.00, and assignment on the 625 Call results in the sale of that futures contract at 6.25. The net result of those two futures transactions is a receipt of 25 cents, not including commissions. The cost of the position, however, 10 cents in this example, is subtracted from the 25 cents received, and the net result is the net profit of 15 cents, or $750.

Note that the maximum profit potential of a bull call spread is equal to the difference between the strike prices less the net cost of the position. Also, the maximum profit is realized at expiration if the underlying futures price is at or above the higher strike.

Bear Call Spread

The sale of one call and the simultaneous purchase of a second call with the same underlying and the same expiration but with a higher strike is known as a bear call spread. Figure 14–2 illustrates a 600–625 Bear Call spread in which one 600 Call is sold for 20 cents, and one 625 Call is puchased for 10 cents. The term *bear* means that the position has a tendency to profit as the underlying futures declines in price. In Figure 14–2, the bear call spread achieves its maximum theoretical profit at expiration only if the futures price is at or below 6.00.

Bear call spreads sometimes are referred to as "credit call spreads," because they are established for a net receipt of premium, or net credit. The spread in Figure 14–2, for example, is established for a net credit of 10 cents, or $500.

Profit or Loss at Expiration. At expiration, there are three possible outcomes. The futures price can be at or below the lower strike, above the lower strike but not above the upper strike, or above the upper strike. The straight line in Figure 14–2 illustrates these possibilities. If the futures price is at or below the lower strike of a bear call spread at expiration, both calls expire worthless and the net premium received, $500 in this example, is kept as income.

If the futures price is above the lower strike but not above the upper strike, then the short call (lower strike) is assigned, and the long call (higher strike) expires worthless. The futures price at expiration at which a bear call spread breaks even is equal to the lower strike price plus the net premium

Figure 14–2 600–625 Bear Call Spread

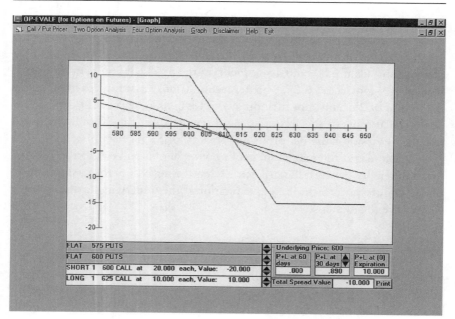

received. In Figure 14–2, the break-even futures price at expiration is 6.10, the lower strike of 6.00 plus the net premium received of 10 cents.

If the futures price is above the higher strike at expiration, the short call is assigned and the long call is exercised. If the futures price is 6.30 at expiration, for example, assignment of the 600 Call results in the sale of a futures contract at 6.00, and exercise of the 625 Call results in the purchase of a futures contract at 6.25. The net result of those two futures transactions is a net loss of 25 cents. The 10 cents net received when the position was established, however, is subtracted from this loss, and the result is the net loss of 15 cents, or $750.

Note that the maximum potential loss of a bear call spread is equal to the difference between the strike prices less the net premium received for establishing the position. Also, this maximum loss is realized at expiration if the futures price is at or above the higher strike.

Bear Put Spread

The purchase of one put and the simultaneous sale of a second put with the same underlying and the same expiration but with a lower strike price is known as a bear put spread. Figure 14–3 illustrates an 575–600 Bear Put spread in which one 600 Put is purchased and one 575 Put is sold.

Figure 14–3 575–600 Bear Put Spread

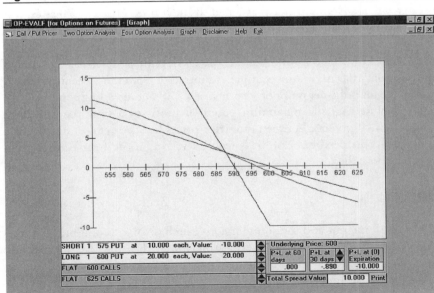

Bear put spreads sometimes are referred to as "debit put spreads," because they are established for a net cost or net debit. The spread in Figure 14–3, for example, is established by purchasing the 600 Put for 20 cents, or $1,000, and simultaneously selling the 575 Put at 10 cents, or $500, for a net cost, or net debit, of 10 cents, or $500, not including commissions. Remember that it is common practice to describe a vertical spread by using the lower strike first regardless of whether calls or puts are involved. Thus, the name for the position in Figure 14–3 is a 575-600 Bear Put spread.

Profit or Loss at Expiration.   At expiration, there are three possible outcomes. The futures can be at or above the higher strike, below the higher strike but not below the lower strike, or below the lower strike. The straight line in Figure 14–3 illustrates these possibilities. If the futures price is at or above the upper strike of a bear put spread at expiration, both puts expire worthless and the full amount paid for the position, $500 plus commissions in this example, is lost.

If the futures price is below the higher strike but not below the lower strike, the long put (higher strike) is exercised and the short put (lower strike) expires worthless. The futures price at expiration at which a bear put spread breaks even is equal to the higher strike price minus the net premium paid for the position. In Figure 14–3, the break-even futures price at expiration is 5.90, the higher strike of 6.00 minus the net cost of 10 cents.

If the futures price is below the lower strike at expiration, the long put is exercised and the short put is assigned. If the futures price is 5.70 at expiration, for example, exercising the 600 Put results in selling a futures at 6.00, and assignment on the 575 Put results in buying a futures at 5.75. The net result of these two futures transactions is a receipt of 25 cents. The cost of the position, 10 cents in this example, is subtracted from the 25 cents received, and the result is the net profit of 15 cents, or $750, not including commissions.

Note that the maximum potential profit of a bear put spread is equal to the difference between the strike prices less the net cost of the position. Also, this maximum profit is realized at expiration if the futures price is at or below the lower strike.

Bull Put Spread

The sale of one put and the simultaneous purchase of a second put with the same underlying and the same expiration but with a lower strike price is known as a bull put spread. Figure 14–4 illustrates a 575–600 Bull Put spread in which one 600 Put is sold and one 575 Put is purchased.

Figure 14–4 575–600 Bull Put Spread

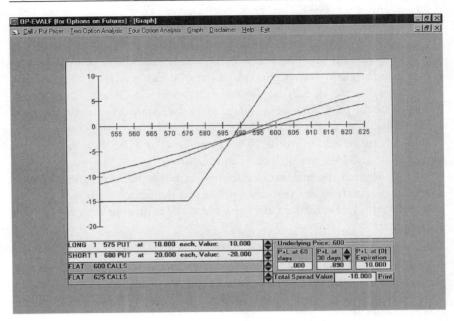

Bull put spreads sometimes are referred to as "credit put spreads," because they are established for a net receipt, or net credit. The spread in Figure 14–4, for example, is established by selling the 600 Put for 20 cents, or $1,000, and simultaneously purchasing the 575 Put at 10 cents, or $500, for a net receipt, or net credit, of 10 cents, or $500, not including commissions. Once again, it is common practice to describe a vertical spread by using the lower strike first regardless of whether calls or puts are involved. Thus, the name of the position in Figure 14–4 is a 575–600 Bull Put spread.

Profit or Loss at Expiration. At expiration, there are three possible outcomes. The futures price can be at or above the higher strike, below the higher strike but not below the lower strike, or below the lower strike. The straight line in Figure 14–4 illustrates these possibilities. If the futures price is at or above the upper strike of a bull put spread at expiration, both puts expire worthless and the full amount received, $500 less commissions in this example, is kept as income.

If the futures price is below the higher strike but not below the lower strike, the short put (higher strike) is assigned and the long put (lower strike) expires worthless. The futures price at expiration at which a bull put spread breaks even is equal to the higher strike price minus the net premium received. In Figure 14–4, the break-even futures price at expiration is 5.90, the higher strike of 6.00 minus the 10 cents received.

If the futures price is below the lower strike at expiration, the short put is assigned and the long put is exercised. If the futures price is 5.70 at expiration, for example, assignment of the 600 Put results in the purchase of a futures contract at 6.00, and exercising the 575 Put results in the sale of that contract at 5.75. The net result of these two transactions is a payment of 25 cents. The credit received for initiating the position, $500 in this example, is subtracted from the 25-cent payment, and the result is a net loss of 15 cents, or $750, not including commissions.

Note that the maximum potential loss of a bull put spread is equal to the difference between the strike prices less the net credit received. Also, this maximum loss is realized at expiration if the futures price is at or below the lower strike.

Now that the terminology and profit and risk potential of vertical spreads have been reviewed, we will return to Bob and his disappointing situation.

BOB'S SITUATION

Bob trades soybean options. Since Bob is a short-term trader who closes positions before expiration, the straight-line expiration profit and loss diagrams in Figures 14–1 through 14–4 do not offer sufficient information for Bob to select a strategy. Although the curved lines in these figures estimate how a spread will behave before expiration, Bob needs a more specific estimate. The Call/Put Pricer and Two Option Analysis pages in OP-EVALF™ are just Bob what needs.

Tables 14–1, 14–2, and 14–3 were created using the Two Option Analysis page in OP-EVALF™ and contain the theoretical values of a 600 Call, a 625 Call, and a 600–625 Bull Call spread, respectively, at different futures prices and different days before expiration. The values in Table 14–3 appear in the Spread Value box on the Two Option Analysis page, but they can also be calculated by subtracting a 625 Call value in Table 14–2 from the corresponding 600 Call Value in Table 14–1. The value of 15¼ cents in Table 14–3, column 1, row 1, for example, is the difference between the 600 Call value of 38 cents and the 625 Call value of 22¾ cents in the corresponding boxes in Tables 14–1 and 14–2, respectively. Bob could use tables such as these to estimate the results of different strategies.

Table 14-1 Theoretical Values of 600 Call at Various Futures Prices and Days to Expiration (Interest Rates, 5%; Volatility, 20%)

Row	Futures Price	Col. 1 60 Days	Col. 2 50 Days	Col. 3 40 Days	Col. 4 30 Days	Col. 5 20 Days	Col. 6 10 Days	Col. 7 Exp.
1	6.30	38	36¾	35¼	33¾	32⅛	30⅝	30
2	6.25	34½	33	31½	29¾	28	26	25
3	6.20	31	29½	27⅞	26	24	21¾	20
4	6.15	27¾	26¼	24½	22½	20⅜	17⅝	15
5	6.10	24¾	23⅛	21⅜	19⅜	16⅞	13⅞	10
6	6.05	21⅞	20¼	18⅜	16⅜	13⅞	10⅝	5
7	6.00	19¼	17⅝	15¾	13⅝	11⅛	7⅞	0
8	5.95	16¾	15⅛	13⅜	11¼	8¾	5⅝	0
9	5.90	14½	13	11⅛	9⅛	6¾	3⅞	0

Table 14-2 Theoretical Values of 625 Call at Various Futures Prices and Days to Expiration (Interest Rates, 5%; Volatility, 20%)

Row	Futures Price	Col. 1 60 Days	Col. 2 50 Days	Col. 3 40 Days	Col. 4 30 Days	Col. 5 20 Days	Col. 6 10 Days	Col. 7 Exp.
1	6.30	22¾	21	19⅛	16⅞	14⅜	11	5
2	6.25	20	18¼	16½	14½	11⅝	8¼	0
3	6.20	17½	15⅞	14	11¾	9¼	6	0
4	6.15	15¼	13⅝	11¾	9⅝	7¼	4⅛	0
5	6.10	13¼	11⅝	9⅞	7⅞	5½	2¾	0
6	6.05	11⅜	9¾	8⅛	6¼	4⅛	1¾	0
7	6.00	9⅝	8¼	6⅝	4⅞	3	1	0
8	5.95	8⅛	6¾	5⅜	3¾	2⅛	⅝	0
9	5.90	6⅞	5⅝	4¼	2⅞	1½	⅜	0

A Review of Bob's Situation

At the start of this chapter, we learned that Bob purchased 10 600–625 Bull Call spreads rather than 10 600 Calls. When Bob was facing this decision, it was 60 days before expiration, July Soybean futures were 6.00, and Bob was predicting a 20-cent rise in soybean futures in 10 days. An examination of Tables 14–1 and 14–3 shows why Bob got a smaller profit from purchasing 10 bull call spreads than from purchasing 10 600 Calls.

Table 14–1 shows that with soybean futures at 6.00 60 days before expiration (column 1, row 7), the price of the 600 Call is 19¼ cents. Ten days later, with the futures price at 6.20 (column 2, row 3), the call price is 29½. Purchasing 10 of these calls at 19¼ and selling them at 29½ results in a profit of 10¼ cents, or $512.50, per option. That amounts to a total profit of $5,125 on 10 options, not including commissions.

Table 14–3 shows that, with the futures at 6.00 at 60 days to expiration and at 6.20 at 50 days, the 600–625 Call spread is 9⅝ and 13⅝, respectively. Buying and selling 10 of these spreads at these prices would result in a profit of 4 cents, or $200, per spread, or $2,000 on 10 spreads.

If Bob had done this simple analysis before making his decision, he would have known what to expect. This analysis does not imply, however, that Bob made the "wrong" decision, because the purchase of 10 of the 600

Table 14–3 Theoretical Values of 600–625 Call Spread at Various Futures Prices and Days to Expiration (Interest Rates, 5%; Volatility, 20%)

Row	Futures Price	Col. 1 60 Days	Col. 2 50 Days	Col. 3 40 Days	Col. 4 30 Days	Col. 5 20 Days	Col. 6 10 Days	Col. 7 Exp.
1	6.30	15¼	15¾	16⅛	16⅞	17¾	19⅝	25
2	6.25	14½	14¾	15	15½	16⅜	17¾	25
3	6.20	13½	13⅝	13⅞	14¼	14¾	15¾	20
4	6.15	12½	12⅝	12¾	12⅞	13⅛	13½	15
5	6.10	11½	11½	11½	11½	11⅜	11⅛	10
6	6.05	10½	10½	10¼	10⅛	9¾	8⅞	5
7	6.00	9⅝	9⅜	9⅛	8⅞	8⅛	6⅞	0
8	5.95	8⅝	8⅜	8	7½	6⅝	5	0
9	5.90	7⅝	7⅜	6⅞	6¼	5¼	3½	0

Calls involved a greater maximum theoretical risk and a greater short-term risk than purchasing 10 of the 600–625 Bull Call spreads. The maximum risk of purchasing 10 of the 600 Calls is the total cost including commissions which, in this example is $9,625. The maximum theoretical risk of purchasing bull call spreads is also the total cost plus commissions. In this example, the cost of 10 of the 600–625 Bull Call spreads is $4,812.50.

Regarding short-term risk, if Bob's forecast is incorrect and soybean futures decline 5 cents in 10 days, then Tables 14–1 and 14–3 indicate that 10 long 600 Calls suffer a greater loss than do 10 600–625 Bull Call spreads. According to Table 14–1, with futures at 5.95 at 50 days, the 600 Call will be 15⅛ cents for a loss of 4⅛ cents per call. Table 14–3 estimates that the 600–625 Bull Call spread will be 8⅜ cents, for a loss of 1¼ cents per spread. Under these circumstances, the bull call spreads would lose substantially less than would the 600 Calls.

The conclusion is that these strategies involve different short-term profit and risk potentials. This means that they are not directly comparable, and a choice between them should not be based solely on cost. Instead, Bob should consider his confidence in his market forecast and his tolerance for risk. This is a subjective process that every trader must do independently.

Using the Greeks

Another way to evaluate Bob's choices is to use the Greeks to analyze the profit and risk potentials of his alternatives. Table 14–4 shows the delta, gamma, theta, and vega of the 600 Call, the 625 Call, and the 600–625 Bull Call spread. Since he has a bullish forecast, Bob's first concern should be delta, and the 600 Call and the 600–625 Bull Call spread have significantly different deltas! Column 1 in Table 14–4 shows that the delta of the 600 Call is +0.512,

Table 14–4 Delta, Gamma, Vega, and Theta: 600 Call, 625 Call, 600–625 Bull Call Spread

	Col. 1 600 Call	Col. 2 625 Call	Col. 3 600–625 Bull Call Spread
Price	19¼	9⅝	9⅝
Delta	+0.512	+0.319	+0.193
Gamma	+0.008	+0.007	+0.001
Vega	+0.962	+0.870	+0.092
Theta	−1.140	−1.024	−0.116

and so the delta of 10 long 600 Calls is +5.12, equivalent to 5.12 long soybean futures. Column 3 shows that the delta of the 600–625 Bull Call spread, however, is only +0.193. This is calculated by subtracting the delta of the 625 Call, +0.319 in column 2, from the delta of the 600 Call. Consequently, the delta of 10 600–625 Bull Call spreads, +1.93, is less than half the delta of 10 long 600 Calls. If Bob had done this analysis, this would have been his first indication that the bull call spreads would underperform relative to the 600 Calls.

Table 14–4 also shows that the gammas of the 600 Call and the 600–625 Bull Call spread are very different. The 600 Call has a gamma of +0.008, and so 10 long 600 Calls have a gamma of +0.080. This means that as the underlying soybean futures contract rises 1 cent, the delta of the 10 long 600 Calls rises by 0.080. Consequently, as soybean futures rise 20 cents from 6.00 to 6.20, the delta of the 10 long 600 Call position rises from +5.12 to approximately +6.72. This is calculated by adding the beginning delta of the call position to the change in futures price times the gamma. In this example, the beginning delta is +5.12, the futures point change is +20, from 6.00 to 6.20, and the position gamma is +0.080. Consequently, the ending delta is 5.12 + (20 × .080) = +6.72. The 10 long 600 Calls started out equivalent to long 5.12 futures and ended up equal to long 6.72 futures.

In contrast, the gammas of +0.001 for one 600–625 Bull Call spread and +0.010 for 10 spreads indicate a much smaller rise in the delta of the spread position. Specifically, with a 20-cent rise in the futures from 6.00 to 6.20, the delta of 10 600–625 Bull Call spreads starts at +1.93 and rises to approximately +2.130 [1.93 + (20 × 0.010)].

To summarize, there are two reasons why the rise in soybean futures caused the 600 Call position to earn a larger profit than the 600–625 Bull Call spread position. First, the long 600 Calls started with a higher delta; second, that delta increased more rapidly as the futures price rose.

Remember, this analysis only explains why one strategy performed better than the other; it does not lead to the conclusion that purchasing 10 of the 600 Calls is a "better" choice. As was discussed above, the 600 Call position involves more risk than does the bull call spread position. Nevertheless, if Bob had done this analysis rather than just considering the "cost" of the positions, he would have realized that the strategies have different profit and risk potentials. He still might have made the same choice, but having done this analysis, he would have been prepared for the outcome.

CAPITAL MANAGEMENT AND STRATEGY ALTERNATIVES

Suppose Bob had approached this trading decision differently. If, for example, he had decided that he was willing to invest and risk $5,000 on this

trade, he could have chosen between alternatives with approximately the same maximum theoretical risk.

Of course, Bob has many alternatives involving calls and puts with different strike prices and expiration dates that are not shown in Tables 14–1, 14–2, and 14–3. For the sake of simplicity, however, these tables will be used to examine only three strategies: buying 600 Calls, buying 625 Calls, and buying 600–625 Bull Call spreads. The purpose of this example is to demonstrate how the price behavior of vertical spreads differs from the price behavior of at-the-money and out-of-the-money options. Although this example uses calls to illustrate several points, the concepts apply equally to puts.

Identifying the Alternatives

Using the prices in Tables 14–1, 14–2, and 14–3, and assuming that Bob has approximately $5,000 to invest and risk, not including commissions, he can evaluate three strategies: the purchase of five of the 600 Calls, the purchase of 10 of the 625 Calls, and the purchase of 10 of the 600–625 Call Spreads. The maximum number of units of each strategy is determined by dividing the capital available by the cost of the strategy and then rounding to the nearest whole number.

The number of 600 Calls that can be purchased, for example, is calculated by dividing the capital commitment of $5,000 by the 600 Call price of 19¼, or $962.50. Rounding the result of 5.19 to 5 indicates that five 600 Calls can be purchased for $4,812.50 (5 × $962.50), not including commissions. By the same process, it is calculated that 10 of the 625 Calls can be purchased at 9⅝ each, or $481.25 each, for a total cost of $4,812.50 (10 × 481.50 = $4,812.50). Finally, 10 of the 600–625 Bull Call spreads, at 9⅝ cents each, can also be purchased for $4,812.50, not including commissions.

Estimating Results

Bob can now use Tables 14–1, 14–2, and 14–3 to estimate the results of these strategies under different market forecasts. Bob's initial forecast will be analyzed first. Subsequently, different outcomes assuming a longer time period and changes in implied volatility will be analyzed.

Bob's initial forecast was that soybean futures would rise from 6.00 at 60 days before expiration to 6.20 at 50 days. Column 2, row 3, of Table 14–1 estimates that, after the predicted move, the price of the 600 Call will be 29½. The corresponding boxes in Tables 14–2 and 14–3 indicate that the prices of the 625 Call and the 600–625 Bull Call spread will be 15⅞ and 13⅝, respectively.

Assuming that these estimates are accurate, the conclusion is that purchasing 10 of the 625 Calls would have given Bob the highest profit. Purchasing these calls at 9⅝ and selling them at 15⅞ yields a profit of 6¼ per option, or a total profit of $3,125 on 10 options, not including commissions. This compares favorably to the purchase and sale of five 600 Calls at 19¼ and 29½, respectively, for a total profit of $2,562.50 total. Purchasing 10 of the 600–625 Bull Call spreads at 9⅝ each and selling them at 13⅝ results in a total profit of $2,000, the lowest profit of these three strategies.

A Different Time Forecast Leads to a Different Strategy

Suppose Bob accurately forecasts the 20-cent rise in soybean futures but his timing is off. If the rise takes 30 days instead of 10, soybean futures will be at 6.20 with 30 days to expiration. In this case column 4, row 3, in the tables provides estimates of the results. Table 14–1 estimates that the price of the 600 Call will be 26. Tables 14–2 and 14–3 estimate that the prices of the 625 Call and the 600–625 Bull Call spread will be 11¾ and 14¼, respectively.

These estimates indicate that a different strategy will yield the highest profit. Purchasing five 600 Calls at 19¼ cents and selling them at 26 cents yields a total profit of $1,687.50. Purchasing 10 of the 625 Calls at 9⅝ and selling them at 11¾ yields a total profit of $1,062.5. And purchasing 10 of the 600–625 Bull Call spreads at 9⅝ and selling them at 14¼ yields a total profit of $2,312.50.

In this second scenario, the bull call spread rose from last place to first place!

The conclusion is that, in choosing between purchasing at-the-money calls, purchasing out-of-the-money calls, and purchasing bull call spreads, assuming a constant amount of capital, short, sharp price rises favor the out-of-the-money calls. Smaller price rises over a longer time period favor the bull call spreads. Purchasing at-the-money calls is preferable when the forecast predicts a price movement somewhere in between.

Until now the examples have assumed a constant volatility. The next example will show the impact of changes in volatility on vertical spreads.

CHANGING THE IMPLIED VOLATILITY

What should traders do when they have a strong opinion about market direction but are worried about an adverse change in implied volatility? Such a situation might arise when a crop report is about to be released.

Refer to Bob's original forecast for a 20-cent rise in soybeans in 10 days. This time, however, assume that Bob is forecasting a decrease in implied volatility from 20 percent to 15 percent. Bob might consider such a change possible if a crop report were due within that time period. Bob could forecast that "after the news is out, the implied volatility will drop." When this new element is included in Bob's forecast, we will see that he chooses a different strategy, even though the price and time elements of the forecast are the same.

Table 14–5 was created using Bob's new assumptions. Soybean futures are 6.20, up from 6.00. The days to expiration have declined from 60 to 50, and the implied volatility has declined from 20 percent to 15 percent. The interest rates and strike prices remain the same. Table 14–5 indicates that the price of 600 Call will be 25⅝. This is 3⅞ cents *lower* than is the case

Table 14–5 Decrease in Implied Volatility

	Initial Inputs		Inputs Changed to Pessimistic Forecast
Inputs:			
Futures price	6.00	→	6.20
Strike price	600 / 625		
Volatility	20%	→	15%
Interest rates	5%		
Days to expiration	60	→	50
Outputs:			
600 Call price	19¼	→	25⅝
625 Call price	9⅝	→	11⅜
600-625 Bull Call spread	9⅝	→	14¼

Strategy Results

	Long 5 600 Calls at 19¼	Long 10 625 Calls at 9⅝	Long 10 Bull Call Spreads at 9⅝
Sale price	25⅝	11⅜	14¼
Purchase price	19¼	9⅝	9⅝
Profit/Loss per option	+6⅜	+1¾	+4⅝
Times quantity	× 5	× 10	× 10
Strategy profit/loss	+31⅞	+17½	+46¼
Profit/loss in dollars	+$1,581	+$ 875	+$2,312

if implied volatility remains constant, as assumed in Table 14–1. The 625 Call price is estimated to be 11⅜, or 4½ cents *lower* than is the case if implied volatility remains constant, as assumed in Table 14–2. The 600–625 Bull Call spread is estimated to be 14¼. That is ⅝ cents *higher* than in Table 14–3, in which implied volatility is constant.

The decrease in implied volatility has greatly affected the price of the 600 Call and the price of the 625 Call. The price of the bull call spread, however, has hardly budged!

Given a forecast including a decrease in implied volatility, the prices in Table 14–5 indicate that Bob should choose to purchase 10 of the 600-625 Bull Call spreads rather than purchasing 10 of the 625 Calls or five of the 600 Calls. Purchasing five 600 Calls at 19¼ and selling them at 25⅝ yields a profit of 6⅜ each, or a profit of $1,593.75, not including commissions. The purchase and sale of 10 of the 625 Calls at 9⅝ and 11⅜, respectively, results in a profit of 1¾ on each, or $875 on 10. Purchasing 10 of the 600–625 Bull Call spreads at 9⅝ each and selling them at 14¼ results in a total profit of $2,312.50, the highest of the three strategies for this forecast.

The conclusion is that one-to-one vertical spreads can be much less sensitive to changes in implied volatility than are single-option positions. When traders think that the implied volatility risk is high, one-to-one vertical spreads may be the strategy of choice!

A LOOK AT THE GREEKS

Table 14–6 presents the Greeks of the three strategies discussed above. The vegas of the three strategies provide a clue that the 600–625 Bull Call spread is least sensitive to changes in implied volatility. The vega of the bull call spread is the smallest, less than one-fifth of the vega of the 600 Call position and just over one-tenth of that of the 625 Call position. But once again, this does not make the bull call spread the "better" choice. The smallest vega is only one aspect of the bull call spread. This strategy also has the smallest delta of the three strategies. This means that in a sharply rising market, this strategy will underperform the other two.

The conclusion to be drawn from Table 14–6 is that the three strategies, despite being almost equal in terms of maximum theoretical risk, still offer trade-offs, i.e., some relatively positive attributes and some relatively negative ones. Although the Greeks are difficult to interpret initially, with some practice, every trader will find that they are of great benefit in making trading decisions.

Table 14–6 Position Greeks

	Long 5 600 Calls Long 10 625 Calls 10 600–625 Bull Call Spreads		
	Col. 1	Col. 2	Col. 3
	Long 5 600 Calls	Long 10 625 Calls	10 600–625 Bull Call Spreads
Price of position	$4,812.50	$4,812.50	$4,812.50
Position delta	+2.56	+3.19	+1.93
Position gamma	+0.04	+0.07	+0.01
Position vega	+4.81	+8.70	+0.92
Position theta	−5.70	−10.24	−1.16

CREDIT SPREADS VERSUS SELLING UNCOVERED OPTIONS

Many traders ask which is better, selling vertical spreads or selling uncovered options? Unfortunately, there is no simple answer to this question because the strategies involve different short-term risks and different maximum theoretical risks. Uncovered short futures options involve substantial or unlimited risk, and this strategy is suitable only for experienced traders who are financially and psychologically prepared to assume those risks. Credit spreads with futures options, however, have limited risk.

Figure 14–5 illustrates a short 220 Corn Call, Figure 14–6 shows a 220–230 Bear Call spread, and Table 14–7 compares the Greeks of the two strategies.

There are many differences between these two strategies. First, the uncovered short 220 Call is sold for 6¼ in this example, and the 220–230 Bear Call spread is sold for 2⅜. Second, the risk of the uncovered 220 Call is unlimited, while the risk of the 10-cent 220–230 Bear Call spread is limited to 7⅜, or $368.75 in this example. Third, Table 14–7 shows how the short-term market exposures, the Greeks, are different.

Table 14–7 reveals that the short 220 Call is more sensitive to all factors than is the bear call spread. Its delta, gamma, and vega are all smaller (higher absolute value), which means it has more risk than does the bear call spread. But its higher theta means that it profits more if factors other than time remain constant.

Which is "better"? There is no "better." These two strategies offer a choice between two sets of trade-offs. Choosing between them is a personal

Figure 14–5 Short 1 220 Call at 6¼

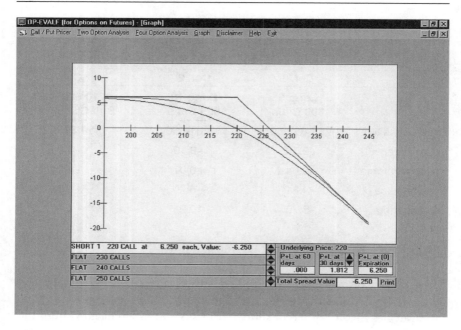

Figure 14–6 Short 1 220–230 Bear Call Spread

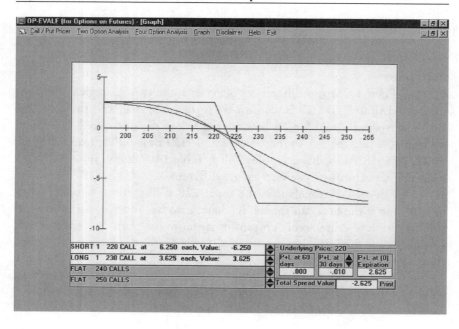

Table 14–7 Short Call versus Bear Call Spread (Futures, 2.20; Days to Expiration, 30; Interest Rates, 5%; Volatility, 25%)

	Short 220 Call	220–230 Bear Call Spread
Theoretical value	6 ¼	3 ⅝
Delta	−0.512	−0.234
Gamma	−0.025	−0.003
Vega	−0.250	−0.037
Theta	+0.774	+0.136

decision that can only be made by traders on an individual basis, depending on their market forecast and tolerance for risk. This may be an unsatisfying answer to those who want a clear choice. Unfortunately, there are rarely "clear" choices in trading, whether it is options, stocks, or futures. One advantage of options is that they provide traders with a wide range of alternatives. But only a trader can decide which alternative is "best" for a particular forecast. And of course, the risk is that the forecast is wrong and a loss will be incurred.

SUMMARY

There are four basic one-to-one vertical spreads. Assuming the same underlying and expiration date, a bull call spread consists of a long call with a lower strike and a short call with a higher strike. A bear call spread consists of a short call with a lower strike and a long call with a higher strike. A bear put spread consists of a long put with a higher strike and a short put with a lower strike. A bull put spread consists of a short put with a higher strike and a long put with a lower strike. Regardless of whether calls or puts are involved, it is common practice to refer to vertical spreads by using the lower strike first.

The prices of vertical spreads behave differently than do at-the-money or out-of-the-money single options, because their Greeks are different. Consequently, the same three-part forecasting technique used for individual options should be used for vertical spreads. The three parts are a price forecast, a time forecast, and a forecast for implied volatility. Different forecasts will lead to the selection of different strategies.

Vertical spreads tend to be less sensitive to changes in implied volatility than single-option positions. This means that vertical spreads may be the preferred choice when a forecast calls for a decrease in implied volatility.

Selling vertical spreads and selling uncovered options are not directly comparable, because they involve different risks, i.e., different Greeks, and have different profit and risk potentials. Although the Greeks are difficult to interpret initially, with practice, any trader will find that they offer valuable information quickly and easily, thereby speeding up trading decisions.

There are no "better" strategies. Traders must make individual judgments about the level of their confidence in forecasts and their tolerance for risk when choosing between alternative strategies.

Fifteen

Straddles and Strangles

O ption traders tend to fall into one of three categories. The first group has heard of straddles and strangles but has no idea what they are. The second group has seen expiration profit and loss diagrams of these strategies but has never traded them. The third group has used them but lost money! The goal of this chapter is to create a fourth group: option traders who have realistic expectations about straddles and strangles and which forecasts they are and are not suited for. Every option strategy has its own set of advantages and disadvantages, and straddles and strangles are no exception.

This chapter discusses long and short straddles and strangles. Each strategy is defined first, and the expiration profit and loss diagrams are presented. Next, a table of theoretical values is used to explain price behavior before expiration. Fourth, some forecasts are tested using the Greeks: delta, gamma, vega, and theta. Finally, straddles and strangles are compared.

The examples in this chapter do not include commissions, other transaction costs, or margin requirements. Since straddles and strangles involve two option positions, transaction costs and margin requirements can be higher than they are for single-option positions. Consequently, these factors can significantly affect the desirability of the strategies discussed in this chapter, and they must be included in the analysis of any real strategy involving real options.

LONG STRADDLE DEFINED

A *long straddle* involves the simultaneous purchase of one call and one put with the same strike price, the same expiration date, and the same underlying. Figure 15–1 illustrates a long 70-strike Live Cattle straddle. This long straddle is established by purchasing one 70 Call for 1.675, or $670, and simultaneously purchasing one 70 Put for the same price for a total cost of 3.35 cents, or $1,340. It is common practice to describe a straddle by using the strike price, because the strike price is the same for both the call and the put. Thus the name for the position in Figure 15–1 is a long 70 Straddle. "Long" indicates that both options are purchased.

Straddle is an appropriate name, because the word *straddle* means taking both sides at the same time, and this strategy has the potential of profiting from either up or down price changes in the underlying futures contract.

Profit or Loss at Expiration

At expiration, there are three possible outcomes. The futures price can be above the strike, below the strike, or at the strike. The straight line in Figure 15–1 illustrates these possibilities. If the futures price is above the higher strike at expiration, the call is exercised, because it is in-the-money. The put expires worthless, because it is out-of-the money. If the futures price is 74.00

Figure 15–1 Long 70 Straddle at 3.35

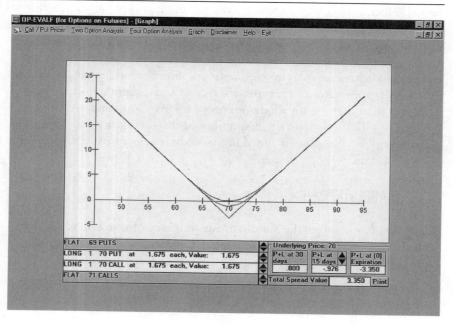

at expiration, for example, exercising the 70 Call results in the purchase of a futures contract at 70.00, and the 70 Put expires worthless. If the futures contract is sold at 74.00, a futures profit of 4 cents, or 4.00, is realized. The cost of the position, 3.35 in this example, is subtracted from the 4.00 futures profit, and the result is a net profit of 0.65, or $260. If the futures price is above the strike but below the upper break-even point at expiration, the result is a loss. In Figure 15–1, the upper break-even futures price at expiration is 73.35. This is calculated by adding the total price paid of 3.35 to the strike price of 70.00.

If the futures price is below the strike price at expiration, the put is exercised, because it is in-the-money. The call expires worthless, because it is out-of-the money. If the futures price is 65.00 at expiration, for example, exercising the 70 Put results in selling a futures contract at 70.00, and the 70 Call expires worthless. If the short futures contract is covered at 65.00, a futures profit of 5.00 is realized. The cost of the position, 3.35 in this example, is subtracted from the futures profit, and the result is a net profit of 1.65, or $660. If the futures price is below the strike but above the lower break-even point at expiration, the result is a loss. In Figure 15–1, the lower break-even futures price at expiration is 66.65, the strike price of 70.00 minus the total cost of 3.35.

If the futures price is exactly at the strike at expiration, both the call and the put expire worthless, and the full amount paid for the straddle is lost.

Expiration profit and loss analysis is beneficial, because it reveals the futures prices where the best possible and worst possible outcomes occur. Expiration analysis, however, does not help short-term traders understand how the strategy behaves before expiration. The following discussion addresses pricing issues that short-term traders should consider.

Buying Straddles

Ralph is confident and unsure at the same time!

December Live Cattle futures are trading at 70 cents per pound, and Ralph is confidently predicting that the price will move sharply in response to a government report this week, but he is unsure about the direction. He is thinking, "News bullish, live cattle up 4 to 5 cents; news bearish, live cattle down 4 to 5 cents; but which will it be?" Consequently, Ralph is considering the purchase of a December Live Cattle 70 Straddle. Today is 60 days before December option expiration. "As long as the market moves," Ralph says, "I'll make a profit if I buy the 70 Straddle."

Table 15–1 tends to confirm Ralph's logic, but a loss can result if the market does not move sufficiently in either direction. Table 15–1 was created by using the Two Option Analysis page in OP-EVALF™. The value in each box is the sum of a 70 Call value and a 70 Put value, assuming the indicated futures price, days to expiration, etc. Ralph's starting position is column 1, row 6, a 70 Straddle value of 3.35.

Table 15–1 estimates how the value of the 70 Straddle will change over a range of futures prices at different days before expiration, assuming that volatility and interest rates remain constant. If, for example, the futures price rises 3 cents in 10 days to a level of 73.00 at 50 days before expiration (column 2, row 3), the straddle is estimated to be 4.00 for a profit of 0.65, or $260, not including commissions. If, however, it takes 40 days for the futures to rise 3 cents, the straddle is estimated to be 3.27 (column 5, row 3) for a loss of 0.08, or $32, not including commissions.

Table 15–1 makes an important point about straddles. Assuming that the futures price is at the strike when a straddle is purchased, down moves generally have to be larger than up moves for a profit to be realized. In the example above, a 3-cent rise in the futures in 10 days resulted in a

Table 15–1 Theoretical Values of 70 Straddle
(1 70 Call and 1 70 Put)
(Interest Rates, 5%; Volatility, 15%)

Row	Futures Price	Col. 1 60 Days	Col. 2 50 Days	Col. 3 40 Days	Col. 4 30 Days	Col. 5 20 Days	Col. 6 10 Days	Col. 7 0 Days
1	75.00	5.52	5.37	5.25	5.12	5.05	5.00	5.00
2	74.00	4.82	4.62	4.45	4.27	4.12	4.00	4.00
3	73.00	4.22	4.00	3.77	3.52	3.27	3.07	3.00
4	72.00	3.77	3.50	3.22	2.92	2.60	2.22	2.00
5	71.00	3.50	3.20	2.89	2.55	2.12	1.62	1.00
6	70.00	3.35	3.07	2.75	2.40	1.95	1.40	0.00
7	69.00	3.45	3.15	2.85	2.50	2.10	1.60	1.00
8	68.00	3.70	3.45	3.17	2.87	2.55	2.20	2.00
9	67.00	4.12	3.90	3.70	3.47	3.25	3.05	3.00
10	66.00	4.70	4.52	4.37	4.22	4.07	4.00	4.00
11	65.00	5.40	5.27	5.17	5.07	5.02	5.00	5.00

profit of 0.65. However, Table 15–1 indicates that, with a 3-cent fall in the futures price in 10 days, a smaller profit results. Column 2, row 9, is 50 days to expiration with the futures price at 67.00, and the estimated 70 Straddle value is 3.90, 0.10 less than the value of 4.00 when the futures price rose 3 cents. The reasons for this asymmetrical price action will be discussed later, when the Greeks are reviewed.

A typical question is, How much of a futures price change in what period of time justifies the purchase of a straddle? Unfortunately, there is no objective answer to this question. Ralph must consider his forecast and make a personal assessment of the potential profits and risks. The creation of value estimates such as Table 15–1 is helpful in making this decision, but an analysis of the Greeks also provides valuable information.

THE GREEKS: LONG STRADDLE

Table 15–2 summarizes the delta, gamma, theta, and vega of a long 70 Call, a long 70 Put, and a long 70 Straddle with a futures price of 70.00 at 60 days before expiration. This information was taken from the Call/Put Pricer page in OP-EVAL3™. The numbers for the Long 70 Straddle are the sums of the numbers for the Long 70 Call and the Long 70 Put. The Greeks of a multiple-part option position are equal to the sum of the Greeks of the individual options in the position. The straddle delta of +0.024, for example, is the sum of the 70 Call delta of +0.508 and the 70 Put delta of –0.484.

What does Table 15–2 reveal about the straddle? First, notice the relatively large vega, the position's sensitivity to changes in volatility. Second, notice the relatively low theta (high absolute value), the position's sensitivity to the passage of time. Third, notice the delta, which is nearly zero.

Table 15–2 Position Greeks: Long 70 Call, Long 70 Put, Long 70 Straddle

	Long 70 Call	Long 70 Put	Long 70 Straddle
Price	1.675	1.675	3.35
Delta	+0.508	– 0.484	+0.024
Gamma	+0.091	+0.091	+0.182
Vega	+0.112	+0.112	+0.224
Theta	–0.100	–0.100	–0.200

The vega of +0.224 indicates that the straddle value will increase or decrease by this amount if volatility rises or falls by 1 percent and other factors remain constant. A large vega should be expected, because the straddle position consists of two long options.

The theta of −0.200 estimates that the straddle value will decrease by this amount if 7 days pass and other factors remain constant. A low theta (high absolute value) should also be expected because of the two long options.

The near-zero delta is the sum of the positive call delta and the negative put delta. It means that for "small" changes in the futures, there will be little or no change in the straddle value. Only after a sufficient move will the gamma effect, the change in delta, come into play, and only then will the straddle value change.

The straddle delta does not equal zero exactly, as many newcomers to options expect it should, because of technical factors in the Black-Scholes option pricing formula. An explanation of these factors is beyond the scope of this book, but it is correct to expect that a straddle delta will be slightly positive when an underlying futures price is exactly at the strike price. This positive delta explains why a straddle has an upward bias and why equal up and down movements in the underlying futures do not change the straddle value equally.

What are the implications for risk of the large vega, the low theta, and the near-zero delta? Simply stated, for straddle buyers, these factors mean that a "big move" must occur in a "short time" with "little or no decline in implied volatility" or a loss will be incurred.

TESTING SCENARIOS

OP-EVALF™ can be used to test various scenarios. Suppose, for example, that in his optimistic scenario Ralph forecasts that the live cattle futures will fall by 5 cents in 7 days and that implied volatility will decline 2 percent. As mentioned above, Ralph's forecast for the change in the futures is based on his belief that the government report will be very bullish or very bearish and that the futures market will react strongly. His forecast for a decrease in implied volatility could be based on his knowledge that implied volatility has risen in recent days, in anticipation of the report, perhaps, and on his belief that implied volatility will "return to normal" after the report. Table 15–3 shows how OP-EVALF™ might be used to test Ralph's optimistic forecast.

Table 15–3 contains three columns of numbers. Column 1 contains the initial inputs — the futures price of 70.00, 60 days to expiration, 15 per-

Table 15–3 Change in Straddle Value: Optimistic Scenario 5-Cent Change in Live Cattle Futures in 7 Days with Implied Volatility Down 2%

	Col. 1 Initial Status		Col. 2 Market Up		Col. 3 Market Down
Inputs:					
Futures price	70.00	→	75.00	→	65.00
Strike price	70.00				
Volatility	15%	→	13%	→	13%
Interest rates	5%				
Days to expiration	60	→	53	→	53
Outputs:					
70 Call price	1.675	→	5.10	→	0.10
70 Call price	1.675	→	0.12	→	5.07
70 Straddle	3.350	→	5.22	→	5.17

cent volatility, etc.—and the initial outputs—the 70 Call value of 1.675, the 70 Put value of 1.675, and the 70 Straddle value of 3.35. Column 2 contains the new inputs of a higher futures price of 75.00, 53 days to expiration, 13 percent volatility, etc., and the new outputs of a 70 Call value of 5.10, a 70 Put value of 0.12 , and a 70 Straddle value of 5.22. Column 3 contains new inputs and new outputs with the futures price down 5 cents to 65.00 in 7 days. In column 3, the 70 Call value is 0.10, the 70 Put value is 5.07, and the 70 Straddle value is 5.17.

What is the conclusion? If Ralph believes in scenario 1, Table 15–3 indicates that he will make 1.87, or $748, if futures rise 5 cents, or 1.82, or $728, if futures fall 5 cents. A different scenario, however, might lead to a different conclusion.

Assume that instead of his optimistic scenario, Ralph believes in a more pessimistic scenario, a 3-cent rise or fall in the futures in 10 days and a 4-percent decrease in implied volatility. Table 15–4 estimates that the 70 Straddle rises to 3.42 for a profit of 0.07, or $28, not including commissions. If the futures price declines 3 cents in 10 days, Table 15–4 estimates that the straddle price will be unchanged at 3.37. If Ralph believes this scenario, Table 15–4 indicates that he should not buy the 70 Straddle! Neither

Table 15–4 Change in Straddle Value:Pessimistic Scenario 3-Cent Change in Live Cattle Futures in 10 Days with Implied Volatility Down 4%

	Col. 1 Initial Status		Col. 2 Market Up		Col. 3 Market Down
Inputs:					
Futures price	70.00	→	73.00	→	67.00
Strike price	70.00				
Volatility	18%	→	14%	→	14%
Interest rates	5%				
Days to expiration	60	→	50	→	50
Outputs:					
70 Call price	1.675	→	3.20	→	0.20
70 Call price	1.675	→	0.22	→	3.17
70 Straddle	3.35	→	3.42	→	3.37

the up market scenario nor the down market scenario is likely to make a profit.

Which scenario should Ralph believe? That is a subjective decision that only he can make based on his conviction about his forecast and his tolerance for risk. The important lesson for all traders is that Ralph's analysis involved a three-part forecast: for the change in the futures price, for the timing of the expected price change, and for the level of implied volatility. In trading straddles, parts 2 and 3 of this analysis are especially important, because straddles involve two options.

SHORT STRADDLE DEFINED

A short straddle involves the simultaneous sale of one call and one put with the same strike, the same expiration, and the same underlying. Figure 15–2 illustrates a short 300 Wheat Straddle which is established by selling one 300 Wheat Call for 12 cents and one 300 Wheat Put for 12 cents, for a total amount received of 24 cents, or $1,200.

Figure 15–2 Short 300 Straddle at 24

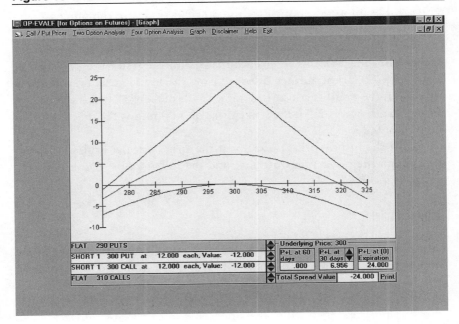

Profit or Loss at Expiration

At expiration, there are three possible outcomes. The futures price can be above the strike, below the strike, or at the strike. The straight line in Figure 15–2 illustrates these possibilities. If the futures price is above the strike price at expiration, the short 300 Call is assigned, because it is in-the-money. The short 300 Put expires worthless, because it is out-of-the money. If the futures price is 3.15 at expiration, for example, assignment of the short 300 Call results in the sale of a futures contract at 3.00, and the 300 Put expires worthless. If the short futures is covered at 3.15, a futures loss of 15 cents, or $750, is realized. This loss is subtracted from the amount received initially, 24 cents, or $1,200 in this example. The result is a net profit of 9 cents, or $450. If the futures price is above the upper break-even point at expiration, the result is a loss. In Figure 15–2, the upper break-even futures price at expiration is 3.24. This is calculated by adding the total amount received of 24 cents to the strike price of 3.00.

If the futures price is below the strike price at expiration, the short 300 Put is assigned, because it is in-the-money. The short 300 Call expires worthless, because it is out-of-the-money. If the futures price is 2.90 at expiration, for example, assignment of the 300 Put results in the purchase of a futures contract at 3.00, and the 300 Call expires worthless. If the futures contract is sold at 2.90, a futures loss of 10 cents is realized. This loss is subtracted from the 24 cents received initially, and the result is a profit of 14 cents, or $700. If the futures price is below the lower break-even point at expiration, the result is a loss. In Figure 15–2, the lower break-even futures price at expiration is 2.76, the strike price of 3.00 minus the initial amount received of 0.24.

If the futures price is exactly at the strike price at expiration, both the call and the put expire worthless, and the full amount received initially is kept as income.

Selling Straddles

Selling straddles is essentially the opposite of buying straddles. Whereas the straddle buyer hopes for a "big move" in either direction and an increase in implied volatility, the straddle seller hopes for no movement at all and a decrease in implied volatility.

Short straddles involve two uncovered short options, and so the risk is unlimited. Consequently, the use of this strategy is suitable only for experienced traders who are financially and psychologically capable of assuming this level of risk and who receive approval from their brokerage firms to use this strategy.

Table 15–1 offers some clues as to the type of forecast that leads to the sale of a straddle. Assume, for example, that the 70 Straddle in Table 15–1 is sold for 3.35 at 60 days before expiration, when the futures price is 70.00 (column 1, row 7). In order for a profit to be realized, the underlying futures price must stay within a 2-cent range between 72.00 and 68.00 (between row 4 and row 8) for 20 to 30 days before the straddle value declines noticeably.

The delta, gamma, vega, and theta of a short straddle are the opposite of those of a long straddle. Therefore, referring to Table 15–2, the delta of a short 70 Straddle is –0.024, the gamma is –0.182, the vega is –0.224, and the theta is +0.200. While the high theta may be enticing to some traders ("Look how much I can make from time decay!"), this potential benefit is balanced by the risk of an increase in implied volatility and the risk of a large move in either direction.

Traders who sell options in general and straddles in particular are well advised to have as much information as possible about implied volatility levels. They should be confident that they are selling options when implied volatility is "high" in their opinion. There are no guarantees that this knowledge will prevent a loss, but the purpose of studying implied volatility levels is to reduce this risk factor as much as possible.

LONG STRANGLE DEFINED

A *long strangle* involves the simultaneous purchase of one call with a higher strike and one put with the same expiration and the same underlying but with a lower strike. Figure 15–3 illustrates a long Live Cattle 68–72 strangle which is established by purchasing one 68 Put for 0.85 and one 72 Call for 0.90 for a total cost 1.75, or $700. It is common practice to describe a strangle by using the lower strike price first. Thus, the name for the position in Figure 15–3 is a long 68–72 Strangle. "Long" indicates that both options are purchased. The origin of the term *strangle* is unknown, but the word starts with the same letters as *straddle* and may have been coined for convenience.

Figure 15–3 Long 68–72 Strangle at 1.75

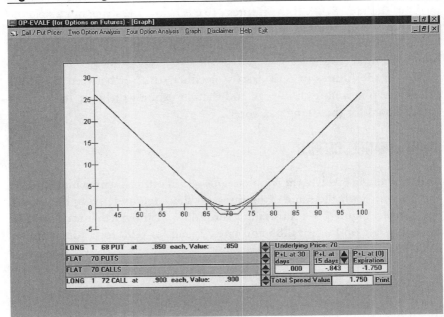

Profit or Loss at Expiration

At expiration, there are three possible outcomes. The futures price can be above the higher strike, below the lower strike, or at or between the strikes. The straight line in Figure 15–3 illustrates these possibilities. If the futures price is above the higher strike at expiration, the call is exercised, and the put expires worthless. If the futures is 75.00 at expiration, for example, exercising the 72 Call results in the purchase of a futures contract at 72.00, and the 68 Put expires worthless. If the futures contract is sold at 75.00, a futures profit of 3 cents, or 3.00, is realized. The cost of the position, 1.75 in this example, is subtracted from the 3.00 futures profit, and the result is a net profit of 1.25, or $500. If the futures price is above the higher strike but below the upper break-even point at expiration, the result is a loss. In Figure 15–3, the upper break-even futures price at expiration is 73.75. This is calculated by adding the total price paid of 1.75 to the higher strike of 72.00.

If the futures price is below the lower strike at expiration, the put is exercised, and the call expires worthless. If the futures price is 66.00 at expiration, for example, exercising the 68 Put results in selling a futures at 68.00, and the 72 Call expires worthless. If the short futures contract is covered at 66.00, a futures profit of 2.00 is realized. The cost of the position, 1.75 in this example, is subtracted from the futures profit, and the result is a net profit of 0.25, or $100. If the futures price is below the strike but above the lower break-even point at expiration, the result is a loss. In Figure 15–3, the lower break-even futures price at expiration is 66.25, the strike of 68.00 minus the total cost of 1.75.

If the futures price is exactly at either strike or between the strike prices at expiration, both the call and the put expire worthless, and the full amount paid for the strangle is lost.

SHORT STRANGLE DEFINED

A short strangle involves the simultaneous sale of one call with a higher strike and one put with the same expiration and the same underlying but with a lower strike. Figure 15–4 illustrates a short 68–72 Strangle that is established by selling one 68 Put for 0.85 and one 72 Call for 0.90 for a total amount received of 1.75.

Profit or Loss at Expiration

At expiration, there are three possible outcomes. The futures price can be above the higher strike, below the lower strike, or at or between the strikes.

Figure 15–4 Short 68–72 Strangle at 1.75

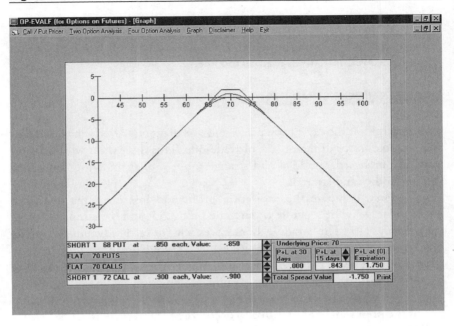

The straight line in Figure 15–4 illustrates these possibilities. If the futures price is above the higher strike at expiration, the short call is assigned and the short put expires worthless. If the futures price is 73.00 at expiration, for example, assignment of the 72 Call results in the sale of a futures at 72.00, and the 68 Put expires worthless. If the short futures is covered at 73.00, a futures loss of 1.00 is realized. This loss is subtracted from the amount received initially, 1.75 in this example, and the result is a net profit of 0.75, or $300. If the futures price is above the upper break-even point at expiration, the result is a loss. In Figure 15–4, the upper break-even futures price at expiration is 73.75. This is calculated by adding the total amount received of 1.75 to the strike price of the call of 72.00.

If the futures price is below the lower strike at expiration, the short put is assigned, and the short call expires worthless. If the futures price is 67.50 at expiration, for example, assignment of the 68 Put results in the purchase of a futures contract at 68.00, and the 72 Call expires worthless. If the futures is sold at 67.50, a futures loss of 0.50 is realized. This loss is subtracted from the 1.75 received initially, and the result is a profit of 1.25, or $500. If the futures price is below the lower break-even point at expiration, the result is a loss. In Figure 15–4, the lower break-even futures price at expiration is 66.25, the lower strike of 68.00 minus the initial amount received of 1.75.

If the futures price is exactly at either strike or between the strike prices at expiration, both the call and the put expire worthless, and the full amount received initially is kept as income.

STRADDLES VERSUS STRANGLES

A comparison of the expiration profit and loss diagrams reveals that straddles and strangles offer different sets of trade-offs. This discussion will focus on long, or purchased, straddles and strangles, but similar reasoning applies to short straddles and strangles.

First, compare the expiration profit and loss diagrams in Figure 15–1 and 15–3. The straddle is purchased for 3.35, and the strangle is purchased for 1.75. The straddle is more expensive, a disadvantage, but its break-even points are 73.35 and 66.63, which are closer together than the strangle's break-even points of 73.75 and 66.65. The relative closeness of the straddle's break-even points is an advantage.

Next, consider the chances that a long straddle will result in the total loss of the premium paid. For this to occur, the futures price must be exactly at 70.00, the strike price, at expiration. For the strangle to incur its maximum loss, however, the futures can be at or between the two strike prices. Whatever the chances are that the long straddle will incur its maximum loss, the chances that the long strangle will incur its maximum loss are greater.

The conclusion is that neither strategy is "better" in an absolute sense. A long straddle costs more than does a comparable long strangle, but its break-even points at expiration are closer together. There is also less of a chance that the maximum loss of a straddle will be incurred. Now consider the profit and risk potential of the two strategies for short-term traders.

Table 15–5 contains 68–72 Strangle values that are comparable to the 70 Straddle values in Table 15–1. The value in each cell in Table 15–5 is the sum of a 68 Put value and a 72 Call value, assuming the indicated futures price, days to expiration, etc. Just as Table 15–1 estimates how the 70 Straddle value changes, Table 15–5 estimates how the 68–72 Strangle value changes over a range of futures prices at different days before expiration, assuming that volatility and interest rates remain constant.

Assuming an initial futures price of 70.00 and 60 days to expiration (column 1, row 6, in both tables), a three-cent rise or fall in the futures price in any time frame yields a higher absolute profit for the straddle. At 50 days with a futures price of 73.00, for example, the straddle value is 4.00, up

Table 15–5 Theoretical Values of 68–72 Strangle
(1 68 Put and 1 72 Call)
(Interest Rates, 5%; Volatility, 18%)

		Col. 1	Col. 2	Col. 3	Col. 4	Col. 5	Col. 6	Col. 7
Row	Futures Price	60 Days	50 Days	40 Days	30 Days	20 Days	10 Days	Exp.
1	75.00	3.75	3.60	3.45	3.30	3.15	3.05	3.00
2	74.00	3.10	2.90	2.70	2.52	2.32	2.12	2.00
3	73.00	2.55	2.32	2.10	1.87	1.60	1.32	1.00
4	72.00	2.12	1.90	1.62	1.35	1.05	0.72	0.00
5	71.00	1.87	1.60	1.32	1.05	0.70	0.35	0.00
6	70.00	1.75	1.50	1.22	0.90	0.57	0.22	0.00
7	69.00	1.80	1.55	1.30	1.00	0.67	0.32	0.00
8	68.00	2.05	1.80	1.55	1.30	1.00	0.67	0.00
9	67.00	2.40	2.20	2.00	1.77	1.55	1.27	1.00
10	66.00	2.95	2.77	2.60	2.42	2.25	2.10	2.00
11	65.00	3.60	3.45	3.32	3.22	3.10	3.02	3.00

0.65, compared to the strangle value of 2.32, up 0.57. In this case the larger investment in the straddle earned a higher absolute profit. However, the profit as a percentage was higher for the strangle. Over a longer time period, the same holds true. At 30 days before expiration with a futures price of 74.00, for example, the straddle value is 4.27, up 0.92, compared to the strangle value of 2.52, up 0.77. As before, the straddle value increased more in absolute terms, but the strangle value increased more in percentage terms.

The situation is comparable in unprofitable outcomes. The strangle incurs a smaller absolute loss but a larger percentage loss. If the futures price is 71.00 at 20 days to expiration, for example, both strategies incur a loss. The straddle value has declined to 2.12, an absolute loss of 1.23 and a 37 percent loss of the initial investment. In comparison, the strangle value declined to 0.70, a lower absolute loss of 1.05 but a higher percentage loss of 60 percent.

This difference in profit measurement when absolute results are compared to percentage results is significant, because it emphasizes the need for traders to define their profit goals in advance of a trade. Any forecast will tend to favor one strategy over another depending on how the profit target is stated.

What do the Greeks reveal?

THE GREEKS: STRADDLES VERSUS STRANGLES

Table 15–6 compares the delta, gamma, vega, and theta of the two long strategies. The numbers for the long 70 Straddle were taken from Table 15–2, and those for the long 68–72 Strangle were calculated in a similar fashion.

What is so striking about the information in Table 15–6 is how close together the numbers are. The vega of the long 70 Straddle, for example, is +0.224, not much greater than the vega of the long 68–72 Strangle of +0.202. Consequently, a rise or fall in volatility will have a similar absolute effect on both strategies. The percentage effect, however, will be greater on the strangle.

Space restrictions prohibit an examination of changes in all inputs on all strategies, and so readers are encouraged to work through a variety of scenarios on their own. Comparing the behavior of straddles and strangles over a range of futures prices, time periods, and volatility levels is a valuable exercise.

SUMMARY

Long straddles involve the purchase of a call and a put with the same underlying, the same expiration date, and the same strike price. Short straddles involve the sale of both. Strangles are different from straddles in that they involve calls and puts with different strike prices. In considering these strategies, it is important to draw an expiration profit and loss diagram first so that

Table 15–6 Position Greeks: Straddle Compared to Strangle (Futures, 70.00; Days, 60; Interest Rates, 5%; Volatility, 15%)

	Long 70 Straddle		Long 68–70 Strangle
Price	3.35	1.75	
Delta	+0.024	+0.026	
Gamma	+0.182	+0.164	
Vega	+0.224	+0.202	
Theta	−0.200	−0.179	

the best and worst possible outcomes are fully understood. Short straddles and strangles involve unlimited risk and are suitable only for experienced traders who are financially and psychologically capable of assuming this level of risk and who receive approval from their brokerage firms to use these strategies.

To study straddles, this chapter used the same method of analysis that readers were taught in previous chapters. First, have a three-part forecast: a target for the underlying futures price, a prediction for the time period, and an outlook for implied volatility. Second, estimate the price of each option in a position and then calculate the estimated profit or loss. Third, evaluate a number of alternative strategies and select the one that best fits your personal risk-reward parameters.

Straddles and strangles involve different trade-offs. Long straddles are more expensive than comparable long strangles, but the break-even points of straddles are closer together and the risk of total loss of the investment for a straddle is lower. Short-term traders should be aware that absolute results and percentage results differ between the two strategies. Consequently, it is important to state a profit target in advance. A comparison of the delta, gamma, vega, and theta of straddles and strangles indicates that changes in individual factors tend to have a greater percentage impact on strangle values.

Sixteen

Ratio Spreads

R atio spreads involve the purchase of one quantity of one option and the sale of a different quantity of a second option of the same type, with the same underlying and the same expiration but with a different strike price. As the name implies, the difference in quantity is expressed as a ratio such as 1 × 2 or 2 × 3. Although there are numerous ratio possibilities, this chapter will focus on "one by two" or "1 × 2" ratio spreads. The method of analysis and the strategy selection for these ratio spreads can be applied to other ratio spreads as well.

Some of the strategies discussed in this chapter involve the sale of uncovered futures options and therefore are suitable only for traders who are psychologically and financially capable of assuming the risks of these strategies and who meet the requirements of their brokerage firms.

The examples in this chapter do not include commissions, other transaction costs, or margin requirements. Since ratio spreads involve two or more option positions, transaction costs and margin requirements can be higher than they are for single-option positions. These factors can significantly affect the desirability of any hedging or trading strategy, and they must be included in the analysis of any real strategy.

1 × 2 RATIO VERTICAL SPREAD DEFINED

A 1 × 2 *ratio vertical spread with calls* involves the purchase of one call and the sale of two calls with the same underlying and the same expiration but with a higher strike price. A 1 × 2 *ratio vertical spread with puts* involves the purchase of one put and the sale of two puts with the same underlying and the same expiration but with a lower strike price.

Note that the term *vertical* is more than a description of the relationship of the strike prices. When applied to ratio spreads, this term means that the greater quantity of options is sold. Although there is nothing in the strict definition of the word *vertical* to connote this meaning, this is common terminology in the options business.

Figure 16–1 illustrates a 600–625 1 × 2 ratio vertical spread with calls. In this strategy, one 600 Call is purchased for 17 cents and two 625 Calls are sold for 7¾ cents each. The spread therefore is established for a "1½-cent net debit" not including commissions. The term *net debit* means that the difference between the amount paid for options and the amount received from the sale of options is an amount *paid*. *Net credit* means that the difference between the amount paid and the amount received is an amount *received*.

Remember, the amount paid or received when a position is established is not necessarily equal to the risk or profit potential of a strategy. Net profit or net loss is the difference between the net revenue from a strategy and the net cost of that strategy. People too often think in terms of "buy first

Figure 16–1 600–625 1 x 2 Ratio Vertical Spread with Calls

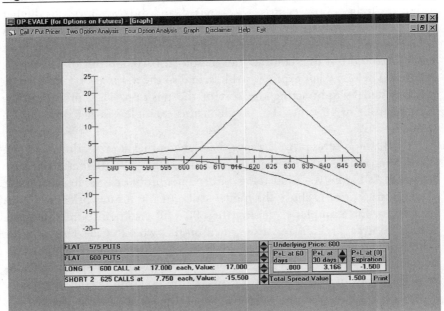

at a cost and sell later for a revenue," but this way of thinking does not always apply to ratio spreads that can be established for a debit or credit and subsequently closed for either a debit or a credit. It can get confusing if you do not take the time to understand each step along the way.

The following explanation of strategy mechanics focuses on ratio vertical spreads with calls, but the explanation is similar when puts are involved.

Profit or Loss at Expiration

At expiration, there are three possible outcomes. The futures price can be at or below the lower strike, above the lower strike but not above the upper strike, or above the upper strike. The straight line in Figure 16–1 illustrates these possibilities. If the futures price is at or below the lower strike at expiration, all calls expire worthless, and the full amount paid for the position, 1½ cents in this example, is lost. This 1½ cents, however, is not the maximum potential risk of this strategy! As will be discussed later, the maximum risk of a ratio spread is unlimited.

If the futures price is above the lower strike but not above the upper strike, the long call (lower strike) is exercised, and the two short calls (higher strike) expire worthless. In Figure 16–1, for example, if the futures price is 6.10 at expiration exercising the 600 Call results in the purchase of a futures contract at 6.00. If that contract can be sold at 6.10, a profit of 8½ cents is realized. The 625 Calls expire worthless, and so the net result of the strategy is calculated by subtracting the cost of the position, 1½ cents, from the futures profit of 10 cents. The result in this example is a net profit of 8½ cents, or $425.

If the futures price is above the higher strike at expiration, the long call (lower strike) is exercised and the two short calls (higher strike) are assigned. As Figure 16–1 illustrates, either a net profit or a net loss can result if the futures price is above the higher strike. If the futures price is 6.30 at expiration, for example, exercising the 600 Call results in purchasing one futures contract at 6.00, and assignment on the two 625 Calls results in the selling of two futures contracts at 6.25 each. The result of these futures transactions is a realized profit of 25 cents on one contract and an open short contract with an unrealized loss of 5 cents. If the open short contract can be covered at 6.30, then the net result of the ratio vertical spread strategy is a profit of 18½ cents. This final net result is calculated by subtracting the initial cost of the strategy, 1½ cents, from the net profit of 20 cents of the two futures contracts.

A net loss of 11½ cents is the result, however, if the futures price is 6.60 at expiration. In this case, exercise of the long 600 Call and assignment of the two short 625 Calls results in two futures transactions with a net loss. A profit of 25 cents is realized on one contract that is purchased at 6.00 and sold at 6.25, but the open short contract has an unrealized loss of 35 cents. If the open short contract is covered at 6.60, the final result of the ratio vertical spread strategy is calculated by adding the net loss from the futures transactions of 10 cents to the initial cost of the strategy of 1½ cents. The combined loss, therefore, is 11½ cents.

The maximum risk of a ratio vertical spread with calls is unlimited. As is illustrated in Figure 16–1, losses increase as the futures price rises.

Break-Even Points and Maximum Profit Potential

In Figure 16–1 there are two futures prices at which the strategy breaks even at expiration. The lower break-even point, 6.01½ in this example, is calculated by adding the net debit paid for the strategy, 1½, to the lower strike, 6.00.

To calculate the upper break-even futures price at expiration, it is necessary to know the maximum profit potential of the strategy. The maximum profit of a 1 × 2 ratio spread with calls is calculated by subtracting the lower break-even point from the upper strike, because the maximum position value is realized if the futures price is exactly at the higher strike at expiration. The higher strike at expiration is where the long call has its highest value without being diminished by the short calls. As the futures price rises above the higher strike, the increase in value of the short calls decreases the position value. Beyond the upper break-even point, a loss results. In this example, the lower break-even futures price of 6.01½ is subtracted from the upper strike of 6.25, and the result is a net profit of 23½ cents.

The upper break-even point is calculated by adding the maximum profit to the upper strike. Above the upper strike, remember, the net position is short one upper-strike call. Consequently, as the futures price rises, this uncovered short call reduces the profit, if any, that would be realized at expiration with the futures price at the maximum profit point. In this example, the upper break-even point is 6.25 plus 23½ cents, or 6.48½.

Price Behavior

Table 16–1 contains theoretical values of a 600–625 1 × 2 ratio vertical spread with calls at various futures prices and days to expiration. This table was created by using the Two Option Analysis page in OP-EVALF™. The value in each box assumes that one 600 Call is purchased and two 625 Calls are sold. Column 1, row 8, in Table 16–1, for example, assumes a futures price of 6.00, 30 days to expiration, and the assumptions about volatility and interests listed in the heading. Although the individual call values are not shown, purchasing one 600 Call at 17 cents and selling two 625 Calls at 7¾ cents each results in a net debit of 1½ cents, not including commissions, and 1½ is the number which appears in this box. Consequently, under the assumptions stated above, the strategy could be established for a net debit of 1½ cents.

Parentheses in Table 16–1 indicate that the strategy can be established for a net credit or closed for a net debit. The number in parentheses appearing in column 1, row 1, for example, indicates that purchasing one 600 Call and selling two 625 Calls results in a net credit of 6½ cents. Alternatively, selling one 600 Call and purchasing two 625 Calls results in a net debit of 6½ cents.

Numbers that appear without parentheses in Table 16–1 indicate the strategy can be established for a net debit or closed for a net credit. The

Table 16–1 Theoretical Values of a 600–625 Ratio Vertical Spread with Calls (Long 1 600 Call and Short 2 625 Calls) (Interest Rates, 5%; Volatility, 25%)

		Col. 1	Col. 2	Col. 3	Col. 4	Col. 5	Col. 6	Col. 7
Row	Futures Price	30 Days	25 Days	20 Days	15 Days	10 Days	5 Days	Exp.
1	6.35	(6½)	(4½)	(2¼)	½	3¾	8½	15
2	6.30	(4½)	(2½)	(½)	2	5½	10	20
3	6.25	(3)	(1)	1	3½	6½	11	25
4	6.20	(1½)	(6¾)	2	4½	7	11	20
5	6.15	(½)	0	2¾	4¾	7¼	10¼	15
6	6.10	1½	1	3¼	5	7	9	10
7	6.05	1	2¼	3½	5	6½	7½	5
8	6.00	1½	2½	3¾	4¾	5½	5¾	0
9	5.95	1¾	2¾	3½	4¼	4½	4	0

Note: Parentheses mean that the spread can be opened for a credit and closed for a debit.
No parentheses means that the spread can be opened for a debit and closed for a credit.

number not in parentheses in column 1, row 9, for example, indicates that purchasing one 600 Call and selling two 625 Calls results in a net debit of 1¾ cents. Alternatively, selling one 600 Call and purchasing two 625 Calls results in a net credit of 1¾ cents.

Table 16–1 can be difficult to interpret. One way to avoid confusion is to use the terms open and close rather than buy and sell. The calculation of profit or loss involves combining the opening debit or credit and the closing debit or credit. Opening a position for a debit number in Table 16–1 is a cash outflow, but opening a position for a credit number is a cash inflow. Closing a position at a debit number is a cash inflow, and closing a position for a credit number is a cash outflow. Let's work through some examples.

In the first example, assume that the ratio vertical spread is opened in column 1, row 8, and closed in column 6, row 7. The position is opened for a debit of 1½. This means that 1½ cents is paid. The position is then closed at a debit of 7½ in the table. This means that 7½ cents is received. The final result is 1½ cents paid and 7½ cents received for a net amount received, or net profit, of 6 cents.

In the second example, assume that the ratio vertical spread is opened in column 1, row 3, and closed in column 6, row 7. The position is opened for a credit of 3 cents, which means that 3 cents is received. The position is then closed at a debit of 7½ in the table, which means that 7½ cents is received. Consequently, the final result is 3 cents received and 7½ cents received for a total received, or profit, of 10½ cents.

In the third example, assume that the ratio vertical spread is opened in column 1, row 9, and closed in column 3, row 1. The position is opened for a debit of 1¾, which means that 1¾ cents is paid. The position is then closed at a credit of 2¼ in the table. This means that 2¼ cents is paid. The final result, therefore, is 1¾ cents paid and 2¼ cents paid for a total paid, or lost, of 4 cents.

As a final example, assume the spread is opened in column 2, row 4, and closed in column 3, row 1. The position is opened for a credit of 6¾, which means that 6¾ cents is received. The position is then closed at a credit of 2¼, which means that 2¼ cents is paid. Consequently, the final result is 6¾ received and 2¼ paid for a net received, or profit, of 4½ cents, not including commissions.

The conclusion from Table 16–1, which is supported by Figure 16–1, is that ratio vertical spreads with calls perform best when the underlying futures contract trades in a narrow range around the strike of the short calls. Traders must therefore forecast this kind of market action in order to choose this strategy.

The Greeks

Table 16–2 summarizes the delta, gamma, theta, and vega of the long 600 Call, the two short 625 Calls, and the ratio vertical spread. The information in columns 1 and 2 was taken from the Call/Put Pricer page in OP-EVALF™, and the numbers in column 3 are the sums of the numbers in column 1 plus two times the numbers in column 2. The Greeks of a multiple-part option position are equal to the sum of the Greeks of the individual options that make up the position. The vega of –0.509 in column 3, for example, is calculated by adding +0.683 and two times –0.596.

What does Table 16–2 reveal about the ratio vertical spread? First, the negative vega indicates that the position will benefit from a decrease in implied volatility and be hurt by an increase in volatility. Second, the positive theta means that the position will profit from time erosion if other factors remain constant. Third, the negative gamma means that the position will be hurt by a sharp move up or down. The ideal scenario for a ratio vertical spread is for the underlying futures contract to trade in a narrow range around the strike price of the short options with declining volatility until expiration.

We can now test some forecasts to estimate how successful the use of a ratio vertical spread with calls might be.

Testing Scenarios

OP-EVALF™ can be used to test various scenarios. Suppose, for example, that Marty, an experienced trader who is prepared to assume the risk of selling

Table 16–2 Position Greeks
600 Call, 625 Call, 600–625 1x2 Ratio Vertical Spread with Calls (Futures Price, 6.00; Days, 30; Interest Rates, 5%; Volatility, 25%)

	Col. 1 Long 1 600 Call	Col. 2 Short 2 625 Calls	Col. 3 600–625 1x2 Ratio Vertical Spread
Theoretical value	17	7¾ (each)	1½ (debit)
Delta	+0.512	−0.296 (each)	−0.080
Gamma	+0.009	−0.008 (each)	−0.007
Vega	+0.683	−0.596 (each)	−0.509
Theta	−2.110	+1.796 (each)	+1.482

uncovered futures options, is forecasting neutral to slightly bullish movement in July Soybeans over the next 25 days. In this example, assume 25 days to expiration of an option on July Soybean futures, a July Soybean futures price of 6.05, a July Soybeans 600 Call price of 18¼ cents, and a July Soybeans 625 Call price of 8 cents. This means that Marty can purchase one 600 Call and sell two 625 Calls for a net debit of 2¼ cents, not including commissions. This situation is consistent with column 2, row 7, in Table 16–1.

Marty forecasts that July Soybean futures will rise gradually to 6.25 in the next 25 days, but because a government report is scheduled for release in 5 days, Marty wants to test some negative scenarios to estimate his risk.

Table 16–1 estimates that if in 5 days July Soybean futures rise 30 cents to 6.35 at 20 days to expiration (column 3, row 1), the spread value will drop to a credit of 2¼ cents for a loss of 4½ cents, not including commissions. This is a risk Marty feels comfortable with, but the numbers in Table 16–1 assume that implied volatility remains constant at 25 percent. Marty wants to estimate the result if implied volatility increases to 35 percent.

Table 16–3 shows how OP-EVALF™ might be used to test this scenario. Column 1 contains the initial inputs: the July Soybean futures price of 6.05, the days to expiration of 25, the volatility of 25 percent, etc. It also includes the initial outputs: the 600 Call value of 18¼ cents (18.287), the 625 Call value of 8 cents (7.965), and the spread value of 2¼ cents debit (+2.358). Column 2 contains Marty's forecast with the futures price at 6.35, volatility of 35 percent, and days to expiration of 20. With the new inputs, the 600 Call is estimated to be trading at 42¼ and the 625 Call is estimated to be trading at 26. The ratio vertical spread therefore is estimated to be trading for a credit of 9¾ cents. This is calculated by assuming that one 600 Call is purchased for 42¼ cents and two 600 Calls are sold at 26 cents each, for a net spread credit of 9¾ cents. Paying 2¼ cents to open the ratio vertical spread and paying 9¾ cents to close it means that a loss of 12 cents, or $600, is incurred. This loss is 7½ cents greater than the 4½-cent loss calculated above from Table 16–1.

Marty can use this information as part of his subjective decision-making process. If Marty does not consider this additional risk too great and if he has confidence in his forecast, he may employ the ratio vertical spread strategy. If, however, this difference in estimated loss changes his attitude toward the risk-reward ratio, he may look for another strategy or may decide to "sit this one out" and do nothing for the present.

We have seen that ratio vertical spreads are suited for neutral market forecasts. The ratio volatility spread that is discussed next is suited for a different market environment.

Table 16–3 Marty's Worst Case Forecast

	Col. 1 Initial Situation		Col. 2 Marty's Forecast
Inputs:			
Futures price	6.05	→	6.35
Strike price	600 / 625		
Volatility	25%	→	35%
Interest rates	5%		
Days to expiration	25	→	20
Outputs:			
600 Call price	18¼	→	42¼
625 Call price	8	→	26
1 × 2 ratio vertical spread	2¼ (debit)	→	−9¾ (credit)

1 × 2 RATIO VOLATILITY SPREAD DEFINED

A 1 × 2 ratio volatility spread with calls involves the sale of one call and the purchase of two calls with the same underlying and the same expiration but with a higher strike price. A 1 × 2 ratio volatility spread with puts involves the sale of one put and the purchase of two puts with the same underlying and the same expiration but with a lower strike price.

When applied to ratio spreads, the term *volatility* means that the greater quantity of options is purchased. This meaning has become common terminology in the options business, because this strategy profits from a "large move" in the underlying futures, i.e., high volatility.

Figure 16–2 illustrates a 300–320 1 × 2 ratio volatility spread with calls. In this strategy, one 300 Call is sold for 12 cents and two 320 Calls are purchased for 5 cents each. This means that the spread is established for a "2-cent net credit," or amount received, not including commissions. The following explanation of strategy mechanics focuses on ratio volatility spreads with calls, but the explanation is similar when puts are involved.

Profit or Loss at Expiration

At expiration, there are three possible outcomes. The futures price can be at or below the lower strike, above the lower strike but not above the upper strike, or above the upper strike. The straight line in Figure 16–2 illustrates these possibilities. If the futures price is at or below the lower strike of a ratio

Figure 16–2 300–320 1 x 2 Ratio Volatility Spread with Calls

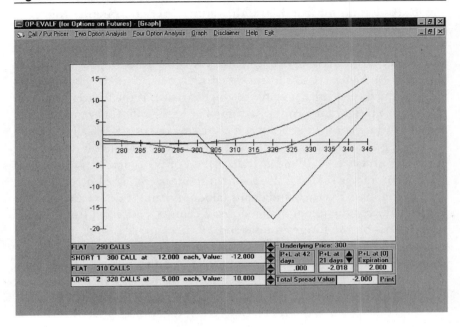

volatility spread with calls at expiration, all calls expire worthless, and the full amount received for the position, 2 cents in this example, is kept as income. This does not imply, however, that establishing a position for net credit guarantees a profit! The maximum risk will be calculated shortly.

If the futures price is above the lower strike but not above the upper strike, the short call (lower strike) is assigned, and the two long calls (higher strike) expire worthless. In Figure 16–2, for example, if the futures price is 3.10 at expiration, assignment of the 300 Call results in selling a futures contract at 3.00. The 320 Calls expire worthless, and so the final profit or loss result is calculated by adding the cost paid or the credit received when establishing the position to the profit or loss from the futures position. If the short futures contract is covered at 3.10, a futures loss of 10 cents is realized. Adding this 10-cent loss to the credit of 2 cents received when the position was established results in a net loss of 8 cents, or $400.

The maximum loss occurs if the futures price is exactly at the higher strike at expiration. With the futures price at 3.20 at expiration in this example, assignment of the 300 Call results in selling one futures contract at 3.00. If this contract can be covered at 3.20, a 20-cent loss is realized. Since the 320 Calls expire worthless with the futures at 3.20 at expiration, the loss of 20 cents is added to the initial credit of 2 cents for a net loss of 18 cents. Figure 16–2 confirms that 3.20 is the futures price at expiration where the maximum loss occurs.

If the futures price is above the higher strike at expiration, the short call (lower strike) is assigned and the two long calls (higher strike) are assigned. As Figure 16–2 illustrates, either a net profit or a net loss can result if the futures price is above the higher strike. If the futures price is at 3.25 at expiration, for example, assignment of the 300 Call results in selling one futures contract at 3.00, and exercising the two 320 Calls results in purchasing two contracts at 3.20 each. These two events result in one long futures contract at 3.20 and a realized loss of 20 cents. If the one long futures contract is sold at 3.25, the final result is calculated by combining credits (amounts received) and debits (amounts paid). In this case, with the futures at 3.25, the initial net credit of 2 cents is subtracted from the net 15-cent loss on the futures transactions. One contract is sold at 3.00 and repurchased at 3.20 for a loss of 20 cents, and the second contract is purchased at 3.20 and sold at 3.25 for a profit of 5 cents. The final result, with the futures price at 3.25 in this example, is a net loss of 13 cents, not including commissions.

A net profit is the result, however, if the futures price is at 3.50 at expiration. In this case, the short 300 Call is assigned and the two long 320 Calls are exercised. These two events cause a realized loss of 20 cents on one short futures contract and create a long futures position at 3.25. If that long futures contract is sold at 3.50, a profit of 30 cents is realized on that contract. Adding the initial net credit of 2 cents to the net 10-cent profit from the futures transactions results in the final profit of 12 cents, or $600, not including commissions.

Break-Even Points and Maximum Profit Potential

In Figure 16–2 the ratio volatility spread breaks even at 3.38 at expiration. This is calculated by adding the maximum potential loss of 18 cents to the higher strike of 3.20. Above a futures price of 3.20 at expiration, the net position is long one 320 Call, because the short 300 Call is offset by one of the two long 320 Calls. The rise in value of the second long 320 Call equals the maximum potential loss of 18 cents at the break-even futures price of 3.38 (3.20 + .18). Above the break-even point, the profit potential is unlimited.

Price Behavior

Table 16–4 contains theoretical values of a 300–320 1 × 2 ratio volatility spread with calls at various futures prices and days to expiration. This table was created by using the Two Option Analysis page in OP-EVALF™. The value in each box assumes that one 300 Call is sold and two 320 Calls are purchased. Column 1, row 8, in Table 16–4, for example, assumes a futures price of 3.00, 30 days to expiration, and the assumptions about volatility and interest rates listed in the heading at the top of the table. Although the individual call values are not shown, selling one 300 Call at 12 cents and purchasing two 320 Calls at 5 cents each results in a net credit of 2 cents, not including commissions, and 2 is the number which appears in this box. Consequently, given the assumptions stated above, the strategy could be established for a net credit of 2 cents.

Parentheses in Table 16–4 indicate that the strategy could be established for a net credit. The number in parentheses appearing in column 6, row 7, for example, indicates that selling one 300 Call and purchasing two 320 Calls results in a credit of 8¼ cents. Table 16–4 can be difficult to interpret. Calculating profit or loss requires knowing the debit or credit when a position is opened and when it is closed and then combining them correctly.

Table 16–4 Theoretical Values of 300–320 Ratio Volatility Spread with Calls (Short 1 300 Call and Long 2 320 Calls) (Interest Rates, 5%; Volatility, 25%)

Row	Futures Price	Col. 1 42 Days	Col. 2 35 Days	Col. 3 28 Days	Col. 4 21 Days	Col. 5 14 Days	Col. 6 7 Days	Col. 7 Exp.
1	3.70	32	31¼	30¾	30¼	30	30	30
2	3.60	23½	22¾	21¾	21	20	20	20
3	3.50	16	14¾	13½	12¼	11	10	10
4	3.40	9¾	8¼	6¾	5	(3)	(¾)	0
5	3.30	4½	3	1½	(¾)	(3)	(6½)	(10)
6	3.20	(1)	(½)	(2)	(3¾)	(6¼)	(9¾)	(20)
7	3.10	(1¼)	(2¼)	(3½)	(4¾)	(6½)	(8¼)	(10)
8	3.00	(2)	(2¾)	(3½)	(4)	(4½)	(4¼)	0
9	2.90	(2)	(2½)	(2¾)	(2¾)	(2½)	(1½)	0

Note: Parentheses mean that the spread can be opened for a credit and closed for a debit.
No parentheses means that the spread can be opened for a debit and closed for a credit.

The conclusion from Table 16–4 that is supported by Figure 16–2 is that ratio volatility spreads with calls perform best when the underlying rises sharply beyond the break-even point. Consequently, traders must be forecasting this kind of market action in order to choose this strategy. If the market trades in a narrow range around the higher strike, ratio vertical spreads with calls will result in a loss.

The Greeks

Table 16–5 summarizes the delta, gamma, theta, and vega of a short 300 Call, a long 320 Call, and a ratio volatility spread with these calls. This information confirms the conclusions from Figure 16–2 and Table 16–4. First, the positive vega indicates that the position will profit from an increase in volatility. Second, the negative theta means that time erosion will cause a loss if factors other than time are unchanged. Third, the positive gamma means that the position will benefit from a sharp move up or down. The ideal scenario for a ratio volatility spread is for the underlying futures to move sharply beyond the strike of the long options. In the case of ratio volatility spreads with calls, this is up. When puts are involved, the desired direction is down.

SUMMARY

Ratio spreads involve the purchase of one quantity of an option and the sale of a different quantity of a second option of the same type, with the same underlying and the same expiration but with a different strike price. In ratio vertical spreads, the larger number of options is sold. In ratio volatility spreads, the larger number of options is purchased.

Ratio vertical spreads involve substantial or unlimited risk, because they involve an uncovered short option. The ideal scenario for a ratio vertical spread is for the underlying futures contract to trade in a narrow range around the strike price of the short options with declining implied volatility until expiration.

The risk of ratio volatility spreads is limited, but it can be greater than the amount paid to establish the position. The ideal scenario for a ratio volatility spread is for the underlying futures contract to move sharply beyond the strike price of the long options.

The short-term price behavior of ratio spreads can be analyzed by creating theoretical value tables similar to those for single options. The numbers in the tables are, however, sometimes difficult to interpret, because ratio

Table 16–5 Position Greeks
            300 Call, 320 Call, 300–320 1 x 2 Ratio Volatility Spread
            (Futures Price, 3.00; Days, 42; Interest Rates, 5%; Volatility, 30%)

	Col. 1 Short 1 300 Call	Col. 2 Long 2 320 Calls	Col. 3 300–320 1 x 2 Ratio Volatility Spread
Theoretical value	12	5 (each)	−2 (credit)
Delta	−0.517	+0.278 (each)	+0.039
Gamma	−0.013	+0.011 (each)	+0.009
Vega	−0.403	+0.343 (each)	+0.283
Theta	+1.043	−0.869 (each)	−0.695

spreads can be established for either a debit or a credit. Consequently, calculating profit and loss can be confusing when a position is opened for a debit and closed at a credit.

    Various market scenarios should be tested, and the information should be used as part of the subjective decision-making process. As with single-option positions, traders should use a three-part forecast when trading ratio spreads. They should have a forecast for the change in the futures price, a forecast for the time period, and a forecast for the implied volatility level.

Seventeen

Conclusion

OPTIONS GIVE YOU OPTIONS

Simply stated, the theme of this book is that options give hedgers and traders more alternatives to profit from their market opinion. Futures contracts offer only three strategies: long, short, and flat. Options, in contrast, offer choices that are far more numerous. Although *flexibility* is an overused and inexact word, that is what options give hedgers and traders. With options, the strategic alternatives include any combination of limited or unlimited risk and limited or unlimited profit potential.

Whether you are a hedger or a trader, learning to use options involves the following steps. First, master the basics: Understand the rights and obligations of long and short options, learn to calculate profit and loss at expiration, and understand exercise and assignment. Second, learn the trade-offs that different strategies offer. No strategy is "better" in an absolute sense. Rather, every strategy has a unique set of trade-offs, which are positive and negative aspects relative to other strategies. Third, learn about option price behavior. Understanding how changing market conditions affect option prices is important, because realistic expectations are necessary to use options successfully. Fourth, both hedgers and traders must learn to think in two steps. The first step is when a position is initiated, and the second step is on or before the expiration date when the position is closed.

Master the Basics

Many option-related terms have one meaning in everyday usage and a different meaning in the world of options. The ability to draw profit and loss diagrams helps one visualize the profit and risk potentials of option strategies. Understanding exercise and assignment is especially important for hedgers, because these events create futures transactions that affect the ultimate purchase or sale price of the underlying commodity.

Learn the Trade-offs

Every strategy offers a unique set of advantages and disadvantages. Buying options allows hedgers to lock in a known maximum or minimum price and leaves intact the opportunity to benefit if prices improve. The disadvantage of buying options, however, is that the price that is locked in is less desirable than the current market price. Option sellers receive a premium that has the potential to improve the ultimate purchase or sale price of the underlying commodity. The premium received from selling options also offers limited protection if prices of the underlying change adversely. The disadvantage of selling options is that no maximum or minimum price is locked in. Table 17–1 summarizes the trade-offs of nine strategies.

Option Price Behavior

Option prices typically change less than one for one with futures prices. Specifically, they tend to change in accordance with the option's delta. Time decay is also an important factor. It is necessary, therefore, to develop realistic expectations about option price behavior so that, given a market forecast, strategy results can be estimated. The computer program OP-EVALF™ that accompanies this text is a tool designed to help with this process. When the various inputs are changed, much can be learned about how option prices change. With experience, both hedgers and traders can use the program to estimate what option prices will be if conditions in the market change as expected. Such estimates can be used along with other information to assess whether a particular strategy is appropriate.

Regarding forecasts, a three-part forecast is necessary for option strategies. There must be forecasts for the change in futures price, for the time period, and for the level of implied volatility.

Implied volatility is a unique aspect of options prices. As was discussed in several chapters in this book, implied volatility is the volatility percentage in an option-pricing formula that returns the market price of an option as the theoretical value. Changes in implied volatility can be interpreted as a shift in general market anxiety. A rise in implied volatility, for instance, might indicate a general concern among option market participants that an upcoming event such as a government report will cause a

Table 17 – 1 Hedging Strategies: The Trade-offs

Long futures. Long hedgers can buy futures to lock in the current price. The disadvantage is that there is no opportunity to benefit if prices decrease.

Short futures. Short hedgers can sell futures to lock in the current price. The disadvantage is that there is no opportunity to benefit if prices rise.

Long call. Long hedgers can buy calls to lock in a maximum purchase price and leave open the possibility of buying at lower prices if prices decline. The disadvantage is that the price that is locked in is above the current market price.

Short call. Short hedgers can sell calls and collect a premium which increases the selling price if the calls are assigned. The premium received also provides limited insurance against declining prices. The disadvantage is that no minimum selling price is locked in; if prices decline more than the premium received, the ultimate selling price can be substantially lower than the current price.

Long put. Short hedgers can buy puts to lock in a minimum selling price and leave open the possibility of selling at higher prices if prices rise. The disadvantage is that the price that is locked in is below the current price.

Short put. Long hedgers can sell puts and collect a premium that decreases the purchase price if the puts are assigned. The premium received also provides limited insurance against rising prices. The disadvantage is that no maximum purchase price is locked in; if prices rise more than the premium received, then the ultimate purchase price can be substantially higher than the current market price.

Bullish collar. Bullish collars reduce the cost of long calls. For long hedgers, a bullish collar locks in a maximum purchase price at a reduced cost relative to purchasing calls outright and still leaves open the opportunity to benefit if prices decline. The disadvantage is that the ability to benefit from falling prices is limited to the strike price of the short put.

Bearish collar. Bearish collars reduce the cost of long puts. For short hedgers, a bearish collar locks in a minimum selling price at a reduced cost relative to purchasing puts outright and still leaves open the opportunity to benefit if prices rise. The disadvantage is that the ability to benefit from rising prices is limited to the strike price of the short call.

Figure 17 – 1 Hedging Strategies: The Trade-offs (*Continued*)

Long futures with ratio call spread.	Long hedgers can use this strategy in two different ways. First, it can be used as a "futures repair" strategy. Without increasing risk, a ratio call spread can be added to a long futures position, and the break-even point will be lowered relative to a point approximately equal to buying another futures contract. The disadvantage is that the upside potential is limited to the strike price of the short calls. Second, if the ratio call spread is purchased at the same time that a futures contract is purchased, market exposure is increased over a limited range. The disadvantage is that upside potential is limited to the strike price of the short calls.

sharp change in futures prices. Whether such a rise in implied volatility is significant is a subjective determination that must be made by each trader. Furthermore, rises in implied volatility are no guarantee that a sharp change in futures prices will occur. Also, there is no rule that indicates whether changes in implied volatility precede, accompany, or follow changes in futures prices. Each trader must observe what has happened in the past and make a judgment about the possibility of similar price action happening again.

As traders consider possibilities, they should keep in mind that implied volatility can change in seemingly contradictory ways just as a futures price can change unpredictably. The old saying "Buy on the rumor and sell on the news" is often used to explain what appears to be contradictory price action in the futures market, such as a price decline immediately after the release of good news or a price rise after bad news is announced. In option markets, contradictory price action can occur in a different form. The price of a particular futures contract may rise, but call prices may remain unchanged or decline. Alternatively, options prices can rise much more than deltas indicate. Such price behavior in option markets is explained by changes in implied volatility, and this is why option traders must pay attention to implied volatility.

As an example, assume that, before the last three crop reports the implied volatility of corn options rose and that after those reports it declined. A trader who is considering initiating a trade prior to the fourth report must evaluate the impact of a similar change in implied volatility. The trader must also make a prediction about whether history will repeat itself a fourth time. There is, of course, no guarantee that it will.

A FOUR-STEP DECISION-MAKING PROCESS

Whether you are a hedger or a trader, the following discussion presents a simple four-step approach for selecting strategies. The goal is to help all option users think clearly so that an appropriate strategy can be chosen.

The four steps are as follows: First, know your situation. Second, state clearly your market forecast. Third, identify your specific objective. Fourth, choose a strategy that will meet your goal if the forecast is accurate.

Know Your Situation

Many hedgers and traders take it for granted that they know their situation. Since the use of options requires specific thinking, however, it is worth reviewing some examples. "I'm bullish" is not a situation; it is a forecast. "I would like to increase income" is not a situation; it is a goal. A situation is "I have no position," "I am long futures with a profit that I am willing to sell," or "I need to buy 20,000 bushels of wheat in March." For different people, the same situation may lead to the selection of different strategies, because they may have different forecasts or different goals.

Hedgers should be careful to include their interest in the underlying commodity as part of their situation. A farmer's situation, for example, might be, "I will harvest 50,000 bushels in September that will be ready for delivery in late October," or "I have 25,000 bushels in storage." A processor's situation might be, "I need 40,000 pounds of soybean oil per month, and I am hedged through March, but after that I am not protected."

State Clearly Your Market Forecast

Being "bullish" or "bearish" is not specific enough for the purposes of hedging or trading with options. "I predict that the futures price will rise from 4.80 to 5.25 in the next 6 to 8 weeks," or "Wheat prices will trade at or below 2.40 between now and expiration and implied volatility will decrease by 5 percent" are clear market forecasts.

Identify Your Specific Objective

Examples of specific objectives are "I want to sell my crop at 5.75," "I would like to leverage my exposure without increasing risk if prices rise as I predict," and "I am willing to buy futures, effectively, at $170 per ton." In contrast, just wanting to "make money" is not specific enough to lead to the selection of a particular option strategy.

SOME EXAMPLES

If a farmer has crops in storage and has a neutral market forecast, selling calls targets the goals of increasing income or selling at a higher price. Alternatively, if the forecast is "bullish but worried," the farmer may buy puts to lock in a minimum selling price while leaving open the possibility of benefiting if prices rise. However, if the farmer thinks that the puts are "too expensive," a bearish collar may be chosen.

Long hedgers can find themselves in a number of situations. They may be unhedged for the next 6 months, or they may be partially or completely hedged. If a long hedger is unhedged and if the forecast is neutral, selling puts provides some upside protection and increases income. If the forecast is bearish, remaining unhedged may be the strategy of choice.

If a long hedger is completely hedged with long futures contracts and the forecast changes from bullish to bearish, lifting some of the hedge and lifting all of the hedge are only two possibilities. Given this situation, a long hedger may purchase puts to limit the risk of the long futures position. If prices decline, the long puts establish a minimum selling price for the futures contracts. If, however, prices rise, the futures contracts still provide a hedge.

TRADING

Trading, as was discussed earlier, differs from hedging, because speculative traders have no interest in buying or selling the underlying commodity on which futures and options are traded. Trading is an endeavor involving a series of short-term purchase and sale transactions that are intended to profit from predicted price changes. It is especially important that option traders have realistic expectations about option price behavior, and their market forecasts must also include three parts: for the futures price, for time, and for implied volatility.

Option traders must think in two steps just as hedgers do. The second step for traders, however, is always an exit strategy. Hopefully, a position will be exited at a profit, but realistically, no trading technique can be expected to return a profit on every trade. Traders therefore must believe that their method of trade selection will generate net profits after a series of trades, and they must trade in a manner consistent with this belief. When establishing a position, traders should set three limits: a profit target, a time limit, and a stop-loss point. Traders should also be disciplined enough to exit the position when any one of the three limits is reached. It is essential that traders be guided by objectivity rather than by emotion. Traders must have confidence that their trading technique will achieve net profits after a series of trades, and they must have the discipline to implement that technique consistently.

SUMMARY

Options can be used to pursue a variety of hedging and trading objectives. Different strategies offer different trade-offs, and the potential profits and potential risks should be understood before one attempts to use any strategy.

The steps in learning to use options are to learn the mechanics, learn to draw profit and loss diagrams, learn about option price behavior, and develop realistic expectations about the results of strategies. Finally, learn a simple four-step strategy selection process that promotes organized thinking and realistic expectations. First, start by stating the situation. Second, have a specific three-part forecast, for the futures price, the time horizon, and the level of implied volatility. Third, state the objectives. Fourth, choose a strategy that matches all three.

By keeping these guidelines in mind, striving to acquire the necessary skills, and gaining experience, any hedger or trader can learn to use options to his or her benefit.

Index

About the Author

James B. Bittman is senior instructor at the Options Institute, the educational arm of the Chicago Board Options Exchange. He is also on the faculty at the Illinois Institute of Technology. Bittman holds a Commodity Options Membership at the CBOT and has profitably traded options for more than 20 years. He has written two successful books on the subject, *Trading Index Options* and *Options for the Stock Investor*.